WORLD WAR 1

THE WESTERN FRONT

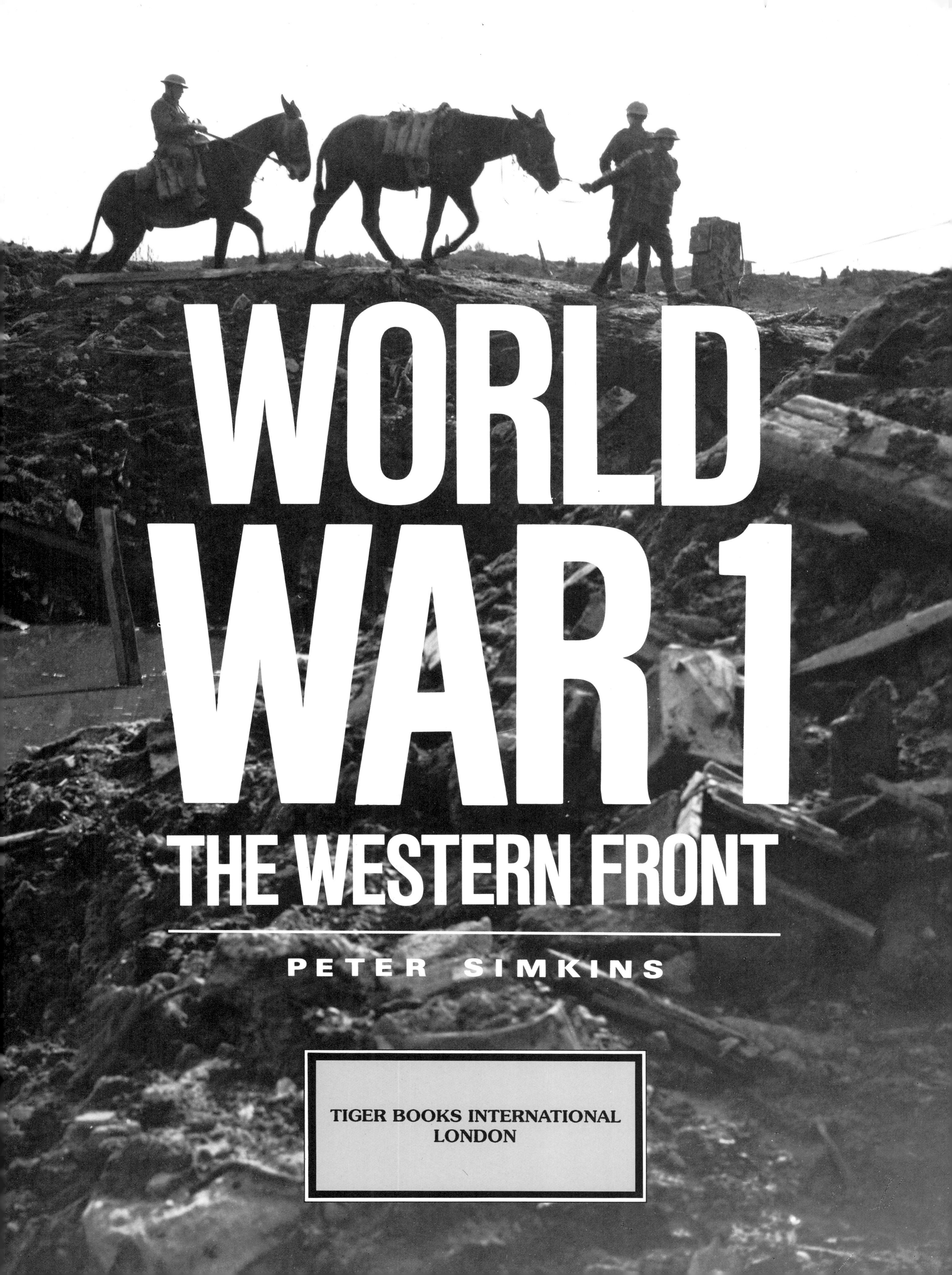

WORLD WAR 1

THE WESTERN FRONT

PETER SIMKINS

TIGER BOOKS INTERNATIONAL
LONDON

Designer	Philip Clucas
Cartographer	Richard Hawke
Photo Researchers	Leora Kahn Gerry Conrad
Commissioning Editor	Andrew Preston
Commissioning Assistant	Laura Potts
Editor	David Gibbon
Production	Ruth Arthur David Proffit Sally Connolly Karen Staff
Director of Production	Gerald Hughes

Photographic Sources
Imperial War Museum, London
Hulton Picture Company, London
Musée de l'Armée, Paris
Bettmann Archive, New York
Prints of illustrations credited to the Imperial War Museum are for sale on application to its Department of Photographs, Lambeth Road, London SE1 6HZ. The Visitors' Room is open to the public by appointment.

Author's Acknowledgement
The author would like acknowledge the assistance of the staff of Colour Library Books and of his colleagues at the Imperial War Museum, especially Jane Carmichael, Mike Hibberd, Laurie Milner and Chris McCarthy, during the preparation of this book.

CLB 2538
This edition published in 1994 by Tiger Books International PLC, London

Printed and bound in Singapore

ISBN 1-85501-403-3

CONTENTS

Left: *Australians outside the Hotel de Ville (or Town Hall) in Bapaume on 19 March 1917. On the night of 25 March, a booby-trap mine, left by the Germans and fitted with a delayed-action chemical fuse, finally exploded, killing a number of Australians and two French Deputies who were sleeping there.*
IWM: E (AUS) 393

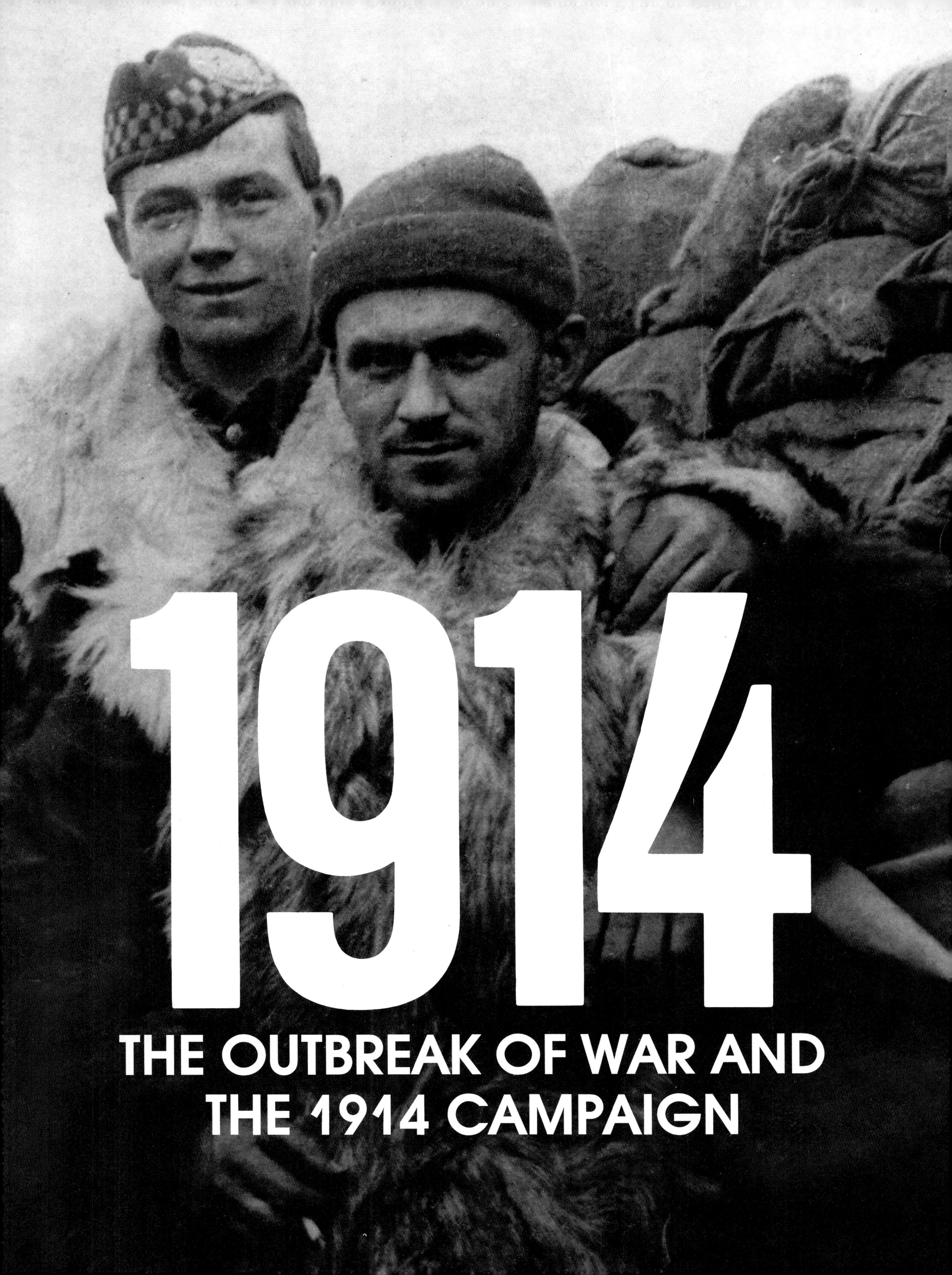

1914

THE OUTBREAK OF WAR AND THE 1914 CAMPAIGN

Previous page: *A group of men from the 2nd Argyll and Sutherland Highlanders wearing goatskin jackets of the type issued to British troops on the Western Front in the winter of 1914-1915.*
IWM: Q 48957

THE POWDER KEG OF EUROPE

The tangled threads of conflicting national ambitions, economic competition, colonial rivalries and new military and naval technology that led to the outbreak of the First World War, and to the formation of the Western Front, can be traced directly back to the defeat of France and the unification of Germany in the Franco-Prussian War of 1870-71. The creation of a German Empire, including the former French provinces of Alsace and Lorraine, upset the old balance of power in Europe, while Germany's rapid and remarkable economic expansion also provoked widespread envy and alarm. Until 1890 the diplomatic skill of the German Chancellor, Otto von Bismarck, kept France isolated, but deteriorating Russo-German relations obliged Germany to strengthen her ties with Austria-Hungary to ensure that she had at least one ally to the east. Although Germany was the dominant partner, she was now bound to a reactionary and ramshackle power which faced serious problems from the nationalist aspirations of her subject peoples in southeastern Europe. The situation in the Balkans was made even more volatile by the decline of Turkey, whose loss of authority in the region provided both Russia – the self-proclaimed protector of the southern Slavs – and Austria-Hungary with territorial and political opportunities which brought them onto a collision course. A third ingredient in the explosive Balkan mixture was the rise of Serbia. Already incensed by the Austrian annexation of Bosnia and Herzegovina in 1908, the Serbs emerged from the Balkan Wars of 1912 and 1913 with increased territory and influence, giving Austria extra cause for concern.

1 *Wilhelm II, Emperor of Germany from 1888 to 1918.*
IWM: Q 81824

Under the erratic and belligerent Wilhelm II, who became Emperor (*Kaiser*) in 1888, Germany pursued a more aggressive international policy. Fear of Germany's military and industrial might spurred Republican France to seek an alliance with Czarist Russia. France was anxious to avenge the defeat of 1870-71 and recover Alsace-Lorraine, while Russia needed a counterweight to the Austro-German alliance which cast a shadow over her western frontier and frustrated her ambitions in the Balkans. In 1892 France and Russia concluded a military agreement, promising to come to each other's aid if either were attacked by Germany. The German Navy Laws of 1898 and 1900, aiming to provide Germany with a fleet which would boost her bargaining powers in world affairs and simultaneously undermine the Royal Navy's long-standing supremacy, inevitably antagonised Britain, and inaugurated a bitter naval arms race that became more intense with the launching of the revolutionary, 'all-big-gun' turbine-driven battleship HMS *Dreadnought* in 1906. German support for the Boers during the South African War of 1899-1902 also persuaded Britain to forsake her isolationist posture and gravitate towards the Franco-Russian alliance. The *Entente Cordiale* of 1904 reinforced Franco-British diplomatic and, later, military links, smoothing the way for a similar understanding between Britain and Russia in 1907. Thus, by 1914 the major European nations were split into two rival alliances, with France, Britain and Russia ranged against the Central Powers – Germany and Austria-Hungary. Any incident involving one of these countries threatened to start a chain reaction, dragging them all into war.

Other factors undoubtedly contributed to the bellicose climate in Europe in 1914. The spread of education in the previous decades was accompanied by the growth of a popular press which glamorised the heroic, empire-building aspects of military life and followed a jingoistic line in foreign affairs. The fashionable concepts of 'Social Darwinism' and 'national efficiency' stressed the survival of the fittest and encouraged a view of war as a purifying agent which could arrest symptoms of national decadence. Almost everyone mistakenly believed that if war came it would be short. Moreover, in the years before 1914 European statesmen collectively failed to reassert the value of diplomatic rather than military solutions

2

2 *King Edward VII takes the salute during his State Visit to Paris in May 1903. Although Edward VII's influence on foreign policy has sometimes been overestimated, his visit to Paris was a symbol of improving relations between Britain and France, and itself contributed to the changing climate of opinion which led to the signing of the Anglo-French Entente in 1904.*
IWM: Q 81788

3 *Russian infantry in review order at a parade held during the State Visit to St Petersburg of President Poincaré of France in July 1914.*
IWM: Q 81723

3

4

4 *The launching of HMS* Dreadnought *at Portsmouth on 10 February 1906. The building of the* Dreadnought *rendered almost all other battleships obsolete, but set in motion a new and more dangerous phase of the 'naval race' between Britain and Germany.*
IWM: Q 41435

to international disputes. Nonetheless, since the work of Professor Fritz Fischer in the 1960s, historians generally agree that, while not exclusively responsible for the eventual European conflict, Germany was certainly the prime mover. Her political and military leaders saw war as an answer to her internal and external problems and as a means of assuring Germany's standing and expansion as a world power. They therefore welcomed war in 1914 and were prepared to exploit any significant crisis in order to engineer its outbreak. As Dr Paul Kennedy has observed, Germany possessed the only *offensive* war plan which included not just a violation of neutral territory but also an attack on another power, regardless of whether or not the latter actually wished to become involved.

THE RIVAL WAR PLANS AND ARMIES

Of all the war plans drawn up by the great powers before 1914, Germany's played the biggest part in shaping the course of the subsequent conflict. As developed between 1897 and 1905 by Count Alfred von Schlieffen, then Chief of the German General Staff, the plan was determined by the possibility that Germany would face a war on two fronts, against France and Russia. Calculating that Russia would be slower to deploy and was unlikely to attack for some six weeks, Schlieffen proposed that Germany should deliver a massive blow in the west to defeat France in a lightning campaign. Once France was beaten, Germany could shift most of her forces to the east to deal with Russia. Afraid that the western offensive

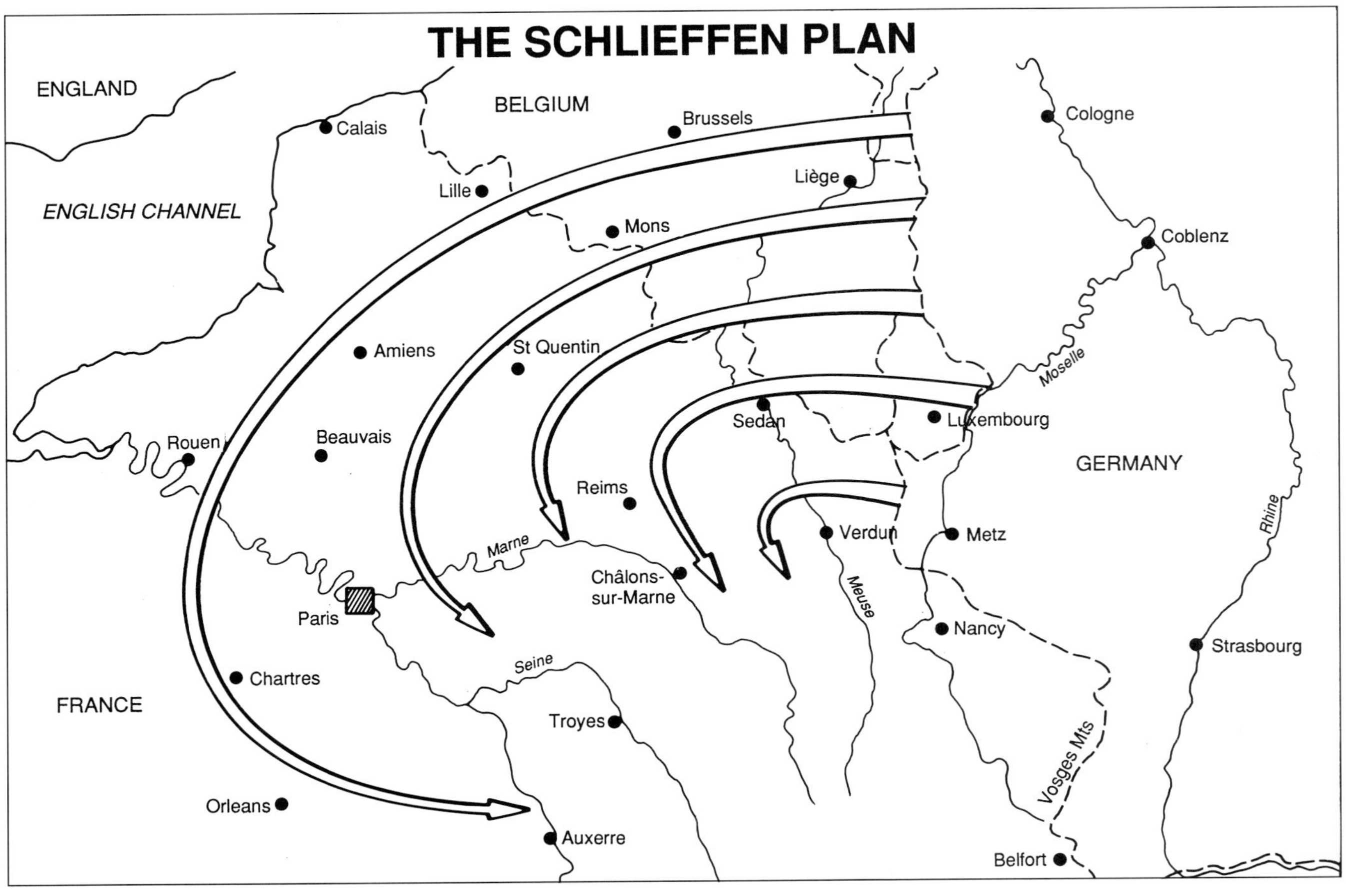

might be delayed by the fortresses on France's northeastern frontier, Schlieffen decided that Germany must attack across a narrow strip of Dutch territory known as the 'Maastricht Appendix' and through neutral Belgium before sweeping into northwestern France. The crucial role in the offensive was assigned to five armies, stretching from Metz to Holland and totalling thirty-five corps. The strongest forces were placed on the extreme right wing, where one army would swing round west of Paris at the outer edge of a gigantic wheeling movement designed to take the French armies in the rear and crush them up against their own frontier. Two weaker armies on the German left wing were to contain the expected French thrust into Lorraine and were even to withdraw slowly, if necessary, so that the French forces on this flank might be enticed beyond the point from which they could intervene against the German encirclement.

Between 1906 and 1914, Schlieffen's plan was modified by his successor, Colonel-General Helmuth von Moltke. Conscientious, but also introspective and lacking in self-confidence, Moltke worried about the danger which a powerful French drive into Lorraine might pose to German communications. Most of the new divisions formed after 1906 were therefore allocated to the left wing, not the right. Under Schlieffen the right wing was seven times stronger than the left; under Moltke it was only three times as strong. Moltke also dropped the idea of advancing through Holland, although the movement through Belgium was retained. This had the effect of constricting the right wing armies into a potential bottleneck, but did not remove the diplomatic risks attendant upon a violation of neutrality. Arguably, the Schlieffen Plan, even in its original form, would still have failed, since it gave too little consideration to over-extended supply lines, poor communications systems, the friction of battle and human exhaustion, as well as misjudging the strength of Belgian resistance and the speed of Russian mobilisation. Equally, however, Moltke may be said to have robbed it of any remaining chance of success without putting anything better in its place.

Germany's military system, based on conscription, enabled her to expand her Army quickly from a peacetime strength of about 840,000 to over 4,000,000 trained men at the outbreak of war. Fit young Germans joined the *Landsturm* at 17, then, at the age of 20, were called to the colours for full-time training for two or three years, according to their arm of service. After this they spent four or five years in the reserve before further periods of service in the *Landwehr* and *Landsturm* until they were 45. On mobilisation, the *Landwehr* and *Landsturm* were available for home defence or lines of communication duties, while reservists were either recalled to regular formations or helped to form reserve divisions and corps which were employed as front-line units. This system gave the Germans an important numerical advantage over the French at vital points in the early weeks of the coming conflict. German infantry training in 1914 was in a state of transition between close-order and open-order tactics, but the Army had a backbone of high-quality NCOs and enjoyed a marked superiority in light, medium and heavy howitzers.

The French, too, had compulsory service, extended in 1913 to three years with the colours and fourteen in the reserve. Having a smaller population than Germany, France was forced to call up a greater

1 *Count Alfred von Schlieffen, Chief of the German General Staff from 1891 to 1905. His war plan, though modified by his successor von Moltke, formed the basis of Germany's strategy in 1914.*
IWM: HU 1777

proportion of her manhood annually, including colonial recruits, to achieve anything approaching parity. As it was, France was able to field some 3,680,000 trained men when war came, though she possessed fewer reserve formations. Following the defeat of 1870-71, French military doctrine had been remoulded. Inspired by the teachings of Lieutenant-Colonel (later General) Ferdinand Foch, first as Chief Instructor (1896-1901) and then as Commandant (1908-11) of the *Ecole Supérieure de Guerre*, the French Army became imbued with the 'will to conquer' and a belief in the virtues of the *offensive à l'outrance* (attack to the limit). A disciple of Foch who did much to promote the offensive gospel was Colonel Louis de Grandmaison, head of the Operations Branch at the War Ministry from 1908 to 1911. The emphasis placed on *élan* (dash) and *cran* (guts) led the French to undervalue medium and heavy artillery, even if their excellent, quick-firing 75mm field gun was superior in numbers, range and accuracy to its German 77mm equivalent.

The French war plan, known as Plan XVII, was drawn up under the aegis of the impassive General Joseph Joffre, who had been appointed Chief of the General Staff in 1911 and was Commander-in-Chief designate if war came. The plan, reflecting the influence of the Foch-Grandmaison school, discarded an earlier proposal for a defensive deployment along the Belgian frontier and embodied Joffre's intention to 'advance with all forces united to attack the German armies'. Of the five French field armies to be deployed, the First and Second on the right wing would attack into Lorraine, just as Schlieffen had wanted; the Third Army, in the centre, would attack towards Metz and Thionville, and the Fifth Army, positioned on the left between Montmédy and Mézières, could either follow the direction of the Third Army or move northeast through Luxembourg and the Belgian Ardennes, depending on the route the Germans took. The Fourth Army, held in semi-reserve, would reinforce the centre or left as circumstances dictated. Plan XVII was less rigid than the Schlieffen Plan but it also suffered from a major flaw. By discounting evidence about the German use of reserve troops alongside regular units, the French seriously underestimated the strength and width of the German move through Belgium.

2 *German infantry on manoeuvres before the First World War.*
IWM: Q 53446

3 *General (later Marshal) Joseph Joffre. Appointed Chief of the French General Staff in 1911, he became Commander-in-Chief of the French Army from the outbreak of war until December 1916. Joffre's belief in the superiority of the offensive was embodied in Plan XVII. When the French plan collapsed in the crisis of August-September 1914, his calm leadership was a major factor in enabling the Allies to halt the Germans on the Marne. However, he failed to find a solution to the subsequent trench deadlock and was eventually replaced by Nivelle after the Battle of Verdun.*

THE RIVAL WAR PLANS AND ARMIES

Neutral Belgium introduced general conscription in 1913, but her forces were in the process of reorganisation and were torn by internal strategic debate. She could mobilise only 117,000 officers and men for her Field Army in 1914. Britain, protected against invasion by the Royal Navy, was still content to maintain a small, long-service volunteer Army, this being considered adequate to police her far-flung Empire. Including its Regular Reserve, Special Reserve and the part-time Territorial Force, the British Army mustered barely 700,000 on mobilisation. Its main striking element was an Expeditionary Force of six infantry divisions and a cavalry division, totalling about 120,000. The Territorial Force of 'Saturday Afternoon Soldiers' had been created from the old Volunteer Force in 1908 and was 268,777 strong in July 1914. Formed primarily for home defence, it offered a framework for an expansion of the Army if the need arose. Like the French, the British Army as a whole was deficient in heavy artillery, yet, man for man, its troops were better trained than any in Europe. Learning from the experiences of the South African War, it had a unique standard of rifle-shooting, with many soldiers capable of firing fifteen aimed rounds a minute. There was no binding agreement to send the British Expeditionary Force (BEF) to the Continent in the event of war, although secret Anglo-French staff talks since 1906 had made this probable. Indeed, because no one had presented a viable alternative, the only plan for the BEF's mobilisation and deployment likely to be put into effect was the detailed scheme prepared after 1910 by the Director of Military Operations, Brigadier-General Henry Wilson, a friend of Foch and a fervent admirer of France. This laid down that the BEF would concentrate on the left of the French, in the Le Cateau-Maubeuge-Hirson triangle. Few bothered to explore the full implications of a Continental commitment, such as the possibility that Britain might ultimately have to raise a mass army.

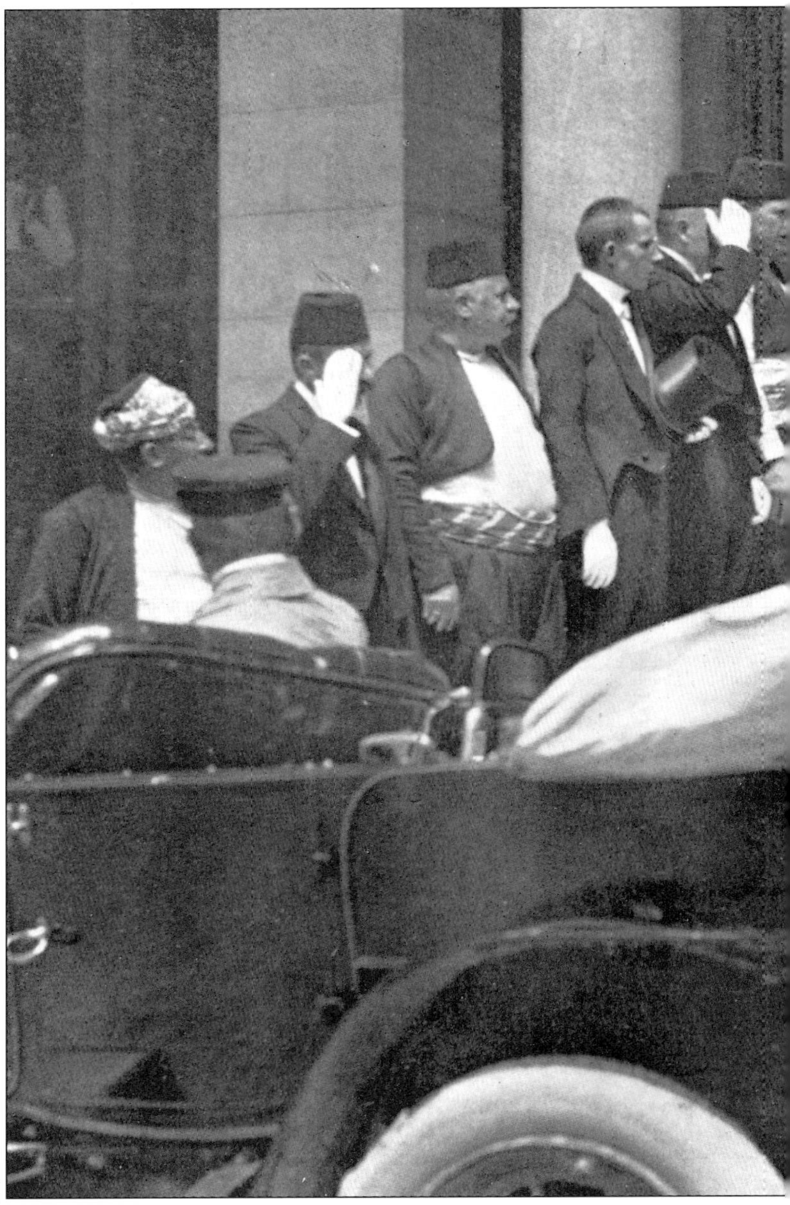

1

EUROPE MOBILISES FOR WAR

On Sunday, 28 June 1914, Archduke Franz Ferdinand, the heir to the Austrian throne, was assassinated with his wife in Sarajevo, the capital of the recently-annexed Austrian province of Bosnia. This incident in the Balkans was the spark which finally ignited the European powder keg.

The assassin, a student named Gavrilo Princip, was a member of the Young Bosnia organisation, a nationalist movement seeking union with Serbia. A secret Serbian terrorist group, the Black Hand, supported the movement but there was no conclusive proof that the Serbian government itself was implicated in the plot. In spite of this, Austria seized the opportunity to humiliate Serbia and reduce the threat she posed to Austro-Hungarian influence in southeastern Europe. After making sure of Germany's unconditional support, Austria gave a ten-point ultimatum to Serbia on 23 July. Although most of the points were accepted, the Serbs refused to agree to

2

1 *Archduke Franz Ferdinand and his wife leaving the City Hall in Sarajevo, a few minutes before their assassination on 28 June 1914.*
IWM: Q 81831

2 *A German officer reads out the Kaiser's order for mobilisation on 1 August 1914.*
IWM: Q 81755

ultimatum calling upon her to stop mobilising, Germany herself ordered mobilisation and declared war on Russia on 1 August. The French also mobilised that day. For all the powers involved, much appeared to depend on their ability to concentrate and deploy their forces before the enemy. The rapid transportation of the mass conscript armies hinged, in turn, on the efficiency of each country's railways. Statesmen and soldiers were reluctant to disrupt the intricate timetables once the machinery was in motion. Thus, if the mobilisation timetables did not cause the war,

3 *The scene in Parliament Square, outside the House of Commons, on Bank Holiday Monday, 3 August 1914, as Londoners wait for the latest news of the European crisis.*
IWM: Q 81792

4 *German troops leave by train on the first stage of their journey to the front, August 1914.*
IWM: Q 81779

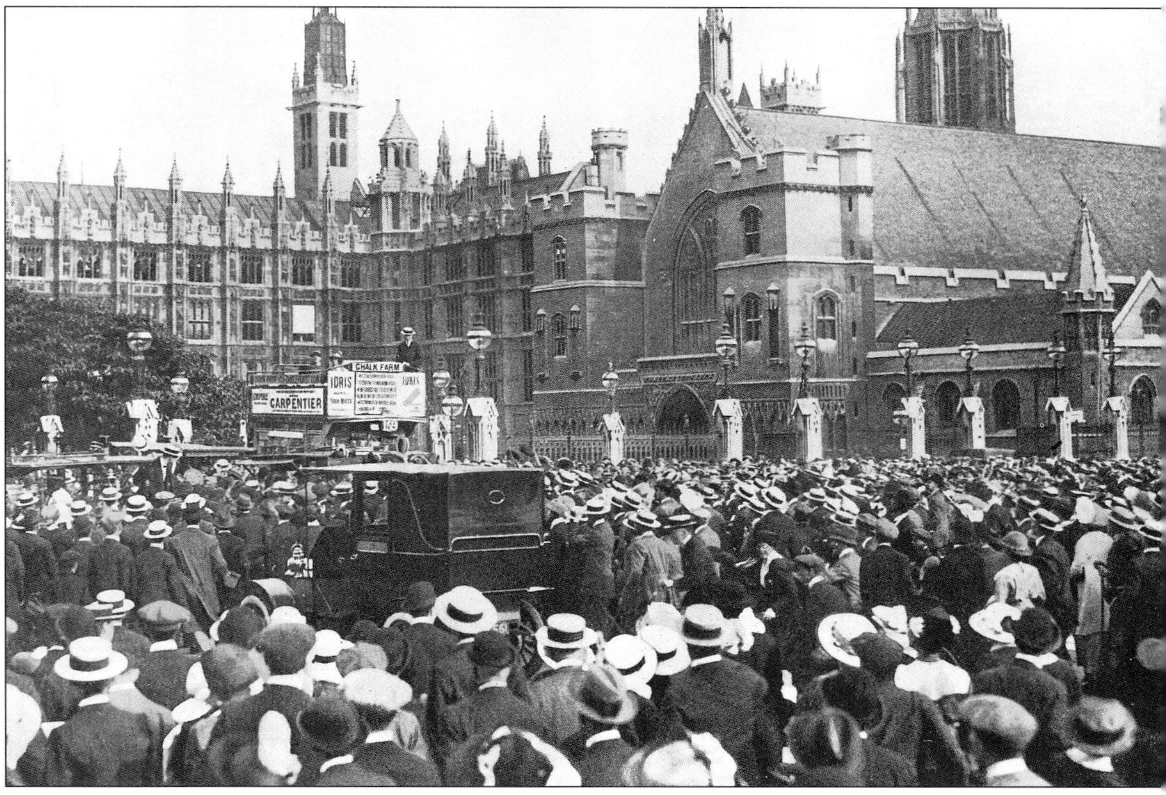

3

4

5

the demand that Austrian officials should be involved in the investigation of the assassination plot. On 28 July Austria-Hungary declared war on Serbia. Two days later Czar Nicholas II ordered general Russian mobilisation in support of the Serbs. The whole network of alliances was consequently called into play, plunging Europe into catastrophe.

When Russia failed to respond to a German they hampered the delicate processes of negotiation as the war clouds gathered. Because of the nature of the Schlieffen Plan this was especially true in Germany's case. On 2 August Germany presented a note to Belgium demanding the right of passage through her territory. This ultimatum, too, was firmly rejected. The following day Germany declared war on France and early on 4 August her troops invaded

5 *Slogans chalked on the side of a railway truck forming part of a German troop train in August 1914.*
IWM: Q 81763

Belgium. The weight of the German forces was awesome. Colonel-General Alexander von Kluck's First Army, on the extreme right, alone numbered 320,000, while next to it in line, Colonel-General Karl von Bülow's Second Army and General Max von Hausen's Third Army respectively comprised 260,000 and 180,000 men. It was the violation of Belgium's frontier that brought Britain into the conflict. Bound by treaty to guarantee Belgian neutrality, and ever sensitive about threats to the Channel ports, Britain declared war on Germany at 11 pm (London time) on 4 August. The cast for the first act of the great European tragedy was now assembled.

1 *Popular enthusiasm for the war is evident in this photograph of a French infantry regiment being given a rousing send-off by a crowd in 1914.*
IWM: Q 81730

2 *A German 42cm 'Big Bertha' howitzer of the type used to bombard the Liège forts in August 1914. The model in service in 1914 had a rate of fire of ten rounds per hour, the projectile weighing 1,800lbs. The weapon's maximum range in 1914 was 10,250 yards, although it was more accurate at about 9,500 yards.*
IWM: Q 65817

3 *The shattered remains of one of the armoured gun cupolas at Fort Loncin, Liège, after the bombardment by German 42cm howitzers. Fort Loncin was situated northwest of Liège. On 15 August 1914 a shell exploded in its magazine and blew up the fort from within. Lieutenant-General Gerard Leman, the Governor of Liège, was in the fort at the time and, although he was knocked unconscious and pinned beneath masonry, he survived to be taken prisoner by the Germans.*
IWM: Q 45995

THE INVASION OF BELGIUM

Moltke's changes to the Schlieffen Plan meant that the armies on the German right wing had to squeeze through the narrow Meuse gateway between the Dutch frontier and the Ardennes. This gap, and the principal crossings of the Meuse, were dominated by Liège and its surrounding ring of twelve forts. The success of the German right wing was therefore conditional upon the swift capture of the Liège forts, for failure here would throw the whole elaborate timetable into disarray at the outset. As head of the mobilisation and deployment section of the General Staff from 1908-13, Erich Ludendorff had devoted much of his attention to preparing a scheme for the assault. Now a Major-General, Ludendorff was Deputy Chief of Staff of von Bülow's Second Army and was temporarily attached to the force of six brigades, under General von Emmich, which had been specially assigned to the operation.

The Liège forts could withstand the fire of guns up to 21cm in calibre but, since 1909, thanks to the Skoda works at Pilsen and the Krupp works at Essen, the Germans had secretly added the huge 30.5cm and 42cm 'Big Bertha' howitzers to their arsenal. Both weapons were capable of hurling massive, armour-piercing shells over seven miles. As yet unaware of the power of these monsters, the Belgians compounded their own problems by a confused and faulty deployment. The cautious Belgian Chief of Staff, General de Selliers de Moranville, had placed the bulk of his forces in a central position behind the River Gette covering Brussels and offering an escape

4 *Belgian Carabiniers, with dog-drawn machine guns, during the retreat to Antwerp on 20 August 1914. The photograph provides a good illustration of the transitional state of the Belgian Army in 1914.*
IWM: Q 70232

5 *Albert I, King of the Belgians. He commanded the Belgian Army in its fighting retreat during the German invasion of his country in 1914. Subsequently, King Albert opposed Belgian participation in Allied offensive operations until the autumn of 1918, when he was made commander of the Flanders Army Group, comprising French, British and Belgian divisions. Under King Albert the Flanders Army Group played an important part in the final Allied offensive on the Western Front. He is pictured here at work in his headquarters at La Panne in 1917.*
IWM: Q 3080

route to Antwerp if needed. King Albert, who became Commander-in-Chief on the outbreak of war, wanted to concentrate further forward on the Meuse, between the Liège and Namur forts, where the Belgian Army could delay the Germans more effectively until the French and British came to its support. In the circumstances, he only had time to hurry a division and a brigade to reinforce Liège and send another division to Namur.

The German assault had an inauspicious start. Attacking in five main columns on 5 August, von Emmich's troops began to suffer heavy casualties and some units lost momentum. Ludendorff took personal charge of the attack in the centre and by 7 August he had penetrated between the forts and entered Liège itself, where he boldly demanded, and secured, the surrender of the Citadel, making him a national hero. Most of the forts held out until 12 August when the giant siege howitzers arrived and opened their terrifying bombardment. Within another four days all the forts had been battered into submission, the last two falling on 16 August. The way was clear for the German right wing armies to advance. Ludendorff left for the Eastern Front to become Chief of Staff of the Eighth Army under General Paul von Hindenburg.

Having waited in vain behind the Gette for the French and British, the Belgian Field Army withdrew, on 18 August, to the fortress of Antwerp. The Germans

1

1 *Belgian troops guarding a bridge over a railway at Louvain, 20 August 1914.*
IWM: Q 53202

2

2 *Ruined and damaged buildings around the Hotel de Ville in Louvain after the burning and looting of the city by the Germans between 25 and 30 August 1914. The burning of Louvain followed alleged incidents in which Belgian civilians were said to have fired shots at rearguards of von Kluck's First Army. The destruction in Louvain was quickly seized upon by Allied propagandists as an example of German 'frightfulness'.*
IWM: Q 53271

3

3 *French infantry in action during the opening weeks of the war.*
IWM: Q 81724

4 *The German 47th Infantry Regiment, part of the 10th Division in Crown Prince Wilhelm's Fifth Army, advancing across a field in northeastern France in August 1914.*
IWM: Q 53422

entered Brussels on 20 August and laid siege to Namur. Again their powerful weapons – including 28cm howitzers – wrought havoc. The city of Namur fell on 24 August and the last of its forts soon afterwards. In trying to keep to their timetable and avoid leaving large forces to protect their rear, the Germans adopted a policy of *Schrecklichkeit* (frightfulness), intended to cow the population by the destruction of property and the execution of civilians. Louvain, with its famous library of priceless medieval manuscripts, was burned in reprisal for alleged civilian resistance against von Kluck's rearguard. Whether or not the defence of Liège and subsequent Belgian demolitions and resistance really delayed the Germans is debatable. The evidence suggests that the Germans crossed Belgium more or less on schedule but might have *gained* four or five days had the opposition been lighter. Much more significant was the fact that the Germans detached up to five corps from the attacking strength of their right wing to invest Antwerp, Namur and Maubeuge.

THE CLASH ON THE FRONTIERS

Plan XVII was set in motion on 6 August. The French VII Corps, commanded by General Bonneau, moved into Upper Alsace, but was soon forced into an ignominious withdrawal by German reinforcements from Strasbourg. A second attempt by a special Army of Alsace, under General Pau, commenced on 14 August. Mulhouse was retaken before the threats to the Allied centre and left compelled Joffre to order another withdrawal so that Pau's troops could be employed elsewhere. The French were able to retain only a tiny portion of Alsace in the eastern foothills of the Vosges.

5 *A German field artillery battery on the march during the advance into France in 1914.*
IWM: Q 56553

The main French advance into Lorraine by the First Army (Dubail) and the Second Army (de Castelnau) also started on 14 August. Schlieffen had envisaged that the German left wing armies should give ground and lure the French on, away from the decisive right wing. However, Crown Prince Rupprecht of Bavaria sought permission for his own German Sixth Army and von Heeringen's Seventh Army to counterattack. Himself tempted by the prospect of enveloping both French flanks, Moltke let the commanders on the spot have their way. At the ensuing actions of Morhange and Sarrebourg on 20

August, the French infantry, clad in their blue coats and conspicuous red trousers, quickly found that the offensive spirit alone would not suffice to overcome modern artillery and well-positioned machine guns. Suffering enormous casualties, the French were checked and then thrown back on their frontier fortifications, although they recovered in time to mount a successful defence of Nancy and the Moselle line. The Germans, therefore, had merely inflicted a reverse rather than a major defeat on the French right and, as the battle here died down, Joffre was again granted the opportunity of switching troops from this sector to more vulnerable parts of the front.

Persisting in the belief that the Germans would not make extensive use of reservists, and ignorant of the real width of the German sweep through Belgium, Joffre wrongly judged that the German centre would be comparatively weak. Ordered to attack northeast into the Ardennes, Ruffey's Third Army and De Langle de Cary's Fourth Army stumbled into the Germans around Virton and Neufchâteau on 21-22 August and also recoiled with heavy losses.

In a belated and ill-conceived effort to coordinate the operations of the German right wing armies, Moltke, on 17 August, placed the aggressive Kluck under the orders of the more tentative Bülow, much to Kluck's disgust. One result of this step was to inhibit von Kluck from swinging his First Army as far west as was necessary to outflank the Allied left. Nevertheless, as the French Fifth Army on this flank marched up to the Sambre and Meuse, between Charleroi and Givet, its commander, Lanrezac, began to understand the true nature of the German strength and movements, even if his warnings caused him to be regarded by some at French General Headquarters as a defeatist. Coming at him through Belgium from the north and east were von Bülow's Second Army and von Hausen's Third Army. French hopes of an offensive to the northeast virtually disappeared on 21 August as Bülow's forces got across the Sambre. Next day, French counterattacks failed and, instead of waiting for Hausen as agreed, Bülow pushed the French back a further five miles. Bülow's uncharacteristic impetuosity partly negated the intended effect of Hausen's crossing of the Meuse on 23 August, since the French Fifth Army was now too far south to be taken easily in the rear, but Hausen's appearance on his right was enough to persuade Lanrezac that he must act promptly to save the Fifth Army from destruction.

THE BATTLE OF MONS

The British Expeditionary Force, commanded by Field-Marshal Sir John French, had by now assembled on the left of the line, in the Maubeuge-Le Cateau area. Field-Marshal Lord Kitchener, who had been appointed Secretary of State for War on 5 August, rightly foresaw that this advanced concentration area would considerably increase the risks of the BEF being swamped by the powerful German forces massing north of the Meuse. He was too late to alter the zone

1 *Men of the 4th Battalion, Royal Fusiliers (9th Brigade, 3rd Division), resting in the Grand Place at Mons after a tiring march on 22 August 1914. The following day the battalion was in action against the German 18th Division, which attacked the positions occupied by the Royal Fusiliers on the Mons-Condé Canal at Nimy, two miles north of Mons itself. During this engagement Lieutenant Maurice Dease and Private S.F. Godley of the 4th Royal Fusiliers both won the Victoria Cross. Dease's award was posthumous, as he was mortally wounded at Mons, while Godley was taken prisoner. The battalion suffered over 150 casualties at Mons but retired in good order at 2pm on the afternoon of 23 August.*
IWM: Q 70071

2 *Colonel-General Alexander von Kluck. Already sixty-eight years old at the outbreak of the First World War, he commanded the German First Army, which had the key role on the extreme right wing in the sweep through Belgium and France in August 1914. It was the First Army that fought the British at Mons on 23 August. Severely wounded in 1915, von Kluck retired the following year.*
IWM: Q 45327

of assembly but, because of anxieties about a possible invasion, kept two Regular divisions at home for a time, leaving Sir John French with only four infantry divisions and a cavalry division at the outset of the campaign. The temper of the mercurial Sir John was not improved when Grierson, the commander of II Corps, died of a heart attack on his way to the front and Kitchener replaced him with General Sir Horace Smith-Dorrien, an officer whom Sir John disliked. In all other respects, the mobilisation and assembly of the BEF proceeded with unprecedented smoothness, and on 22 August the British divisions moved up to the drab industrial region of Mons, ready to advance further into Belgium as part of the Allied offensive on the left wing. They were also directly in the path of Kluck's First Army sweeping down from the northeast.

Sir John French soon learned that Lanrezac had been unable to prevent the Germans from crossing the Sambre the previous day. The BEF was dangerously exposed but Sir John agreed to stand at Mons for twenty-four hours to cover Lanrezac's left. Smith-Dorrien's II Corps held the line of the Mons-Condé Canal and a small salient around the town. To its right, and echeloned back at a sharp angle to the southeast, was I Corps under Lieutenant-General Sir Douglas Haig. As yet, Kluck was largely unaware of the British presence on his own immediate line of advance. Consequently, on the morning of 23 August, his units ran head-on into the BEF and were condemned to ill-coordinated and piecemeal frontal assaults, which began with probes by the German IX Corps against

3 *A German pontoon bridge over the Mons-Condé Canal at Jemappes on 24 August. The bridge was constructed by engineers of the 6th Division of the German First Army on 23-24 August, following the British withdrawal. Note the smoke from a house which is still burning the day after the battle. The picture was taken by a local photographer from Jemappes by order of the Germans.*
IWM: Q 70073

3

1 Troops of the German 18th Division, part of IX Corps in von Kluck's First Army, passing through Mons on the heels of the retreating BEF on 24 August 1914.
IWM: Q 70072

2 The 1st Battalion, The Cameronians (Scottish Rifles), halted at a farm on 24 August 1914, the day after the Battle of Mons. The officer on the extreme left, Major C.B. Vandeleur, is looking up through binoculars at a German aircraft. Seated next to Vandeleur is Lieutenant-Colonel P.R. Robertson, the battalion's commanding officer.
IWM: Q 51478

the salient on Smith-Dorrien's right and then developed westwards along the canal as III and IV Corps arrived. Attacking in dense formations, the Germans were decimated by the BEF's superb musketry, although the British swiftly came to appreciate the weight and accuracy of German artillery fire. With Haig's I Corps scarcely involved, II Corps held its own until, in the late afternoon, sheer pressure of numbers caused it to withdraw some two miles to positions which had been shrewdly selected earlier in the day.

In the first British battle in Western Europe since Waterloo, the BEF had acquitted itself well, delaying von Kluck for twenty-four hours at a cost of 1,600 casualties, almost all in II Corps. That night, however, Lanrezac – menaced on his right near Dinant, on the Meuse – ordered the general retirement of his Fifth Army, without consulting either Joffre or Sir John French. The British had to fall back in conformity with their allies, slipping away just as von Kluck resolved to make renewed attempts to envelop the BEF's open left flank.

2

1

3 General Sir Horace Smith-Dorrien, who commanded the British II Corps at Mons and Le Cateau in August 1914. Although his decision to stand and fight at Le Cateau on 26 August further strained an already tense relationship with Sir John French, the Commander-in-Chief of the BEF, Smith-Dorrien was placed at the head of the newly formed Second Army in the December reorganisation of the British forces on the Western Front. However, he was blamed for the failure of a diversionary attack near Mount Kemmel in March 1915, and was replaced by Plumer in May.
IWM: Q 70054

THE GREAT RETREAT AND THE MIRACLE OF THE MARNE

All along the vast battlefront the Allied armies were in retreat, though they were not routed or destroyed and remained capable of determined rearguard actions. As Plan XVII collapsed around him and the appalling truth about the German employment of Reserve units became clearer, the unflappable Joffre was at his best. With his mind still fixed on an eventual resumption of the offensive, he calmly drew troops from the French right and from his own reserves to form a new Sixth Army, under General Maunoury, on the threatened Allied left. Moltke, in contrast, was growing increasingly nervous and irresolute in his remote headquarters at Coblenz. Fast succumbing to the allure of a possible double envelopment of the

3

4

5

Allies, and having unwisely let the German left wing armies have their head, he hammered another nail into the coffin of the Schlieffen Plan on 25 August by sending two corps from the all-important right wing to help stem the advancing Russian tide in East Prussia. Taking into account the other formations still detached to cover or invest various fortresses, the combined strength of the three German right wing armies had been reduced by over a quarter and their primary objective had not yet been achieved.

Marching over twenty miles a day under the blazing August sun, Allied and German soldiers alike shared the hardships of hunger, thirst, blistered feet and, above all, fatigue. After Mons the two corps of the BEF had become separated by the Forest of Mormal. On 26 August Smith-Dorrien felt that the Germans were too close to II Corps for him to disengage without a battle so, against Sir John French's wishes, he fought a holding action at Le Cateau. Once more the BEF's disciplined rifle fire exacted a heavy toll of the enemy. Despite losing 7,182 officers and men and 38 guns, II Corps was able to continue its retirement in reasonably good order, but Smith-Dorrien's relations with Sir John French were irreparably strained. The decision to stand at Le Cateau was justified, however, for the resistance he met there led von Kluck to overestimate the BEF's strength and deterred him from immediate pursuit. Kluck also wrongly concluded that the BEF was retiring to the southwest rather than southwards, thus permitting it to retreat almost unmolested for five more days. The temporary easing of pressure did not greatly change the pessimistic outlook of the British Commander-in-Chief. Depressed by the BEF's losses and disillusioned with the French – especially Lanrezac – Sir John was now certain that he could only preserve the BEF by removing it from the line of

4 *Part of the British 5th Cavalry Brigade during the retreat from Mons.*
IWM: Q 60698

5 *The 11th Hussars resting near Gournay, to the east of Paris and just south of the River Marne, on 4 September 1914, at the end of the retreat from Mons. They are in the grounds of a chateau at Champs, about a mile from Gournay. The chateau was the property of the wife of Major-General Charles Townshend, who surrendered to the Turks at Kut al Amara in Mesopotamia in April 1916. The officer standing in the foreground is Captain F.G.A. Arkwright of 'A' Squadron. He was killed in an accident in October 1915 while serving with the Royal Flying Corps.*
IWM: Q 51200

1 *General Joseph Galliéni. Having served as Governor of Madagascar from 1896 to 1905, he was nearing retirement when he turned down the post of Chief of the French General Staff in 1911, recommending Joffre, once his subordinate in Madagascar, for the appointment. He was recalled to service on the outbreak of war in 1914 and became Military Governor of Paris on 26 August. It was Galliéni who spotted that von Kluck's wheel east of Paris at the beginning of September offered the Allies the chance of an attack against the exposed German right flank. This was a vital contribution to the Allied success on the Marne. Galliéni stayed on as Governor of Paris until he was appointed Minister of War in October 1915. He was unhappy about the conduct of operations but lacked the political influence to have Joffre removed, so Galliéni himself resigned in March 1916. He died in May of the same year. He was posthumously created a Marshal of France in 1921.*
IWM: Q 65476

2 *Colonel-General Helmuth Graf von Moltke, Chief of the German General Staff from 1906 to 1914. His failure to exercise adequate control over the operations of his right wing armies, and his subsequent loss of nerve under pressure, led to the German reverse on the Marne and to his own replacement by von Falkenhayn.*
IWM: Q 81806

3 *The first-line transport of the 1st Battalion, The Middlesex Regiment, under shrapnel fire on the road between Signy and Signets on 8 September 1914, during the Battle of the Marne. The man in the centre of the photograph has been wounded in the head and his face is covered with blood. Nine horses were killed and a watercart was riddled with shrapnel.*
IWM: Q 51489

battle and withdrawing behind the Seine. It required a hurriedly-arranged personal visit to France by Kitchener on 1 September to stop him doing so.

Since losing contact with the BEF, Kluck had been released from Bülow's direct control on 27 August and had initially pushed on southwest towards Amiens. By 28 August he had discounted the BEF and was much attracted by the idea of wheeling inwards to drive Lanrezac away from Paris and to roll up the left of the French Fifth Army. A reluctant Lanrezac was ordered by Joffre to face to the west and execute a counterattack between St Quentin and Guise, an operation in which Haig was forbidden to participate by Sir John French. As things turned out, Lanrezac conducted the whole affair with no little skill and, on 29 August, the French I Corps, under the dynamic General Franchet d'Esperey, administered such a bloody rebuff at Guise to the élite Guard Corps of the German Second Army that Bülow appealed to Kluck for support. This cry for help gave Kluck the excuse he needed. On 30 August, and before referring the matter to Moltke, he ordered the wheel inwards, a manoeuvre which would cause his First Army to pass northeast of Paris, not west as planned. Moltke, out of touch and losing his grip on his subordinates, limply acquiesced. The shift in the axis of advance of the German right

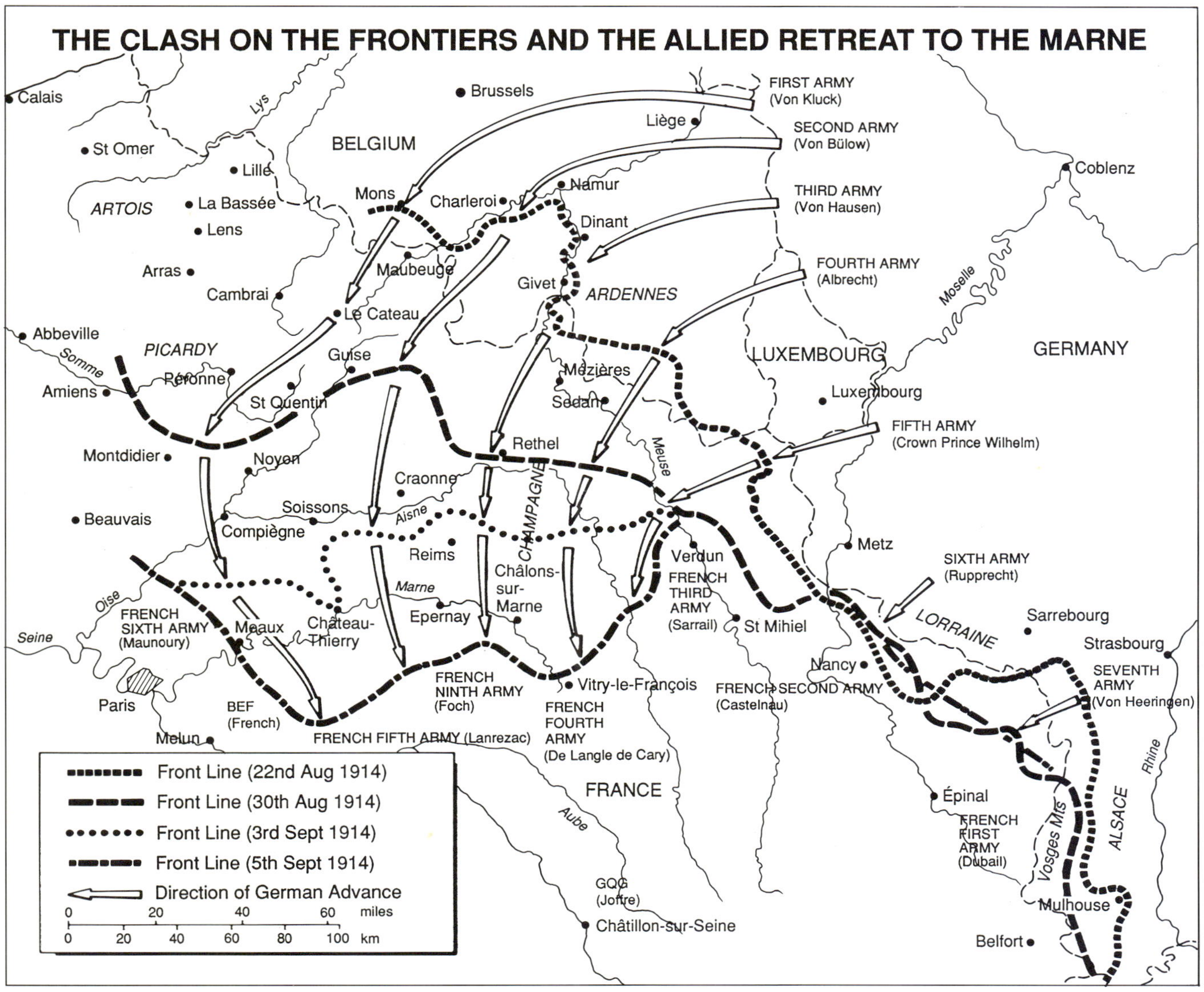

4 *Lieutenant-General Sir Douglas Haig (left), commander of the British I Corps, confers with Major-General Charles Monro, commander of the 2nd Division, in a street in France. When Haig was placed at the head of the First Army, Monro took over I Corps and himself went on to command both the First and the Third Armies on the Western Front. Second from right in this picture is Brigadier-General John Gough, Haig's gifted chief of staff and brother of Hubert Gough, then leading the 2nd Cavalry Division. 'Johnnie' Gough, who had won the VC in Somaliland in 1903, was mortally wounded by a sniper's bullet while visiting the front line near Fauquissart in February 1915. Here he is talking to Brigadier-General E.M. Perceval, the CRA (or senior artillery officer) of the 2nd Division.*
IWM: Q 54992

wing was the last in a series of fatal modifications to the Schlieffen Plan, as it rendered Kluck's flank vulnerable to counterattack by Maunoury's Sixth Army, which was now north of the French capital.

The full implications of Kluck's change of course were not grasped by the Allies for another three or four days. Kluck reappeared on the BEF's heels, causing lively rearguard actions like the one at Néry on 1 September, when 'L' Battery of the Royal Horse Artillery won three Victoria Crosses. On 3 September the BEF crossed the Marne, having retreated 200 miles to date, but by the following day, thanks to invaluable aerial reconnaissance reports, the vital opening offered by Kluck's exposed flank had been perceived by General Galliéni, the Military Governor of Paris. On 4 September, with Kluck ahead of Bülow and across the Marne, Galliéni persuaded Joffre to stop the retreat and order a general counterattack by the Allied left.

Between 5 and 7 September Kluck responded to Maunoury's attacks on his sensitive flank by skilfully reversing three of his corps and pivoting to the west to confront the French Sixth Army on the Ourcq. Reinforcements despatched from Paris in taxicabs could not prevent Maunoury's forces from being driven back, although Kluck's latest movement westwards widened the gap between himself and von

4

1 *'D' Company of the 1st Battalion, The Cameronians (Scottish Rifles), crossing a pontoon bridge over the River Marne at La Ferté sous Jouarre on 10 September 1914 during the BEF's advance to the Aisne. The Marne is between 200 and 300 feet wide at this point, but the pontoons immediately available only sufficed to span about 75 feet of the river. The Royal Engineers, however, collected boats, barges and extra planking to enable the 19th Brigade to cross.*
IWM: Q 51493

2 *A position held by the Machine Gun Section of the 1st Cameronians at St Marguerite, towards the left of the British line on the Aisne, on 19 September 1914.*
IWM: Q 51498

Bülow. The latter was in fact coping well with the French Fifth Army, now under Franchet d'Esperey, and the newly formed Ninth Army, under Foch. However, the BEF recrossed the Marne on 9 September, advancing slowly into the gap on the German right. A worried von Bülow thereupon ordered a retreat, his decision being endorsed by Lieutenant-Colonel Hentsch, a staff officer representing the thoroughly demoralised Moltke. Kluck had no choice other than to retire northwards with Bülow to the Aisne.

The Allied success on the Marne was strategic rather than tactical. Paris was saved and the German hopes of a lightning victory in the west had been trampled underfoot, but the German armies were very far from beaten. Perhaps the most important single factor in the 'miracle of the Marne' was Joffre's ability to keep his nerve while Moltke and Bülow lost theirs. After the Marne 'Papa' Joffre's reputation was at its peak, his authority apparently unchallengeable. Moltke's fate was different. On 14 September the conduct of German operations was taken over by General Erich von Falkenhayn even if, to preserve morale, Moltke retained his post in name only until 3 November.

3

STALEMATE ON THE AISNE

The positions to which the German right wing armies retired were, for them, reassuringly strong. In particular, four miles north of the Aisne lay the Chemin des Dames Ridge, which ran parallel to the river between Soissons and Craonne and which took its name from the road built along its crest for the daughters of Louis XV. Steep, and with a series of spurs stretching out like fingers towards the Aisne, the Chemin des Dames was a formidable defensive obstacle. Nevertheless, it was precisely in this direction – on the BEF's axis of advance – that the gap still existed between the armies of Kluck and Bülow. Unfortunately for the Allies, the pace of advance of the BEF and its neighbouring French armies was not equal to the opportunity. In the BEF's case there were several reasons why its daily progress averaged ten miles or less after 9 September. Many historians have criticised its senior commanders and GHQ for lack of drive or excessive caution about the security of flanks,

3 *General Erich von Falkenhayn (left), who effectively took over as Chief of the German General Staff from von Moltke on 14 September 1914, even though the latter retained the post in name until 3 November to avoid any possible slump in the German Army's morale which Moltke's sudden removal might have precipitated. Falkenhayn himself was to hold the post until 29 August 1916. He firmly believed that the war would be won on the Western Front but, while prepared to employ ruthless means, such as gas, he was never sufficiently single-minded in his pursuit of his strategic goals. This picture was taken later in the war when he was commanding the German Ninth Army, which played an important part in the defeat of Romania. Between November 1917 and February 1918 he commanded Army Group F in Palestine, conducting a skilful defence against the British forces there before he was succeeded by Liman von Sanders.*
IWM: Q 23726

but the BEF was also marching across ground intersected by rivers; the troops were tired after their recent exertions; a change of front on 11 September caused congestion on the roads, and clouds and rain hindered aerial reconnaissance. On 13 September all three corps of the BEF (III Corps having been constituted on 30 August) succeeded in crossing the Aisne and pushed forward up the spurs and valleys ahead of them. They were fractionally too late. Freed by the fall of Maubeuge on 8 September, von Zwehl's VII Reserve Corps had hurried to the Aisne as the vanguard of a new German Seventh Army which was to fill the gap on the German right. In sharp contrast to the speed of the Allies, VII Reserve Corps – admittedly fresher than the BEF – covered some forty miles in twenty-four hours and, while nearly a quarter of its infantry dropped out on the march, its leading division reached the crest of the Chemin des Dames just two hours before the arrival of the advanced elements of Haig's I Corps. It was one of the critical moments of the war. On 14 September, a day of confused fighting, the British tried to storm the ridge, encountering well-entrenched infantry and heavy German artillery fire. Some units of I Corps, on the right, managed to force their way across the Chemin des Dames to glimpse the Ailette valley to the north and, although later driven out of their most forward positions, held on near the crest. To their left II and III Corps made less progress, so by nightfall the British line extended southwest from the Chemin des Dames towards the Aisne at Missy and then ran west to Crouy, two miles from Soissons. The Germans made determined attempts to push the British back over the river but the BEF's musketry stood it in good stead, and a fortnight later the line was virtually unchanged. A stalemate developed on the Aisne as the defensive qualities of modern artillery, machine guns and rifles became increasingly dominant and each side dug in. Trench warfare had begun to impose itself on the Western Front.

4

4 *French villagers standing reverently round the grave of a Seaforth Highlander killed in action at La Ferté sous Jouarre in September 1914.*
IWM: Q 53263

1 *French cavalry riding past troops of the British 19th Infantry Brigade near St Remy on 5 October during the 'race to the sea'. The British soldiers seen in this picture are from the 1st Cameronians (Scottish Rifles), who have emerged from their bivouacs in a wood. The 19th Brigade's movement to the north was made chiefly at night, with the men resting under cover in daylight. This was intended to help conceal the line of march, particularly from enemy aircraft.*
IWM: Q 51503

2 *British infantry advancing across a field in Belgium on 13 October 1914.*
IWM: Q 53321

3 *British cavalry scouts on a country road in Flanders in the autumn of 1914.*
IWM: Q 60708

THE RACE TO THE SEA

The growing deadlock along the front from the Aisne eastwards led to a succession of attempts by both sides to get round the other's open flank to the west and north. These manoeuvres became known – graphically, if a trifle misleadingly – as the 'race to the sea'. On 17 September Maunoury's Sixth Army struck north astride the Oise but was checked near Noyon by the German IX Reserve Corps, brought down from Antwerp. On 22 September, de Castelnau's Second Army, transferred from Lorraine, advanced westwards across the Avre, only to be halted in turn by a German corps arriving from Reims. Joffre created a new Tenth Army, under General de Maud'huy, which then made a push further to the north. Instead of turning the German right, de Maud'huy was hard pressed to hold Arras against an offensive early in October by three corps drawn from the German First, Second and Seventh Armies. All this activity between the Aisne and Belgium did not necessarily halt operations in other areas. Towards the end of September, repeated German assaults at Verdun were repulsed, though Crown Prince Wilhelm's Fifth Army achieved some progress in the Argonne forest, while a troublesome German bridgehead was also consolidated at St Mihiel, on the western bank of the Meuse. The Western Front was rapidly assuming the shape which, with some variations, was to become so familiar in later months and years.

Not wishing to get bogged down in the inconclusive struggle on the Aisne, Sir John French, on 27 September, exhorted Joffre to permit the BEF to disengage and take up its former position on the left of the Allied line. This made good sense, for the lightly-gunned BEF and its cavalry would be of more use on the open flank and its natural lines of communication with the Channel ports would be shortened, enabling it to be reinforced quickly and in reasonable security and secrecy. After weighing the possible benefits against the problems of a British move across his own lines of communication, Joffre agreed. On 1 October the BEF began its shift to Flanders, a region with which it would remain closely associated for the rest of the war.

During the first three weeks of October 1914, the British II Corps advanced towards La Bassée and, to its north, in front of Armentières, Major-General Pulteney's III Corps moved towards Lille. On Pulteney's left, the Cavalry Corps, under Major-General Edmund Allenby, took Messines and Wytschaete, linking up with the British IV Corps which arrived at Ypres following the capitulation of Antwerp. Joffre had appointed Foch as commander of a Northern Army Group, entrusting him with the coordination of

4

4 *The No.1 gun of a French 75mm field battery firing at Le Maisnil, south of Armentières, on 21 October 1914. The barrel is at full recoil.*
IWM: Q 51511

operations between the Oise and the sea, albeit without direct powers over his allies. Foch would need all his powers of leadership in the coming battles as Falkenhayn, for the moment, was showing great sureness of strategic touch and deftly using the available railway links to ensure superior speed of reinforcement and redeployment. In General Galliéni's words, the Allies were 'always twenty-four hours and an army corps behind the enemy'. Thus it was the Allies, in late October and early November, who were in the greater danger of being outflanked. While the German Sixth Army, recently switched from Lorraine, contested the line from La Bassée to Armentières and Menin, a reconstituted Fourth Army, under Duke Albrecht of Wurttemberg, approached Ypres. It contained four new Reserve Corps, composed principally of enthusiastic young volunteers from universities and technical colleges. Hastily trained as they were, they provided the Germans with a potential trump card in their next attempt to turn the Allied left and sweep down the coast.

THE FALL OF ANTWERP

As the 'race to the sea' developed in late September and early October, the Germans could no longer defer the problem of subduing Antwerp, which had posed a threat to their rear ever since the Belgian Field Army

1 *Belgian civilians leaving their homes while shelling is in progress, during the early stages of the fighting around Messines, October 1914.*
IWM: Q 60764

1

2

2 *Burning oil tanks at Antwerp in October 1914.*
IWM: Q 51926

3 *Men of a Belgian rearguard covering the retreat of their forces to Antwerp after blowing up a bridge in Termonde in September 1914.*
IWM: Q 53248

4 *Part of the Howe Battalion from the 2nd Naval Brigade of the British Royal Naval Division in a street in Vieux Dieu, an eastern suburb of Antwerp, on 6 October 1914. They are posing for the camera with a local civilian before going into the trenches south of the city, between Forts 5 and 8. Most of these men were from the Royal Naval Volunteer Reserve.*
IWM: Q 14772

3

had retired to the fortress city. All the Germans could spare for the task was a mixed force equivalent to five or six divisions, commanded by General von Beseler and comprising mostly Reserve, *Ersatz* or *Landwehr* units. The strength of the Belgian 'national redoubt', however, was illusory. Apart from 65,000 men of the Field Army, its 80,000 other garrison troops were of poor quality; its 48 forts and smaller redoubts were obsolete and outgunned, and recently-dug trenches were shallow, damp and dangerously exposed to artillery fire. Hoping to assist the Allied struggle in France and menace German communications to the south, the Belgians mounted sorties from Antwerp on 24 August and 9 September. While the second briefly halted the movement of some German units to the main battlefield, neither sortie actually did much more than add to the exhaustion and demoralisation of the Belgian troops, but against his better judgement, King Albert was persuaded by Joffre to organise a third. It had hardly got under way when, on 28 September, the Germans signalled the start of their attack on Antwerp by bombarding its outer forts.

4

5

Lacking the wherewithal to invest the entire perimeter, von Beseler attacked only the southeast sector of the defences, where he could also protect the lines of communication of the German right wing armies. Four days of infantry assaults and bombardment by super-heavy siege guns sufficed to achieve the first breach in the outer ring of forts and convince the Belgians that they must prepare to evacuate Antwerp. Reports from the British Minister in Belgium stirred the British government into last-minute action. Winston Churchill, the First Lord of the Admiralty, who went to Antwerp in person on 3 October, secured Belgian agreement to prolong the defence for a few days provided they soon received firm assurances that substantial relieving forces would be sent. The French promised the 87th Territorial

5 *German infantry resting in Termonde, southwest of Antwerp, in September 1914.*
IWM: Q 53288

1 *The 2nd Battalion, Scots Guards, part of the British 7th Division, digging trenches near Ghent on 9 October 1914. The Scots Guards took up positions astride the Ghent-Antwerp road with the object of assisting the retirement of the Belgians from Antwerp.*
IWM: Q 57168

Division and a Marine Brigade under Rear-Admiral Ronarc'h, while the British War Office despatched Lieutenant-General Sir Henry Rawlinson with the Regular 7th Division and 3rd Cavalry Division. In fact, the only reinforcements to reach Antwerp were the Royal Marines and naval volunteers of the newly formed Royal Naval Division, who arrived between 4 and 6 October, but, even as they were being deployed, the Germans were enlarging a bridgehead across the River Nethe, sealing the fate of the city. The bulk of the Belgian Field Army retired yet again, this time to the Nieuport-Dixmude line along the River Yser. A rearguard, composed of the Belgian 2nd Division and the Royal Naval Division, left Antwerp during the night of 8-9 October and on 10 October the Military Governor, General Deguise, formally surrendered the city to the Germans.

Rawlinson's force, which had by now disembarked at Zeebrugge and Ostend, could only concentrate at Ghent to cover the withdrawal of the Belgians and Royal Naval Division. Designated the IV Corps, it then itself fell back southwest to join the French 87th Territorial Division in covering the town of Ypres. Though meagre and belated, the British intervention at Antwerp had nevertheless helped to delay the fall of the fortress for up to five days, gaining precious time for the arrival in Flanders of the main British force. Just how valuable this contribution was to the Allies in the context of the campaign as a whole would shortly be revealed.

1

THE BATTLE OF THE YSER

During the next five weeks, in the last phase of the 'race to the sea', both sides made further desperate attempts to turn the enemy's flank in Flanders, although space for manoeuvre was now running out. After evacuating Antwerp the Belgian Field Army established itself on the River Yser from Dixmude to

2

2 *The German flag flying from the Hotel de Ville in Ghent on 13 October 1914. Belgian, French and British troops had begun to withdraw from Ghent during the afternoon and evening of 11 October, and the Germans entered the city a few hours later.*
IWM: Q 53317

3

3 *German prisoners with their Belgian captors at Furnes in the autumn of 1914. Furnes, a West Flemish town about four miles from the coast, between Nieuport and the French border, became the home of the Belgian General Headquarters after the fall of Antwerp and until the end of 1914.*
IWM: Q 51939

4

4 *Belgian troops in the trenches at Pervyse, October 1914.*
IWM: Q 51950

5

5 *The ruined village of Dixmude, as seen from the Belgian lines late in 1914.*
IWM: Q 51940

the coast north of Nieuport, the position being held by five Belgian divisions and Admiral Ronarc'h's French Marine Brigade. Proclaiming this to be 'our last line of defence in Belgium', King Albert rejected Foch's appeals to leave the coast and join the Allied operations inland. It was a wise decision. On 14 October Falkenhayn ordered that the German Sixth Army should stay temporarily on the defensive south of Ypres until the reconstituted Fourth Army, with its four new Reserve Corps of young volunteers, was ready to launch the decisive thrust against the Allied left between Menin and the sea, aiming to capture Calais. Its right, or coastal, flank would be covered by von Beseler's III Reserve Corps, containing the troops released from the siege of Antwerp.

On 18 October a determined attack by the III Reserve Corps drove back Belgian outposts east of the Yser. The following day the XXII Reserve Corps, from the Fourth Army, added its weight to von Beseler's efforts, but the German assaults on 19 and 20 October were blocked at Dixmude and also at Nieuport, where they came under fire from British and French warships. Foch reinforced the crucial Nieuport sector by sending the French 42nd Division to aid the Belgians – a timely move, since the Germans gained a bridgehead across the Yser at Tervaete early on 22 October. Supported by super-heavy artillery, the Germans struck repeatedly at Dixmude, which was now in danger of being outflanked. These assaults, too, were beaten off, yet growing losses made it uncertain how long the

1

1 *French dead outside a ruined church in Pervyse on 1 November 1914.*
IWM: Q 51955

2 *Belgian soldiers crossing a flooded area near Ramscapelle on 26 November 1914.*
IWM: Q 51985

2

dogged Belgian resistance could continue. Accordingly, at high water on 28 October, Belgian engineers opened the gates of the old Furnes lock at Nieuport, letting the sea into the low-lying area east of the embankment of the Nieuport-Dixmude railway.

The effects of this extreme measure were not felt immediately, for by noon on 30 October the Germans had advanced south of Nieuport, taken Ramscapelle and secured a footing in Pervyse. That night, however, the steady rise of the flood waters caused von Beseler to order III Reserve Corps to retire across the Yser to avoid being trapped. XXII Reserve Corps followed suit two days later. The check near the coast forced Falkenhayn and Duke Albrecht to make their supreme effort inland and concentrate their attacks against the sector around Ypres.

SACRIFICE IN FLANDERS: THE FIRST BATTLE OF YPRES

While the fighting on the Yser was approaching its peak, the BEF had basically managed to maintain its line at La Bassée, Ploegsteert and Messines. Now the farming country round the Belgian market town of Ypres became the only area where either side could still hope to outflank the other. As Haig's I Corps arrived from the Aisne on 20 October it was ordered to advance north of Ypres, near Langemarck, but ran head-on into the German XXIII and XXVI Reserve Corps coming from the northeast. Thus, instead of making the telling thrust, the Allies were quickly embroiled in a see-saw encounter battle during which they were forced to commit their available units bit by

3

3 British cavalry passing through the Grote Markt or Grand Place at Ypres on 13 October 1914. Most of the local civilians watching them would soon disappear from the town. The troops belong to the 3rd Cavalry Division, which reached Ypres that day.
IWM: Q 69527

4

4 French troops passing through the outskirts of Ypres, October 1914.
IWM: Q 57214

5

5 An armoured car of the Royal Naval Air Service on the Menin Road, near Ypres, at the spot which was later called 'Hell Fire Corner'. The photograph was taken on 14 October 1914, the day on which the 2nd Scots Guards marched into Ypres from Roulers. Part of the battalion did not actually go into Ypres but turned off along the Menin Road to bivouac in the grounds of the Chateau Biebuyck, known to British troops as the White Chateau. Some German cavalrymen were seen in the distance and shots were fired. The crew of the armoured car, hearing the shots, drove up to investigate. 'Hell Fire Corner' was at the intersection of the Menin Road with the Potijze-Zillebeke road and the Ypres-Roulers railway.
IWM: Q 57194

bit merely to hold their ground. Unhappily for the Germans, the outstanding courage displayed by their young volunteers did not compensate for their lack of training. Attacking shoulder to shoulder in thick skirmish lines, they died in their thousands around Langemarck, causing the Germans to remember the battle as the *Kindermord von Ypern* (the Massacre of the Innocents at Ypres). The front remained semi-fluid but trenches were spreading across the farmland.

1

2

1 *A London furniure van, requisitioned by the British Army to augment its motorised transport, stands in front of the Cloth Hall at Ypres in October 1914.*
IWM: Q 57283

2 *Men of the 2nd Battalion, Royal Scots Fusiliers, digging trenches at Terhand, north of the Menin Road, near Gheluvelt, on 20 October 1914. After the troops involved in the morning's reconnaissance in force towards Menin had received orders to retire, the whole of the British 7th Division's front east of Gheluvelt, between Zandvoorde and Zonnebeke, came under attack from the Germans during the afternoon. The 7th Division beat off two German assaults before dark, but the enemy at one point advanced to within fifty yards of the British trenches and, for much of the night, continued his efforts to break through in this sector.*
IWM: Q 50336

3

4

By the evening of 24 October the Germans had realised that the attacks of the Reserve Corps were unlikely to succeed and therefore began to prepare a fresh assault by a special task force of seven divisions, under General von Fabeck, which would attempt to break through, slightly further south, between Messines and Gheluvelt.

Von Fabeck's attack started on 29 October, reaching its crisis point on 31 October when the Germans breached the British defences at Gheluvelt. As at Langemarck a few days earlier, the Germans lost cohesion after penetrating the British lines, revealing shortcomings in their training. In a true 'soldier's battle', decided largely by the initiative of junior commanders and other ranks, the Germans were driven out of Gheluvelt by a counterattack from 357 officers and men of the 2nd Worcestershires, although Messines Ridge was lost by Allenby's cavalry and the

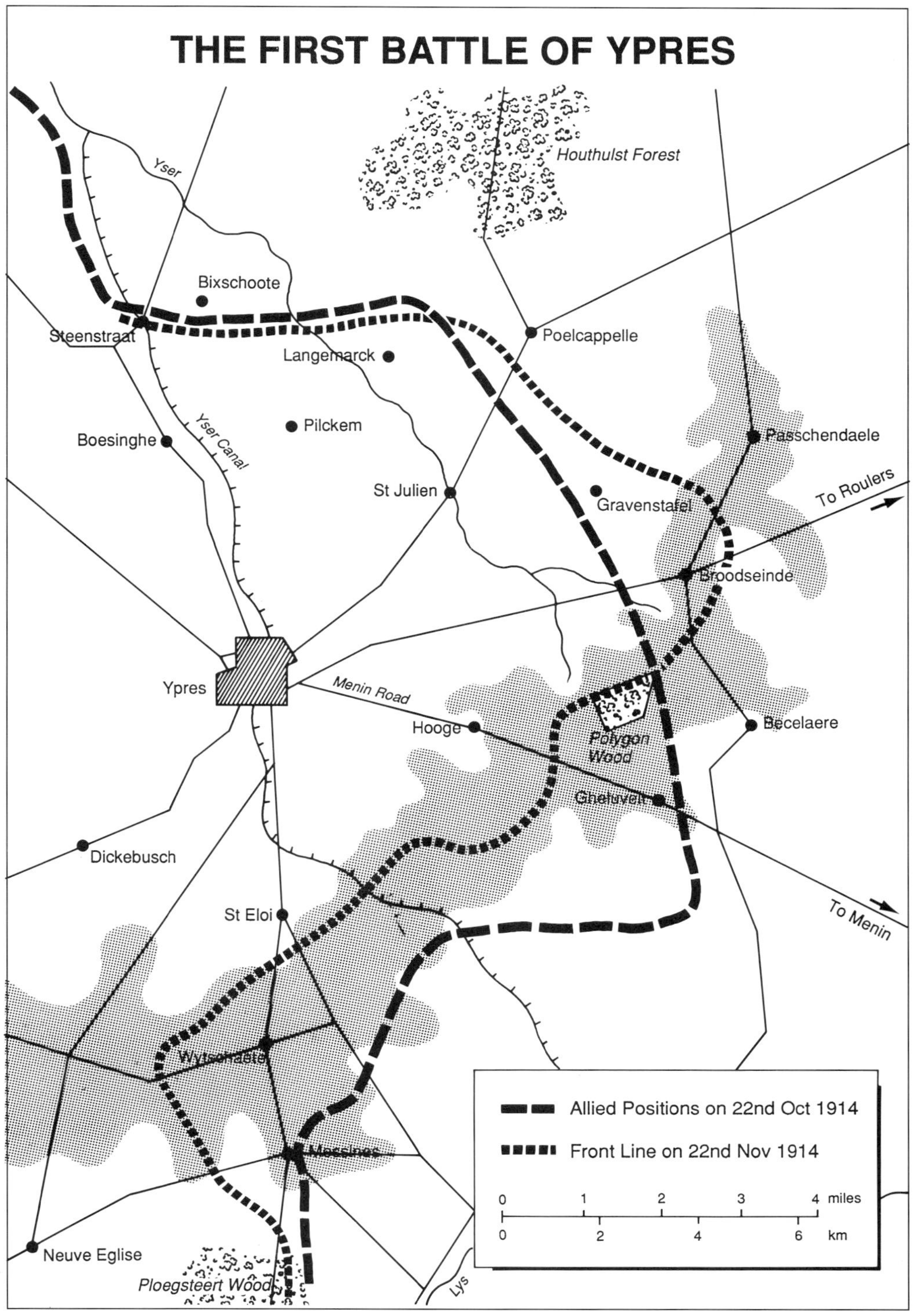

French during the following forty-eight hours. The deployment of increasing numbers of French troops on the BEF's flanks stabilised the situation until the next German onslaught on 11 November. Again Falkenhayn was close to triumph. A composite Prussian Guard Division, using the same obsolete tactics as the youthful Reserve Corps, broke through to the north of the Menin Road, only to be stopped by point-blank fire from the British 2nd Division's artillery and by a hurriedly assembled body of men which included engineers, cooks and brigade headquarters clerks. Unaware that this was the last line of British resistance, the Prussian Guard wavered and were then pushed back from the *Nonne Bosschen* (Nun's Wood) in a brisk counterattack led by the 2nd Oxfordshire and Buckinghamshire Light Infantry. Within a few days snow was falling to douse the flames of battle.

The final act of the 1914 campaign had been played out. The war plans of both sides were in shreds. Falkenhayn himself tacitly acknowledged failure at Ypres by transferring eight infantry and four cavalry divisions to the Eastern Front by early December. The Germans occupied much valuable territory in France and Belgium, but Schlieffen's nightmare of a prolonged two-front war had become

3 *Damage to the Cloth Hall in Ypres, caused by German shelling in October-November 1914.*
IWM: Q 57288

4 *Major-General Hubert Gough (left), commander of the British 2nd Cavalry Division, talking to Lieutenant-General Edmund Allenby, commander of the Cavalry Corps, by a roadside near Messines during the First Battle of Ypres.*
IWM: Q 60681

1 *Field-Marshal Sir John French, Commander-in-Chief of the British Expeditionary Force from August 1914 to December 1915. He was personally brave and generally popular with the troops, qualities which helped his leadership to hold the BEF together in the early months of the war. Nevertheless, his volatile temperament made him basically ill-suited for prolonged command of the BEF, and he quarrelled not only with his French allies but also with his own subordinates, such as Smith-Dorrien, and with Kitchener, blaming the latter for the shell shortages in the spring of 1915. He was replaced by Haig after failures in his handling of the reserves at the Battle of Loos.*
IWM: Q 28858

reality. At Ypres the Allies were left holding a precarious salient with the Germans on the dominating ridges to the east and south. For the original BEF Ypres was the biggest field of sacrifice. The German drive to the Channel ports had been blocked but the price was another 50,000 casualties. The old, pre-war professional British Army was gone for ever.

THE TRENCH DEADLOCK IN THE WINTER OF 1914-1915

By the onset of winter in 1914, the deadlock on the Western Front was complete, with the opposing trench lines stretching from the Swiss frontier to the Belgian coast. At first, in their haste to seek protection from the remorseless artillery, machine gun and rifle fire, troops had dug holes anywhere they could, or occupied handy ditches and drains. Such defences did not always command a satisfactory field of fire or offer concealment from enemy artillery observers but, as movement ceased on both sides, the troops often had to remain just where they were until a tactical opportunity arose to improve their positions. In the meantime, the rudimentary trenches were extended and linked to form a continuous defensive front; basic shelters or 'dugouts' were constructed in the forward trenches; belts of barbed wire and parapets and breastworks of sandbags were put up to give added protection; earth buttresses or 'traverses' were built at regular intervals along the line to guard against enfilade fire, and support and communication trenches were excavated to facilitate movement in the rear. The armies soon became accustomed to the daily 'wastage' of casualties and the almost incessant toil involved in static trench warfare, also adjusting to the routine of tours of duty in the front, support and reserve lines interspersed with periods of so-called 'rest'. Even so, the trenches of that first winter of the war were primitive compared with those of later years.

From the start, the trenches of the respective armies differed to some degree in both pattern and conception. The French, while committed to driving the invader out, did not ignore defence altogether. A reasonable supply of labour enabled them to construct a relatively solid system which, in January 1915, Joffre decreed should be divided into active and passive sectors. In both types of sector the front and flanks would be covered by fire from a line of strongpoints, behind which was sited a support line containing shelters for counterattack companies. Joffre then ordered the preparation of a similar second position, about two miles back, in case of local advances by the enemy. Their large numbers of quick-firing 75mm guns helped the French to avoid over manning the front line and to keep most of the trench garrisons in the support line, where they were less exposed to sudden atack. The Germans, for their part, had yet to develop the formidable defences which reflected their chosen strategic stance in the west for much of the war. In 1914 they believed that the very existence of

2

2 *Men of the 1/14th Battalion, The London Regiment (London Scottish), photographed shortly after their baptism of fire between Messines and Wytschaete on 31 October 1914, when the unit became the first Territorial Force battalion to go into action on the Western Front. The London Scottish suffered 394 casualties in this fighting.*
IWM: Q 60737

a second position might weaken the determination of their troops in the firing line. The Germans, therefore, relied initially on a single line, which it became a matter of honour to defend at all costs. If lost it had to be recaptured at once. Not surprisingly, the actual conditions in France and Flanders swiftly caused some modification of these views and, during the winter of 1914-1915, greater depth was given to their defences with the installation of concrete machine gun posts 1,000 yards behind the front.

The Germans, having anticipated siege operations against fortresses, were fairly well equipped with the weapons needed for trench warfare, including heavy guns and howitzers, high-explosive shells, grenades and trench mortars. The British, in contrast, had to improvise, making grenades out of jam tins and mortars out of shell cases and drainpipes. Another problem to contend with was that the 21 miles of front held by the BEF, between the La Bassée Canal and Wytschaete,

3 *Two French soldiers using a box periscope in a front line trench in the Argonne in the winter of 1914-1915.*
IWM: Q 53604

3

ran through the wet, low-lying countryside of Flanders, where the shallow trenches were frequently flooded. Constant immersion in water and mud caused feet to swell and become inflamed to such an extent that it was agony for a soldier to keep his boots on at all. Growing non-battle casualties from frostbite and 'trench foot' did not make it any easier to maintain a regular system of reliefs from the rigours of front-line duty.

1 *Two men of the 1st Cameronians in a waterlogged trench at Bois Grenier in the early spring of 1915.*
IWM: Q 60233

All the armies were short of shells, particularly for the heavy artillery which appeared to offer the most likely way of unlocking the trench stalemate. Even field-gun ammunition was nearly exhausted. The French, needing 50,000 rounds of 75mm ammunition per day, were producing only 11,000 per day by mid-November 1914. Pre-war British estimates had allowed for the expenditure of ten rounds of 18-pounder ammunition per gun per day, about one-eighth of what was actually used on days of intense fighting in 1914. By January 1915 some British field guns were limited to four rounds a day. At home, measures had already been taken to increase output, but the placing of British industry on a proper war footing could not

2 *The 2nd Battalion, Royal Scots Fusiliers, part of the British 7th Division, in the trenches at La Boutillerie, north-east of Neuve Chapelle, in the first winter of the war. Note the use of loopholes for rifles.*
IWM: Q 49104

TRENCH DEADLOCK

1 *A British 18-pounder field gun concealed in a shelter near Armentières on 7 December 1914. The need for camouflaged gun positions grew as the use of aircraft for artillery cooperation purposes developed on both sides.*
IWM: Q 51542

2 *A French wiring party moving along a recently constructed trench in the Argonne sector late in 1914.*
IWM: Q 53490

3 *The Machine Gun Section of the 11th Hussars stripping and cleaning a Vickers gun in a trench east of Zillebeke, near Ypres, in February 1915. Unable to perform their normal duties because of the trench deadlock, British cavalry units frequently undertook front line duties alongside the infantry during the First World War, fighting dismounted. This service was particularly valuable in the first winter, when the BEF was recovering from the casualties it had suffered at Ypres in October-November 1914.*
IWM: Q 51194

1

2

3

4 

be achieved overnight. Fortunately for the Allies, the Germans were in similar difficulties. As Falkenhayn later wrote, the failure of a single ammunition train in the winter of 1914-1915 'threatened to render whole sections of the front defenceless'.

While all the armies had suffered terrible casualties, the effects were perhaps felt most keenly in the small BEF, which could least afford the loss of highly-trained soldiers. Some 3,627 of its officers and 86,237 of its men were killed, wounded or missing between August and December 1914, most of these losses occurring in the infantry of the first seven divisions, which originally numbered only 84,000. True, reinforcements were also reaching the BEF. The Indian Corps had arrived in October and the Regular 8th Division in November. They were followed in December and January by the 27th and 28th Divisions, composed of Regulars from overseas garrisons, and in February by the !st Canadian Division. Twenty-three Territorial battalions were also in France by the end of 1914. On 26 December the BEF was reorganised into two Armies, the First Army being commanded by Haig and the Second by Smith-Dorrien. In Britain, Lord Kitchener – one of the few political or military leaders to predict a long and costly war – had initiated a massive expansion of the Army, calling for volunteers to form a series of 'New Armies', each duplicating the six infantry divisions of the original BEF. Over 1,186,000 men enlisted in the first five months. These recruits would take months to train and the reinforcements now arriving on the Western Front required time to adapt to the conditions and methods of trench warfare. For several weeks the BEF's fighting edge was blunted and morale sagged. Some ground was lost to the Germans in minor operations at Givenchy in December and near the Cuinchy Brickstacks in January, evidence that the infantry was no longer fully capable of the 'fifteen rounds rapid' fire in the minute of the original BEF. At Christmas in 1914 there was a spontaneous unofficial truce in Flanders, when British and German troops fraternised openly between the front lines, exchanging souvenirs and taking photographs. As the war became ever more impersonal and insatiable in its demands for men and material, there would be no more such incidents on this scale, although a 'live and let live' attitude existed on both sides in many 'quiet' sectors throughout the conflict.

4 *Two Territorials of the London Rifle Brigade pose for the camera with Saxon troops of the 104th and the 106th Regiments in No Man's Land near Ploegsteert Wood during the unofficial truce at Christmas 1914.*
IWM: Q 70075

THE WESTERN FRONT: THE TERRAIN

THE TERRAIN

The Western Front, that ribbon of death across France and Belgium, varied in length as the tactical situation changed, and it fluctuated considerably in 1918 when movement was restored to the battlefield. However, in its most static phase, from December 1914 to March 1917, it measured about 475 miles. Of this length of front, the British, in the winter of 1914, originally held only 21 miles in Flanders between Wytschaete and Givenchy. By March 1918 the BEF was responsible for 126 miles, extending from the Forest of Houthulst, north of Ypres, to Barisis, south of the Oise, an increase which reflected its massive expansion and growing role in land operations as the war progressed. In the latter respect, the length of front held was not the sole yardstick, for, whereas the French were content to maintain passive sectors on some portions of their line, the BEF's aggressive stance – as embodied in its raiding policy – was one of the factors which caused the Germans to station opposite the British nearly half of their available divisions in the west during 1916-1917.

The nature of the terrain also differed widely from sector to sector. On the extreme left the line ran from the dunes and locks on the Belgian coast near Nieuport, and along the Yser, where the inundations of 1914 inhibited movement. It then looped through the farmland just to the east of Ypres, forming the infamous Salient which was overlooked by the low Passchendaele and Messines Ridges, both in German hands for much of the war. From here it continued south through the wet Flanders plain to the La Bassée Canal, with the Germans enjoying superior observation from Aubers Ridge, to the south of Armentières. In low-lying Flanders, water is invariably found less than two feet below the surface, so breastworks rather than trenches were the rule in this region. Beyond the La Bassée Canal the line ran across the cheerless mining landscape near Loos, an area dotted with dreary villages, pitheads and slagheaps. However, after the industrial town of Lens, which was held by the Germans, the front began to traverse the rolling chalk uplands of Artois. Between Lens and Arras lies Vimy Ridge. Another key German defensive position until 1917, its western slopes are comparatively gentle, although it falls away steeply to the Douai plain on its eastern side. South of Arras the line continued through

2

1

1 *A trench in the sand dunes in Belgium, on the extreme German right wing, near the Dutch frontier, in September 1915.*
IWM: Q 51006

another 50 miles or so of similar undulating and open countryside, punctuated by scattered woods, on either side of the winding Somme. Here, particularly in the stretch from Gommecourt to Montauban, the Germans had occupied the high ground, fortified the villages and dug deep in the chalk to make this sector one of their principal strongholds on the Western Front.

Below the Somme the country is more broken and wooded. Having reached the tip of the great German-

2 *Canadian troops manning a breastwork in the front line near Ploegsteert Wood on 19 October 1915.*
IWM: Q 29023

3 *The front line on the Aisne Canal, captured by the Germans from the British 8th Division in May 1918. Berry au Bac can be seen in the background.*
IWM: Q 55312

4 *German dugouts in the Argonne sector, April 1918.*
IWM: Q 55271

THE WESTERN FRONT: THE TERRAIN

1 *Men of the Lancashire Fusiliers carrying duckboards across a muddy area near Pilckem, in the Ypres Salient, on 10 October 1917.*
IWM: Q 6049

2 *A German sentry on the Hartmannsweilerkopf in the Vosges.*
IWM: Q 58194

3 *View from close to the Albert-Bapaume road near La Boisselle, on the Somme battlefield, looking along a captured German trench towards the ruins of Ovillers. The picture was taken in September 1916.*
IWM: Q 4123

1

2

held salient near Noyon, scarcely 60 miles from Paris, the front line swung away almost at a right angle to the east, threading along the Chemin des Dames Ridge, north of the Aisne, and then the heights north of Reims. Next it passed over the bare and arid chalk fields of the Champagne *pouilleuse* (literally 'lousy'), the French Army's pre-war training area, before entering the Argonne forest, a region intersected by streams and thickly-wooded ridges. At Verdun the line followed a horseshoe-shaped curve around the Meuse heights north of the fortress city, turning sharply south once more towards the St Mihiel salient, where the Germans retained a bridgehead across the Meuse for four years. The remaining 150 miles of front ran eastwards again to Nancy, which the Germans failed to capture, and finally through the mountainous Vosges and the southwestern corner of Alsace to the Swiss frontier. Though representing about one third of the entire Western Front, this last stretch from St Mihiel to Switzerland did not favour large-scale offensive operations and, apart from fierce but sporadic actions by crack mountain troops for important peaks such as the Hartmannsweilerkopf, it was a relatively quiet part of the line manned by low-grade units.

TRENCH SYSTEMS

TRENCH SYSTEMS

For much of the war, until the more elastic defence in depth on a zonal pattern was adopted in the winter of 1917-18, the standard British trench system on the Western Front consisted of three roughly parallel lines, known respectively as the front, support and reserve trenches. These lines were continuous but usually dug in a zigzag or 'dog-tooth' form, not only to protect the troops from flanking or enfilade fire but also to limit the blast and splinter effects of grenades, mortar bombs and shells. As a result, the trench was essentially divided into many short sections, each screened from the next by an earth buttress, or traverse, which projected into the trench at a right angle from the front or rear. The straight sections between the traverses were called fire bays.

The front, support and reserve lines were linked at frequent intervals by communication trenches, along which passed all reliefs and supplies. Where the opposing trenches were relatively close, forward saps were also dug, enabling two or three soldiers to crawl out from the front line at night and man a listening post so that enemy activity could be monitored. Belts of barbed wire, sometimes well over one hundred feet thick, guarded the trenches of both sides. No Man's Land – the scarred and stinking stretch of contested ground between the opposing front lines – was 100-400 yards wide on average, although it narrowed in places to only a few feet and extended elsewhere to as much as 1,000 yards, depending on the terrain and the tactical importance of local natural features.

Trenches in the front line were generally about seven feet wide at the top and two to three feet wide at the bottom, with a depth of between seven and ten feet. The parapet at the front of the trench facing the enemy had a wall of sandbags running along its top to give the occupants a little extra protection against bullets. A similar line of sandbags was placed on the parados, or rear wall of the trench. Lengths of slatted timber, called 'duckboards', were laid along the floor of the trench above the drainage channels and sumps. The sides of the trench were reinforced with revetments of timber, wattle, wire, corrugated iron or sandbags. The latter were particularly common as their use demanded fewer specialist skills, while they were also easier to replace and did not throw off potentially lethal splinters when struck by shells.

Because of the threat posed by snipers, routine

1

2

1 *An early British trench at Frelinghien, near Armentières, in November 1914. It is held by men of the 1st Battalion, The King's Own (Royal Lancaster Regiment).*
IWM: Q 56719

2 *A barbed wire obstacle, mounted on a timber frame, in a trench near Cambrin, east of Béthune, occupied by the 1/7th Sherwood Foresters in September 1917. In the event of a German attack or trench raid, the wire could be lowered, as seen here, to block the progress of the enemy along the front line.*
IWM: Q 6020

3 *Part of the French front line below the crest of Vimy Ridge in December 1915. This particular section of the line was captured by the Germans the following month.*
IWM: Q 49225

3

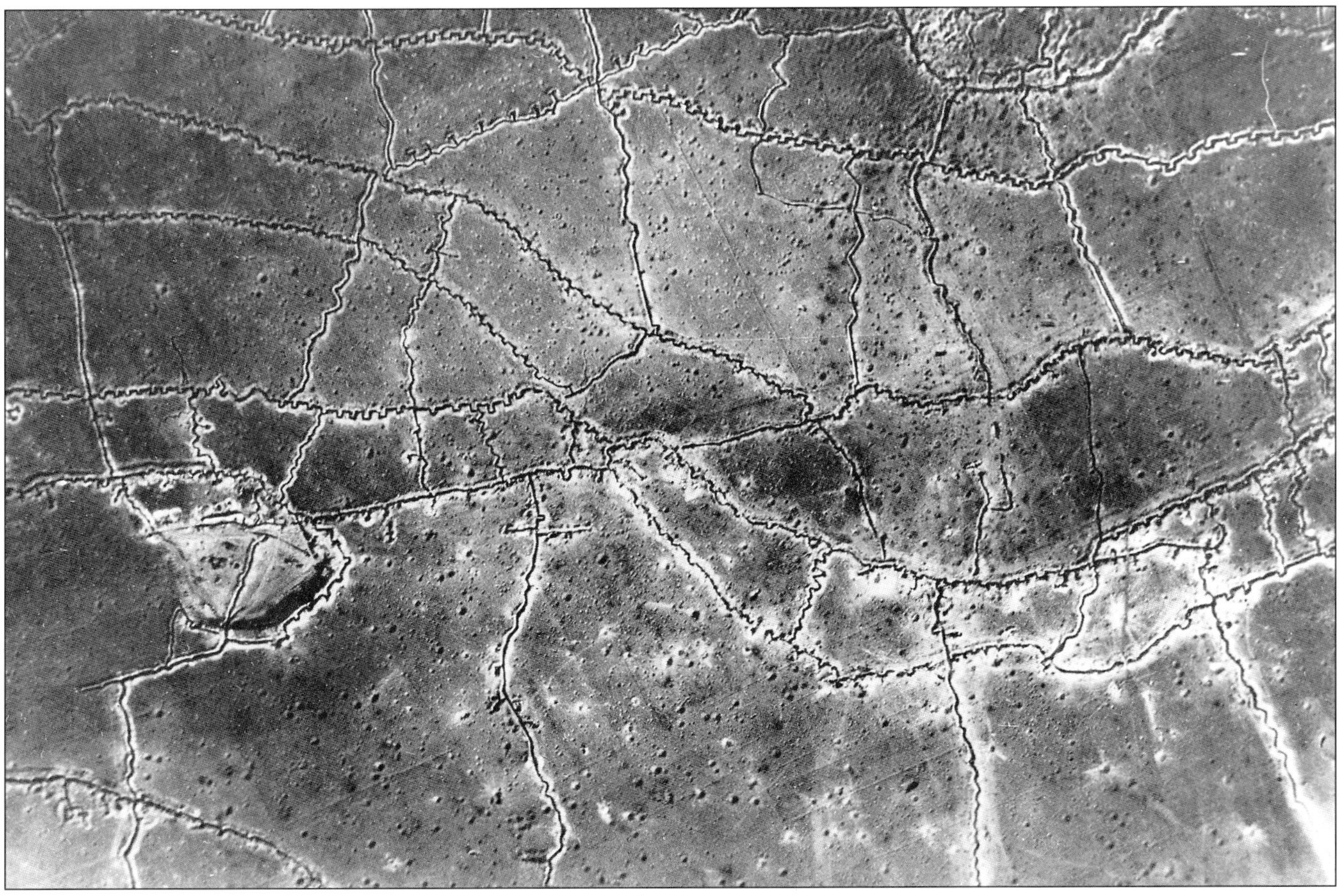

1 *Aerial photograph of the Western Front in the Auchy sector, between Loos and La Bassée, on 14 November 1915. The irregular 'dog-tooth' pattern of the trench lines is clearly visible in this picture.*
IWM: Q 65490

2 *Electrically-driven earth-boring machines being used by the Germans in the construction of dugouts on the Western Front.*
IWM: Q 55394

3 *Soldiers of the 1st Canadian Division at Ploegsteert, near Armentières, on 20 March 1916. The trench shown here is of the breastwork type, consisting of a wall of sandbags, timber and corrugated iron built up above ground level.*
IWM: Q 442

4 *German troops at the entrance to a dugout in a front line trench at Hill 60, southeast of Ypres, in June 1916.*
IWM: Q 45247

5 *A soldier of the 12th (Service) Battalion, The East Yorkshire Regiment, using a box periscope for observation in a trench in the Arleux sector, northeast of Arras, on 9 January 1918. The battalion had been raised in 1914 as the 'Hull Sportsmen' but was disbanded a month after this photograph was taken.*
IWM: Q 10617

observation of the enemy front line was usually carried out with the aid of simple periscopes. However, to permit soldiers to see directly over the top when necessary, a fire step was provided at a height of about three feet from the trench floor. The fire step was manned by sentries throughout the day and night, and by most of the rifle strength of the company or platoon concerned at the critical periods of dawn and dusk 'stand to'. In Flanders, where the wet conditions made it impossible to dig deep, 'trenches' tended to consist of breastworks of sandbags and wood, raised above ground level to a height of six or seven feet. In some cases these defensive walls were up to twenty feet thick.

As a rule, living accommodation in the trenches was extremely primitive. Small, cave-like structures or 'dugouts', sometimes reinforced with timber and corrugated iron and reached by a short flight of steps, were cut into, and below, the walls of the trench to offer shelter to officers and senior NCOs. The majority of soldiers had to make do with a waterproof sheet for covering or, at best, might curl up in a tiny niche or 'funk hole' scraped out of the side of the trench. The Allies, committed to an offensive policy, never regarded their trenches as permanent, and therefore discouraged the construction of elaborate accommodation in the front line. The Germans, who adopted a defensive stance on the Western Front for long spells of the war, built much more sophisticated shelters for their troops where time and terrain allowed. For example, in the chalk of the Somme sector, German dugouts were frequently some forty feet underground and, apart from being sufficiently spacious to house a whole infantry platoon in almost total security from shell fire, they had electric light, piped water supplies and efficient air ventilation. Here, too, the officers' dugouts could be relatively luxurious, with timber wall panelling and floor surfaces, painted ceilings, and even carpets.

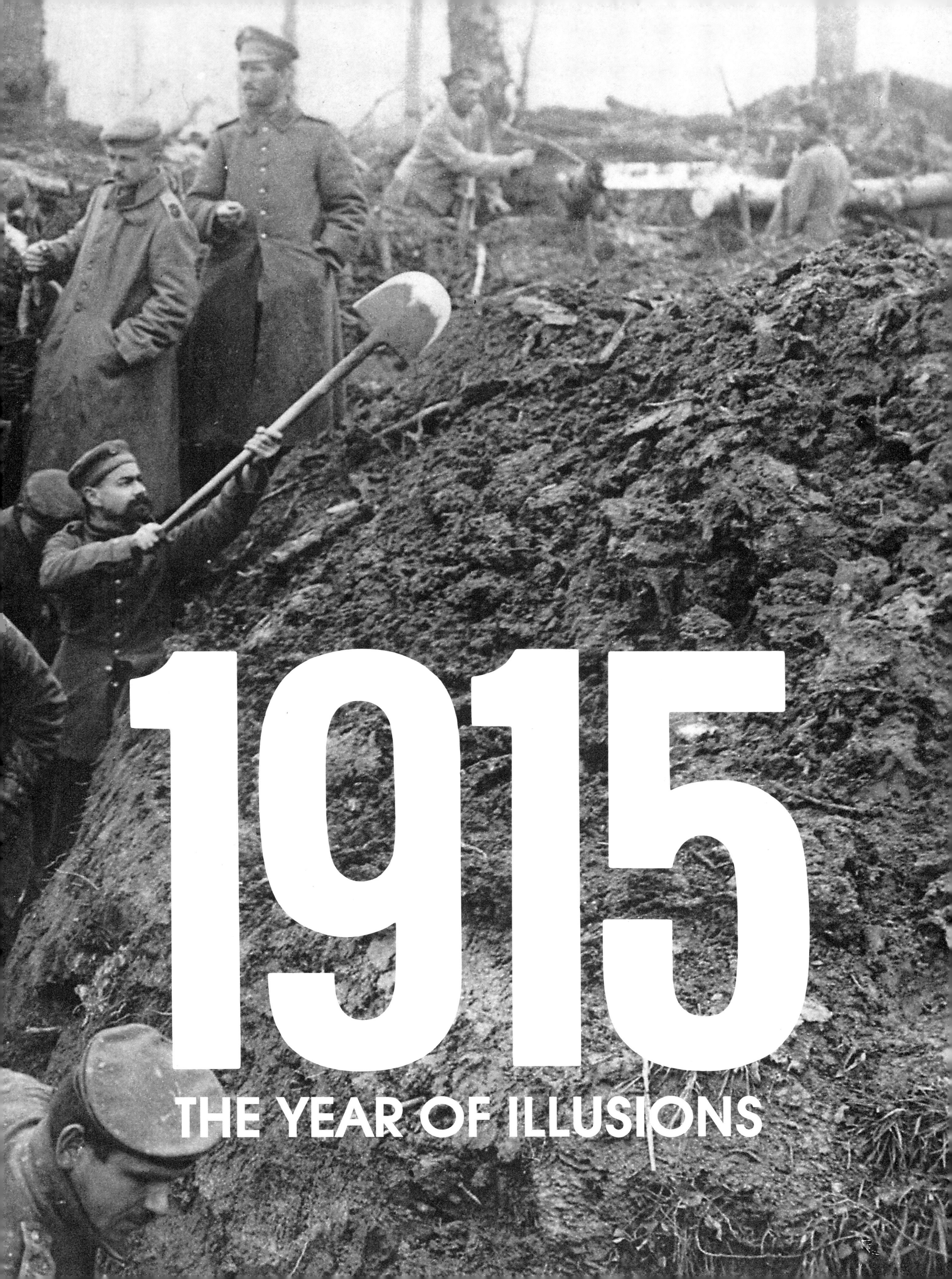

1915

THE YEAR OF ILLUSIONS

STRATEGIC OPTIONS

Falkenhayn's reluctant decision to yield to the demands of the Eastern Front in November 1914 compelled the Germans to adopt a largely defensive strategy in France and Flanders during the first winter of the war. The operations against Russia not only diverted manpower away from the Western Front but also artillery and shells and, for a time, the Germans barely had sufficient artillery ammunition for day-to-day tactical requirements, let alone a big offensive in the west. Nevertheless, Falkenhayn remained convinced that the war would ultimately be won in that theatre. In December he told the Chief of the Austro-Hungarian General Staff that once the Russians were driven back across the Vistula he envisaged resuming the offensive in France, possibly at the beginning of February 1915.

Several factors conspired to frustrate Falkenhayn's intentions. Austria-Hungary badly needed a notable victory to dissuade potentially predatory neighbours, such as Italy and Romania, from entering the war against the Central Powers. Without extra German support, particularly in the Carpathians, there was even a danger of the Austrians being tempted to seek a separate peace. Both the Kaiser and Bethmann-Hollweg, the German Chancellor, therefore backed Hindenburg and Ludendorff, who urged that the Eastern Front should be given priority in 1915. Whereas the heavy fighting and huge casualties in the west had produced only a trench stalemate, Hindenburg and Ludendorff – with smaller resources – had twice halted Russian attempts to invade Germany and had also seized a sizeable piece of Russian Poland, so it seemed sensible to reinforce success rather than failure. The best that Falkenhayn himself hoped for in the east was a victory 'big enough to check the enemy for a long time' but, for the moment, he had to swim with the prevailing current of German strategic opinion.

The German decision to switch to the defensive in the west was a cardinal error. By failing to launch a series of hammer blows, as soon as they were able to do so, against a weakened and now partly inexperienced BEF, the Germans shunned a genuine, if fleeting, chance of victory in the winter of 1914-15. As it was, the Allies were given time to reorganise. The British, especially, gained a breathing space in which to train Kitchener's new formations and to strengthen the BEF with additional Regular units from India and other overseas garrisons as well as with Territorial and Dominion troops. The respite had an undesirable consequence for both sides in that it allowed the opposing trench systems on the Western Front to become more firmly established, making them much harder to breach when offensive operations did resume.

The French faced a relatively simple strategic choice as 1914 drew to a close. Most of Belgium, and a substantial area of France, was in German hands, including regions which contained a large proportion of France's heavy industry and raw materials. The obvious French desire to liberate their national territory and recover Alsace-Lorraine could only be assuaged by a policy of attack. Joffre believed it was possible to break through the enemy's trench system but did not necessarily expect instant success. His view was that a preliminary series of attacks would force the Germans to use up reserves, and so diminish their powers of resistance that continued pressure would finally cause their line to disintegrate. A pet phrase ascribed to

1

Previous page: *Troops of the German Fifth Army digging trenches in the Argonne in November 1915. This heavily wooded sector, full of hills and ravines, was eminently suitable for defensive warfare.*
IWM: Q 45584

1 *General Joseph Joffre (centre), the French Commander-in-Chief, with General Noel de Castelnau (left) and General Paul Marie Pau (right) in February 1915. De Castelnau, an aristocrat and a devout Catholic, had been Deputy Chief of the General Staff under Joffre before the war, helping to shape Plan XVII. He commanded the French Second Army in the 1914 fighting and was elevated to lead the newly created Central Army Group in the summer of 1915. An advocate of large-scale offensives, he conducted the French operations in Champagne in September 1915, becoming Joffre's chief of staff at French General Headquarters in December that year. His advice was of key importance in determining the nature of the defence of Verdun in 1916. General Pau, who had lost an arm during the Franco-Prussian War, commanded the Army of Alsace in 1914.*
IWM: Q 53625

2 *A French 120mm gun in a camouflaged position in the Argonne Forest, December 1914. The gun is clearly an elderly model as it has an obsolete breech mechanism and no recoil system*
IWM: Q 53470

3 *French soldiers collecting wood in the Argonne Forest in the winter of 1914-1915.*
IWM: Q 53520

4 *French infantrymen in full marching order.*
IWM: Q 53517

Joffre was *Je les grignote* (I keep nibbling at them). In his nibbling strategy lay the seeds of three years of attrition.

First Joffre had to decide where to attack. The fighting of 1914 had left the Germans in possession of a big salient between Arras and Reims, with its snout, at Noyon, poking menacingly towards Paris. Something clearly had to be done about this, but the vital railway links to the German forces in northern France also offered tempting objectives. In the event Joffre decided to pinch out the Noyon Salient by striking at it from two directions. An advance from the Artois plateau eastwards against one side of it would push the Germans back across the plain of Douai and threaten the supply lines to such key points as Cambrai and St Quentin. A second advance northwards from

1 *Men of the 27th German Infantry Regiment in a fire trench near Arras during the winter of 1914-1915. Note the apertures in the parapet and the timber revetting.*
IWM: Q 51081

2 *French troops marching through a ruined village near Nancy early in 1915.*
IWM: Q 53605

Champagne would cut the lateral railway feeding the German centre, and might expose the routes running through the gap between the Ardennes and Holland. A third offensive, from the Verdun-Nancy front, might also sever the Thionville-Hirson railway, causing the Germans to loosen their grip in this sector, as the routes north of the Ardennes forests could not sustain the whole fighting front by themselves. Apart from cutting the enemy communications close to the Rhine crossings on this flank, any real progress here might even enable the French right wing armies to take the war into Germany in a kind of abridged version of Plan XVII.

JOFFRE'S WINTER OFFENSIVES

There was nothing fundamentally wrong with Joffre's overall plan, which determined the shape of Franco-British strategy in the west throughout the next twelve months and, in a revised and enlarged form, was to serve the Allies well in the latter half of 1918. In the first winter of the war, however, it was undermined by inadequate means and flawed execution. Short of fresh troops and suitable equipment, Joffre was initially obliged to restrict his main blows to the fronts of the French Tenth Army in Artois and the Fourth Army in Champagne, although other armies were to mount diversionary attacks, with local objectives, in support.

The Artois part of Joffre's two-pronged winter offensive was launched on 17 December under Foch's direction as commander of the Northern Army Group. De Maud'huy's Tenth Army had the task of breaking through the German defences around Souchez to secure the dominating feature of Vimy Ridge, situated to the north of Arras and overlooking the Douai plain and the Lens coalfield. XXI Corps, under Maistre, was to attack towards Angres and the spur of Notre Dame de Lorette which rose on the other side of the Souchez valley, opposite the northwestern end of Vimy Ridge; Pétain's XXXIII Corps was required to take Carency, a village that barred the western approaches to Souchez. The operations were dogged from the start by lack of sufficient heavy artillery, forcing the French to stagger their opening attacks and thus enabling the Germans to concentrate their defensive firepower. Heavy rain turned the ground into clinging mud, clogging the rifles of the infantry, and fog hampered artillery observation, causing repeated postponements of further French attacks. Largely as a consequence of the bad weather, the Artois offensive was effectively terminated as early as 4 January 1915. Minor gains to the north of Notre Dame de Lorette and on the southern edge of Carency were all that Foch and de Maud'huy could show for 7,771 French casualties.

In Champagne the offensive by the Fourth Army, under De Langle de Cary, began on 20 December. Attacking German positions along a front of approximately twenty miles, the French had some quick successes on the right, where the Colonial Corps and XVII Corps took important strongpoints in the German front line, but XII Corps, on the left, made little progress in the face of heavy machine-gun fire from the flanks. The offensive continued into January, when the poor weather and the sheer exhaustion of the troops brought about an enforced pause, used by the Germans to fortify their support positions wherever the front line had been pierced or seriously threatened. The second main phase of this First Battle of Champagne commenced on 16 February 1915 and lasted until 17 March, though limited attacks went on for another fortnight. Despite subjecting the Germans to the full fury of rapid 'drum-fire' from their 75mm guns, the French won no more than a handful of isolated villages on the forward slopes of the hills. The

3 *General Louis-Ernest de Maud'huy (right), who commanded the French Tenth Army in the winter of 1914-1915.*
IWM: Q 53488

4 *French prisoners, escorted by German dragoons, on the march in the St Mihiel sector, 8 December 1914.*
IWM: Q 53454

only appreciable result of the Champagne operations had been an estimated 240,000 French casualties. The railway communications supplying the German centre remained intact.

None of the French subsidiary offensives did much to brighten the picture. Operations by Maunoury's Sixth Army north of Soissons won some ground at Crouy and Vauxrot but prompted such a violent and telling counterattack that the French were driven back, in January, to positions on the left bank of the Aisne. The Third Army, under Sarrail, lost around 12,000 men in attacks between the Argonne and Meuse designed to cover the right flank of the Fourth Army's offensive in Champagne. On the extreme Allied right wing, the *Chasseurs Alpins* of General Putz's newly created Army of the Vosges – subsequently the French Seventh Army – fought a vicious battle against German *Jäger* units for possession of the Hartmannsweilerkopf, a peak offering superb observation over the Alsace plain. It was in French hands by 26 April, but the four-month struggle in the Vosges cost Putz 20,000 troops. On all sectors the need for heavy artillery to demolish the enemy trenches, strongpoints and shelters was strikingly demonstrated, and even Foch started to revise his tactical ideas. Considering his own background as an engineer, Joffre was slow to come to terms with what were essentially siege warfare conditions, and his lack of tactical imagination was now becoming increasingly manifest. Whatever had been learned, the French winter offensives were expensive failures and Joffre's claim, in March, that French troops displayed 'an obvious superiority in morale' had a hollow ring.

1 *The headquarters of the 21st Infantry Brigade (7th Division, IV Corps), commanded by Brigadier-General H.E. Watts, during the Battle of Neuve Chapelle. A haystack was chosen as the site of the headquarters as a building would have been a more likely target for German gunners. Though in reserve during the initial stages of the assault, the brigade was involved in heavy fighting during a German counterattack on the morning of 12 March.*
IWM: Q 49220

THE TEST AT NEUVE CHAPELLE

The BEF could do little to support the French operations until the early spring of 1915. At the beginning of the year, Sir John French himself felt that the Eastern Front was perhaps more likely to prove the decisive theatre, yet he was conscious of the need to keep up the pressure in the west and to restore the BEF's offensive spirit after a miserable winter in the trenches. With the War Council at home now discussing possible operations in the Dardanelles and Balkans, it was clear to the senior British commanders in France that resources might be diverted elsewhere if the BEF did not take positive action soon. The replacement of Sir Archibald Murray by Lieutenant-General Sir William Robertson as the BEF's Chief of Staff on 25 January injected a brisker approach into the work of General Headquarters, and by mid February approval had been given to a plan for an attack by Haig's First Army at Neuve Chapelle, the object of which was to secure Aubers Ridge and threaten the important road and rail junction of Lille. For a fortnight or so there was a chance that the French Tenth Army would mount a simultaneous offensive from the Artois plateau against Vimy Ridge. This was postponed because the slow arrival of reinforcements, and the proposed despatch of the Regular 29th Division to the

2 *The machine gun post in the German front line which inflicted heavy losses on the 2nd Middlesex and 2nd Cameronians on the morning of 10 March 1915. The emplacement was only destroyed during the second British bombardment that day.*
IWM: Q 49208

Dardanelles, prevented the BEF from carrying out the necessary relief of the French IX Corps at Ypres. Sir John thereupon decided to proceed independently, if only to show the French that the BEF was capable of more than merely holding the line.

Haig's diligent preparations for the first big British set-piece attack of the war furnished the BEF with a blueprint for future trench assaults. Over 3,000 detailed trench maps were produced with the help of photographic reconnaissance by the Royal Flying Corps and were distributed to the attacking units, enabling them to rehearse the first phase of the

3

3 *Shells of a German barrage bursting close behind the British front line trenches at Neuve Chapelle to prevent reinforcements being brought up.* IWM: Q 49217

4

4 *The village of Neuve Chapelle, shortly after it had been captured by the 25th Brigade of the British 8th Division during the battle in March 1915.* IWM: Q 49216

1

2

3

1 *Soldiers of the 1st Battalion, The Queen's Own Royal West Kent Regiment (13th Brigade, 5th Division), in a primitive trench near Ypres in the spring of 1915. After taking part in the capture of Hill 60 on 17 April, the battalion was rushed to the northern flank of the Salient to help reinforce the crumbling front after the German gas attack of 22 April. The battalion was involved in counterattacks on Mauser Ridge between 23 and 26 April. Despite the unit's losses, it was permitted only a few days' rest before being moved back to the Zillebeke area. On 5 May the Royal West Kents launched an unsuccessful counterattack on Hill 60, which the Germans had recaptured earlier that day.*
IWM: Q 61569

operation; assembly trenches were dug; advanced dumps for stores and ammunition were established, and precise artillery timetables were issued for the first time. One-sixth of the BEF's total stocks, 100,000 shells, were made available to the artillery. The gunners were limited to a 35-minute preliminary bombardment, after which they would lift their fire from the German front trenches and lay down a barrage to block the forward movement of enemy reinforcements.

The short, hurricane bombardment began at 7.30 on the morning of 10 March, surprising and stunning the defenders, with the result that the Indian Corps and Rawlinson's IV Corps quickly seized the German front trenches. However, there were delays on both flanks caused, on the right, by the loss of direction of the 1/39th Garhwal Rifles and, on the left, by the failure of two recently arrived howitzer batteries to destroy a 400-yard stretch of trenches. In little over three hours, growing congestion in the centre and in the rear areas took the initial sting out of the attack, while German strongpoints behind the front line also impeded further progress. The British and Indian troops had overrun the German defences on a front of

4

4,000 yards, gained 1,200 yards at the deepest point, captured Neuve Chapelle and eradicated the German salient west of the village, but during the next three days they could not exploit their early success. Late on 12 March Haig ordered that the attack should be stopped and the new line consolidated. The BEF's casualties in the battle numbered nearly 13,000 officers and men and German losses were about 12,000.

Neuve Chapelle revealed many of the fundamental problems of trench warfare offensives. Given methodical preparation, it was generally possible to break into the enemy lines. The harder part was to get one's reserves and artillery forward speedily enough to assault subsequent positions and break out of the opposing defences before the enemy brought up substantial reinforcements. Poor battlefield communications also made it difficult to control an attack, particularly when telephone cables were cut by shells and battalion runners became casualties. One vital lesson of Neuve Chapelle – the effectiveness of surprise hurricane bombardments – was largely ignored by the British over the next thirty months, with often tragic consequences. On the credit side, the BEF's offensive capabilities, after this battle, were taken far more seriously by both the French and the Germans.

CLOUD OF DEATH: THE SECOND BATTLE OF YPRES

While the Allies were preparing for another round of offensive action in May, the Germans struck against the northern flank of the Ypres Salient on 22 April 1915, using poison gas for the first time on the Western Front. Here Falkenhayn displayed that strange confusion of purpose which was to mar his term of office as Chief of the German General Staff. The Eastern Front still had priority so, notwithstanding the offensive potential of gas and the significance of Ypres to both sides, the actual employment of gas against the Salient was largely in the nature of an experiment. No fresh reserves were allocated to Duke Albrecht of Württemberg's Fourth Army, and the stated objectives of the XXIII and XXVI Reserve Corps were limited to Langemarck, Pilckem Ridge and the line of the Yser Canal as far as Ypres, though it was vaguely hoped that German possession of the high ground near Pilckem would make it 'impossible for the enemy to remain longer in the Ypres Salient'. On the Allied side, to free French units for Artois, the British Second Army had recently taken over more of the line northeast of Ypres, but the French 45th (Algerian) Division and 87th Territorial Division held the sector between Poelcappelle and the Yser Canal, the very area chosen by the Germans for their attack.

Shortly after 5pm on 22 April, in the wake of a brief but savage bombardment, the Germans opened the valves of 5,730 cylinders to release greenish-yellow clouds of chlorine gas which, as they drifted towards the French positions, merged to form a bluish-white mist. Totally unprotected against the gas, the French divisions broke in panic, leaving a gap of nearly five miles on the left of the 1st Canadian Division. By dusk Langemarck and Pilckem had fallen and the Germans were within two miles of Ypres itself, but the attacking troops were not eager to follow their own gas cloud too closely and, without sufficient reserves, the Germans were unable to capitalise on their only opportunity to achieve a breakthrough in the west in 1915. That night the British and Canadians somehow improvised a patchwork defensive line. A second gas attack was delivered on 24 April at St Julien, where the Canadians, using handkerchiefs, towels or bandages soaked in water or urine as makeshift respirators, bravely prevented a further serious collapse of the front.

As the general responsible for coordinating Allied operations in Flanders, Foch did not enjoy his most distinguished period of command at Ypres in April and May 1915. Still over-imbued with irrational confidence in the offensive spirit, he ordered Putz, the local French commander, to participate in counterattacks which the latter, having lost many guns to the advancing Germans, could not realistically execute. From 23 to 26 April the British launched a series of assaults which, because they were made with minimal help from the artillery or the French, all incurred severe losses and failed to recover the lost ground. On 27 April, with the Germans now in a position to bombard parts of the Salient from the left rear, Smith-Dorrien sensibly suggested a withdrawal to a more tenable line along the canal and through the Ypres ramparts. Sir John French, whose moods were swinging unpredictably between gloom and optimism, was currently encouraged by a pledge of additional divisions from Foch. His reservations about Smith-Dorrien resurfaced and, in rejecting the proposal, he handed over responsibility for all British troops around Ypres to Plumer, the commander of V Corps. This latest upset in a tense relationship drove Smith-Dorrien to resign, depriving the BEF of an able tactician.

2 *The ramparts of Ypres, near the Menin Gate, in 1915. By the time this picture was taken the remaining structures of the town were honeycombed with military quarters of every description. The ramparts themselves eventually contained hundreds of dugouts, in which thousands of troops found temporary billets during the course of the war. Many of the dugouts were used as dressing stations or unit headquarters.*
IWM: Q 28949

3 *Panoramic photograph of Hill 60, southeast of Ypres, on 10 April 1915, only one week before its capture by the British 5th Division. This feature, which is the slight elevation on the left of the picture, had been formed from the earth excavated when the cutting was made for the Ypres-Comines railway, seen here running diagonally across the photograph. A similar spoil heap, known as 'The Caterpillar' because of its long, irregular shape, can be seen on the opposite side of the line. Although small, Hill 60 provided good all-round observation and therefore became a position of some tactical importance. The struggle for Hill 60 cost the 5th Division over 3,000 casualties. However, it was lost again to the Germans on 5 May, partly as a result of enfilade fire from 'The Caterpillar', which had not been taken by the British, but mainly due to gas attacks. The British regained possession in June 1917.*
IWM: Q 44172

4 *The 1st Battalion, Royal Scots Fusiliers, in a trench running through the houses of St Eloi village, south of Ypres, in the spring of 1915.*
IWM: Q 49819

1

1 *French troops wearing goggles and an early form of pad respirator for protection against poison gas in 1915.*
Hulton-Deutsch Collection: H63054

Plumer took over command of the Second Army on 6 May. Ironically, Foch had by then confessed that, because of the imminent Artois offensive, substantial French reinforcements would not be forthcoming and between 1 and 3 May Plumer was allowed to pull back as Smith-Dorrien had urged. However, as a sop to GHQ's doubts about yielding ground and Sir John's desire to leave space for any belated French manoeuvre, Plumer's new line was a compromise, stopping some three miles short of Ypres.

During May the Germans made four more gas attacks and captured some ground on the Frezenberg and Bellewaarde Ridges, but at the end of the battle on 25 May the outline of the Salient was much as Plumer had traced it earlier that month. The fighting had cost the BEF 58,000 casualties and the Germans nearly 38,000. For a second time the BEF had just held the Germans at bay around Ypres though, until the summer of 1917, the new Salient, less than three miles deep, was even harder to defend than before. With the Germans on three sides, and in possession of the vital ridges, the Salient became a vast target for the German gunners and a place of continual danger and seemingly endless sacrifice for the BEF.

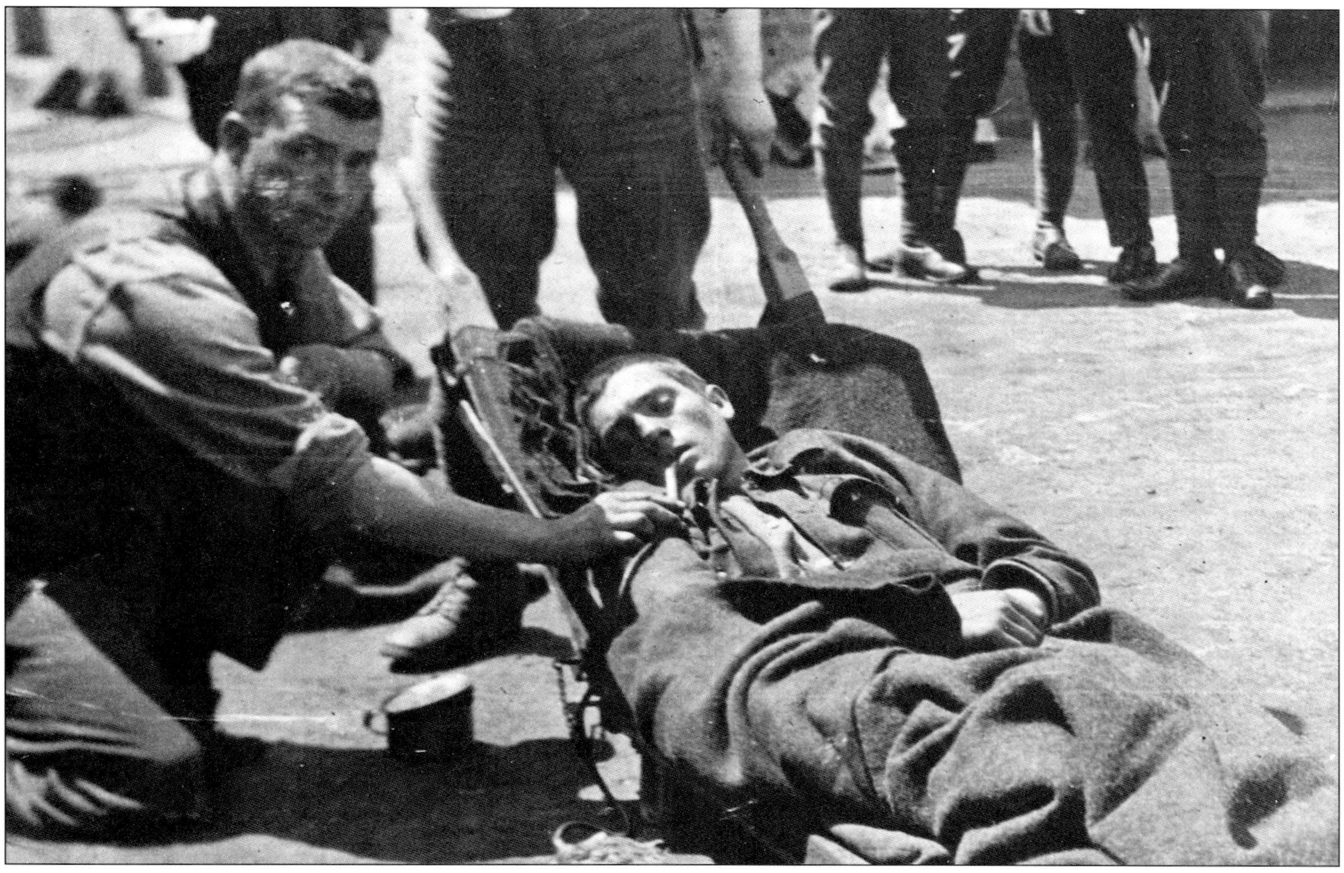
2

2 *A seriously gassed soldier is given oxygen at the North Midland Field Ambulance station at Hazebrouck, June 1915.*
IWM: Q 51886

3

3 *View from the Menin Gate at Ypres in May 1915. The pre-war Gate was not, like its successor, an archway, but was marked by two lions on stone pedestals, one on either side of the road. The road to Menin from Ypres was a constant target for German artillery, and in this photograph a shell has landed near the Gate, killing both the driver and a horse of a British transport wagon as well as destroying nearby buildings.*
IWM: Q 61637

During the operations leading to the capture of Neuve Chapelle in October 1914 the Germans fired shells containing a chemical which induced violent sneezing. They first employed tear gas, fired in liquid form in 15cm howitzer shells, against the Russians at Bolimov on the Eastern Front on 31 January 1915. The experiment was not a success, as the liquid failed to vaporise in the freezing temperature, although the French were bombarded with an improved tear gas mixture at Nieuport in March that year. Poison gas was added to the horrors of the Western Front on 22 April 1915, when the Germans released chlorine clouds from cylinders against French positions in the Ypres Salient, creating a five-mile hole in the defences. The British used gas in an attack for the first time at Loos, on 25 September 1915, but a shift in the wind blew it back over their own front line in some places. The difficulties of controlling the direction of gas released from cylinders prompted both sides, from 1916 onwards, to make increasing use of gas-filled rounds, fired from artillery pieces, mortars or other devices such as the British Livens projector.

Three main types of gas were employed in the First World War. Chlorine, and the more powerful phosgene, attacked the lungs, causing them to fill

1

2

1 *Aerial photograph of a British cloud gas attack in progress between Carnoy and Montauban on the Somme front in June 1916, shortly before the Allied offensive. Montauban, which was then still in German hands, is at the top left of the picture, below Bernafay Wood, and Carnoy, which was behind the British lines, can be seen at the bottom right.*
IWM: Q 55066

2 *Men of the 2nd Battalion, Argyll and Sutherland Highlanders in the Bois Grenier sector in June 1915. They are wearing early pad respirators for protection against poison gas. These were issued to the battalion in May 1915 and represented a slight improvement on the improvised masks, such as moistened handkerchiefs and towels, which had been used by British and Canadian troops at Ypres during the last week of April. The bottles held by the soldiers probably contain water, hypo or soda solution for moistening the cotton wool and muslin masks.*
IWM: Q 48951

1

3

1 *New Zealanders wearing Small Box Respirators during musketry training in March 1918.*
IWM: Q 10509

2 *A German soldier shows how a frying pan can be used as a gas alarm in 1917.*
IWM: Q 55224

3 *A gas alarm bell in a British trench at Beaumont Hamel in December 1916.*
IWM: Q 1717

4 *A German transport driver and his horses wearing anti-gas respirators. Special respirators were produced by the British, French and Germans to reduce the risk of gas casualties among transport animals working near the front lines. These generally took the form of a long fabric bag, treated with a chemical absorbent and stiffened with canvas or a similar material so that it would not collapse against the nostrils when not in use.*
IWM: Q 55085

2

with fluid and suffocate or 'drown' the victim. Mustard gas, introduced in 1917, severely blistered and burned the body, both internally and externally, producing agonising pain and sometimes resulting in temporary blindness.

The earliest gas masks issued to British troops in the spring of 1915 consisted of a pad of cotton waste, wrapped in muslin or veiling, and soaked in a water, hypo or soda solution. These were replaced in the summer by the 'P' helmet, a grey flannelette hood which was impregnated with sodium phenate and glycerine, and which was placed over the head and tucked into the collar of the soldier's tunic. In January 1916 the 'PH' helmet, dipped in sodium phenate and hexamine to provide better protection against phosgene, was introduced, followed shortly afterwards by the 'PHG' version with improved goggles. The best British gas mask was the Small Box Respirator which made its appearance on the Western Front in August 1916 and soon became standard issue. The actual face mask was fitted with goggles, a nose-clip and flanged mouthpiece and connected, by a flexible tube and outlet valve, to a canister filled with charcoal and absorbent chemical granules. The effectiveness of anti-gas measures was such that, after April and May 1915, deaths from gas were relatively rare. On the British side, 9 per cent of all wounded soldiers treated by medical units from 1915 to 1918 were gas casualties, but of these only 5,899, or 3.18 per cent, died.

4

5

5 *Projectiles being loaded and electric leads being fitted to a battery of Livens' Projectors on the Western Front. Developed by Captain W.H. Livens of the Royal Engineers in 1916, the projector was a steel tube – originally a cut-down gas cylinder – about eight inches in diameter and fitted with a strong base plate. Fired electrically, it could hurl a projectile containing thirty pounds of gas up to a mile. Livens' Projectors, which were placed in the ground at an angle of forty-five degrees, were not very accurate individually, but they were frequently installed just behind the front lines in batteries of twenty and, when fired simultaneously, could achieve a high concentration of gas in a small area. They were used by the BEF on a large scale for the first time at the Battle of Arras in April 1917.*
IWM: Q 14945

ASSAULT IN ARTOIS

The Allied spring offensive in Artois was given added meaning by the situation on the Eastern Front, where the Central Powers delivered a shattering blow in Galicia on 2 May against the Russian forces between Gorlice and Tarnow. For Joffre and Foch, a more immediate concern than offering indirect help to the Russians was the projected attack by the French Tenth Army, now under General d'Urbal, on a narrow, four-mile front with the object of taking Vimy Ridge prior to an advance into the Douai plain. An overwhelming six-day bombardment by over 1,200 guns prepared the way for the main assault on 9 May. In the vital central sector, allotted to Pétain's XXXIII Corps, the speed and depth of the advance surpassed all predictions. After only ninety minutes, the Moroccan and 77th Divisions had penetrated two-and-a-half miles and were on top of the ridge. Unhappily, d'Urbal had stationed his nearest reserves about seven-and-a-half miles in the rear, with the inevitable outcome that he was unable to provide early support to the divisions in the centre. By evening

2

1

1 *Men of 'C' Company of the 2nd Battalion, The Lincolnshire Regiment, occupying a mine crater in the German lines near Delangre Farm on 9 May 1915, during the Battle of Aubers Ridge. Acting Corporal Charles Sharpe, a member of this battalion, won the Victoria Cross on 9 May for clearing the Germans out of some 300 yards of trench, during which action most of his original bombing party fell. At Aubers Ridge the 2nd Lincolnshires, part of the British 8th Division, suffered 284 casualties, including 32 officers and men killed or died of wounds, 175 wounded and 77 missing.*
IWM: Q 50418

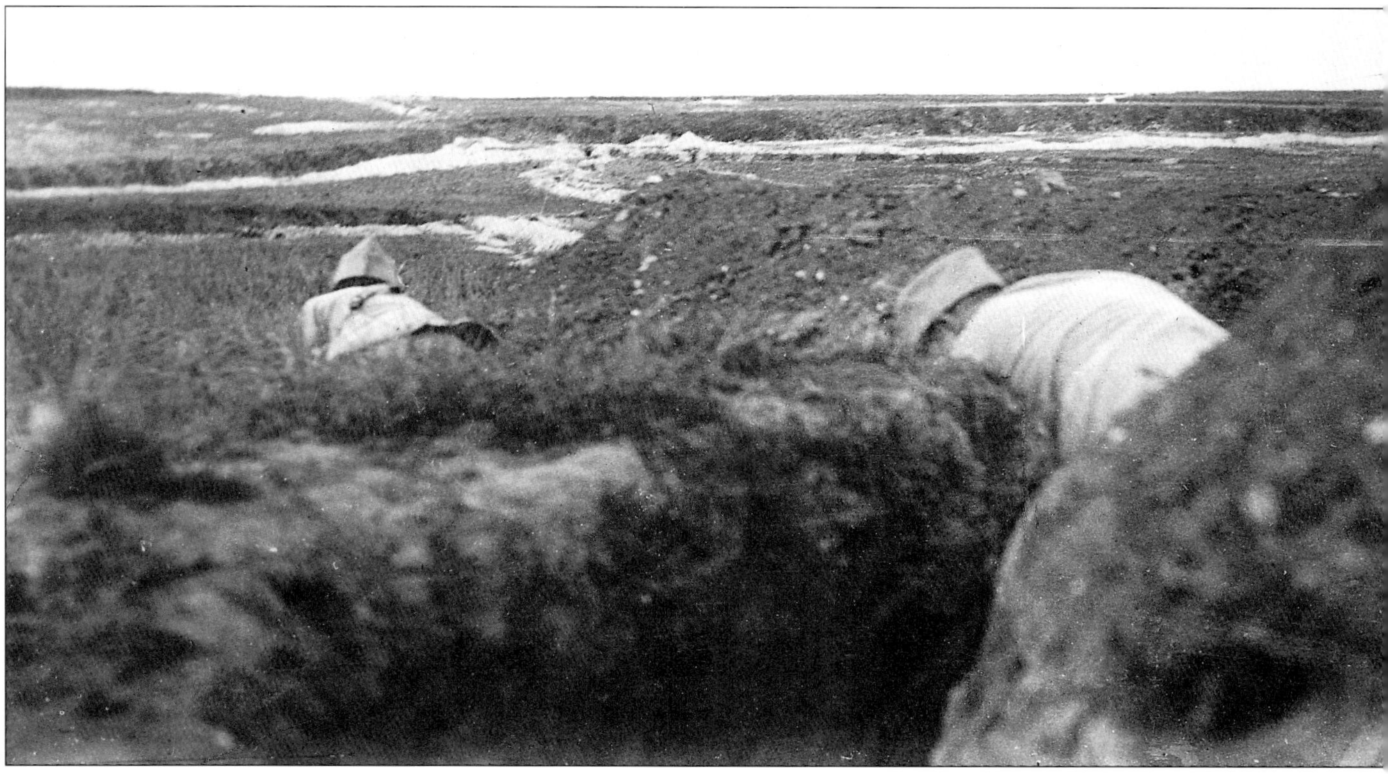

3

Pétain's troops had been counterattacked and driven off the crest. The high point of the offensive had been passed in more ways than one. The fighting, predominantly at close quarters in the network of German trenches and strongpoints, went on until 18 June, settling into the familiar pattern of attrition. Some gains were made by the French, the greater part of the imposing spur of Notre Dame de Lorette being captured. Tantalisingly, the Moroccan Division once more reached the crest of Vimy Ridge on 16 June but was again unable to keep all the ground won. In five weeks the French had lost another 100,000 men while inflicting around 60,000 casualties on the Germans. A foothold on Vimy Ridge and the recapture of another five square miles of French soil was small compensation to Joffre and Foch for overall failure.

The British contribution in support of the offensive on 9 May was an unmitigated disaster. In a large-scale version of its March thrust, Haig's First Army attacked either side of Neuve Chapelle in a further attempt to reach Aubers Ridge, 3,000 yards to the east. With the success of the short artillery bombardment in March still very much in mind, but also because of the shortage of heavy guns and ammunition, the British preliminary bombardment was limited to forty minutes' duration. The problem was that it lacked the weight to deal with German defences which had been strengthened after the March battle in this sector. The inadequacies of the bombardment enabled the Germans to man their trench parapets and strongpoints without the pause usually needed for the defenders to scramble up from their dugouts. The attack resulted in 11,600 casualties for minimal gains and Haig had no alternative but to break off the battle after one day.

Under constant pressure from Joffre to continue operations, Sir John French agreed that the First Army should make a new attack at Festubert, just north of the La Bassée Canal, on 15 May. On this occasion the objective was confined to a line only 1,000 yards away and the assault was to be preceded by a longer, sixty-hour bombardment. GHQ's declared intention of gradually wearing down the enemy 'by exhaustion and loss until his defence collapses' marked the real beginning of a more deliberate policy of attrition by the British on the Western Front. The BEF suffered 16,000 casualties at Festubert between 15 and 27 May, against only 5,000 on the German side, but a three-quarters-mile gain on a 3,000-yard front was sufficient to encourage greater reliance on prolonged artillery

4

2 *French troops in a trench on the heights of Notre Dame de Lorette, near Souchez, in the spring of 1915. The photograph reveals something of the extensive view which the Lorette spur commanded and indicates why it became such an important tactical feature during the 1915 battles in Artois. Much of the Lorette spur, a continuation of Vimy Ridge on the northern side of the Souchez valley, was taken by the French Tenth Army in May and June 1915.*
IWM: Q 49240

3 *A French staff officer keeps under cover as he crawls forward, only some 80 yards away from the Germans, whose trenches can be seen as a line of white chalk in front of the opposite bank. The picture was taken at the foot of the Lorette spur, near Souchez, on 15 May 1915.*
IWM: Q 49241

4 *A French officer in a communication trench on the heights of Notre Dame de Lorette in the summer of 1915. Note the foot sticking out from the wall of the trench.*
IWM: Q 49243

1

2

bombardments before future infantry assaults. Both the British and the French misinterpreted the lessons of May and took a tactical wrong turning in judging that, henceforth, a combination of wider frontages of attack, longer and heavier bombardments and 'wearing-out fights' would be the necessary preconditions for any breakthrough. These conclusions were to cost them dear.

THE FLAMES OF SUMMER

The Allied setbacks on the Western Front in May helped to foment a political crisis in Britain. Details of the BEF's ammunition shortages at Aubers Ridge were made available by Sir John French to Colonel Repington, the Military Correspondent of *The Times,* and used by the Northcliffe press as the basis of a hostile, if rather unfair, campaign against Kitchener and the War Office, criticising their performance in the field of munitions production. Coupled with the resignation of Lord Fisher from the Admiralty over the conduct of the Dardanelles operations, the 'Shells Scandal' led to the formation of a coalition Cabinet in Britain and, on 26 May, the creation of a Ministry of Munitions, under David Lloyd George, was announced. By placing armaments production on a systematic footing more suited to the demands of a mass industrialised war, the latter measure had colossal implications for the course of the war on the Western Front, even if the full benefits would not be felt by the BEF for another year or so.

The expansion of the BEF gathered pace during the spring and summer. Between February and September, six Territorial and fifteen New Army divisions were added to it, as well as the 2nd Canadian Division which, with its predecessor, was to form the Canadian Corps. In May the BEF took over an extra five miles of front between the La Bassée Canal and Lens, followed in August by another fifteen miles on the Somme, south of Arras, where a Third Army was organised under General Sir Charles Monro. The French Army, in June, was itself organised into Northern, Central and Eastern Army Groups, respectively commanded by Foch, de Castelnau and Dubail. As a reward for his services in Artois, Pétain was promoted to command the French Second Army.

As the Allied leaders considered their next major moves, fighting flared up intermittently in various sectors. The French, at a cost of 64,000 casualties, tried unsuccessfully in April to eliminate the troublesome St Mihiel salient which threatened to outflank Verdun. From 20 June to 14 July they lost a further 32,000 in the neighbouring Argonne. One of the most famous soldiers of the century, Erwin Rommel, saw action in this sector in 1915 as a young company commander in the 124th Infantry Regiment from Württemberg.

Having first employed flamethrowers near Verdun in February, the Germans launched a 'liquid fire' attack against the inexperienced British 14th Division at Hooge, in the Ypres Salient, on 30 July. The new terror weapon was successful here because of the close proximity of the opposing trench lines, but conditions were seldom as favourable to it again. In any event, the ground lost at Hooge was recaptured by the British 6th Division in a model minor operation on 9 August.

Joffre's proposals for the Allied autumn offensives were circulated at the beginning of June. They were similar to his plans of the previous winter in that they called for convergent thrusts from Artois and Champagne against the Noyon salient and its communications. Joffre decided to give the main role to the French Second and Fourth Armies in Champagne, where there were fewer fortified villages to overcome. In Artois, the Tenth Army would again attempt to take Vimy Ridge, while the British were asked to attack immediately north of Lens, across an area full of mines, slagheaps and villages – exactly the kind of obstacles that had prompted the French to make their principal effort east of Reims.

Conscious of their continuing deficiencies in heavy

3

1 *One of the remarkable photographs, taken by Private F.A. Fyfe, which are among the very few to depict soldiers at close quarters in the heat of action during the First World War. It shows British troops at about 6am on the morning of 16 June 1915 during the attack towards Bellewaarde Farm, between 'Y' and Railway Woods, just north of Hooge in the Ypres Salient. The men are taking cover while a shell bursts in the background. Private Fyfe, a press photographer in civilian life, took the picture with a pocket camera, even though such unofficial photography was forbidden by the military authorities.*
IWM: Q 49751

2 *Another of the extraordinary action photographs taken by Private F.A. Fyfe at 'Y' Wood near Hooge on 16 June 1915. The troops seen here include men of the 1/10th Battalion, The King's (Liverpool Regiment), otherwise known as the Liverpool Scottish. Private Fyfe was then serving as a bomber in the battalion's 'Z' Company. The unit formed part of the British 3rd Division. The men are a few yards in front of those shown in the previous picture and are sheltering under the parapet of the German front line trench. The flag in the top centre has been put up to confirm that the trench is in British hands and that the troops are moving on.*
IWM: Q 49750

3 *View over No Man's Land in the Bois Grenier sector, south of Armentières, in June 1915. The British lines are marked with an 'O', the German lines with an 'X'. The landscape in the fighting zone has not yet taken on the desolate appearance that it would present in later years of the war.*
IWM: Q 69482

1 *A trench known as 'The Appendix' or 'The Apex' in Sanctuary Wood in August 1915. It was then occupied by the 1st Battalion of the Honourable Artillery Company. This trench was a sort of deep gully which jutted out towards the German lines, and from which it was possible to fire both to the front and to the rear.*
IWM: Q 49378

2 *French troops filling sandbags on the Champagne front in 1915.*
Musée de l'Armée: 15494

artillery, Sir John French and Haig protested vigorously about the part assigned to the BEF, but Allied reverses in Gallipoli, in Italy and on the Eastern Front in August persuaded Kitchener that he must order Sir John to comply with the French plan, 'even though by so doing we may suffer very heavy losses'. German numerical inferiority in both Champagne and Artois was counterbalanced by their construction of a second defensive system some two to four miles behind the first. The Allied offensives were delayed until 25 September to allow the French to build new roads, light railways and jumping-off trenches in the bare fields of Champagne, yet Falkenhayn refused to be disturbed by the stream of reports about French preparations coming from von Einem, the German Third Army's commander, and left for a tour of the front with the Kaiser on 21 September. While Falkenhayn stayed cool, the French were supremely optimistic. 'Your *élan* will be irresistible', proclaimed Joffre in a stirring eve-of-battle message to his troops.

THE SECOND BATTLE OF CHAMPAGNE

The infantry attack in Champagne was launched in pouring rain at 9.15am on 25 September, three-and-a-half hours earlier than the French assault in Artois. Despite the weather, the French troops went forward with colours flying while bands played the *Marseillaise*. Early progress was encouraging. The massive four-day preliminary bombardment had badly damaged the German front trenches and had cut the wire in many places. This, and the violence of the infantry assault, enabled the French leading waves to reach the German first position in relatively good order and break through at four points. In the centre of the attack front the Moroccan Division was held up around the heights of the Bois de Perthes, yet the 10th Colonial Division, to its left, advanced up to 3,000 yards in under an hour, reaching the German second position. On the right of the Moroccans, the 28th Division made similar gains. Units on the extreme flanks also made a little headway but nowhere else did the progress match that achieved on either side of the Bois de Perthes, and casualties were becoming heavy.

Falkenhayn was made aware of the potential seriousness of the situation when his tour brought him to the Fifth Army's headquarters at noon. His immediate response was to send von Einem a division from the Vosges and to hasten elements of X Corps – which had recently arrived, with the Guard Corps, from the Eastern Front – towards the German Third Army's battle zone. The German defences in Champagne may have been dented, but with the bulk of his artillery already pulled back behind the second position, and with the wire in front of that position still comparatively intact, Einem was by no means facing a catastrophe. Nevertheless, Joffre felt that the French gains of the first day could be exploited and made two reserve divisions available to de Castelnau, as well as ordering Dubail to transfer to the Central Army Group all the 75mm ammunition that the Eastern Army Group could spare.

On 26 September the French edged towards the German second position, reaching it along a front of nearly eight miles. However, apart from securing one shallow foothold in the second position, the Champagne offensive lost its forward impetus at this stage. The next set of German trenches confronting the French had been cleverly located, where possible, on reverse slopes, denying the French gunners direct observation. Over the following three days the French infantry threw themselves into a series of furious attacks against the German second defence line, but only a few tiny lodgements were made. Mounting losses, dwindling ammunition supplies and Pétain's brave decision to stop the attacks on his own initiative compelled Joffre to order a pause in the offensive. Renewed assaults on 6 October were equally fruitless. Joffre's major blow in Champagne had neither lived up to his hopes nor fulfilled his grandiose promises. The Germans had suffered 85,000 casualties in Champagne but French losses totalled nearly 144,000. Thus the French could not even find consolation in the dubious balance sheets of attrition.

3 *The bodies of French infantrymen on the battlefield after an attack in Champagne in the autumn of 1915.*
Musée de l'Armée: K19169

4 *Weary French soldiers welcome a brief period of rest during operations in Champagne, 1915.*
Musée de l'Armée: S18

THE BATTLE OF LOOS

Haig's qualms concerning the lack of heavy artillery for the British First Army's part in the Allied Artois offensive were mostly offset by the availability of chlorine gas, some 5,000 cylinders of which were distributed to Lieutenant-General Hubert Gough's I Corps and to Rawlinson's IV Corps in September. Rawlinson was still none too optimistic about the prospects of the attack and favoured a battle of attrition in which the Germans would be drawn into expensive counterattacks, whereas Haig now saw the possibility of a strategic victory rather than a mere subsidiary tactical success. Aiming to break through the German first and second positions between Loos and Haisnes, and then push on east to the Haute Deule Canal, he decided to hurl all six divisions of the I and IV Corps into the main assault, on the understanding that XI Corps, in general reserve, would be handed over to him as soon as it was required. Sir John French, who was also uneasy about the coming battle, wished to keep the reserves under his own control until the assault developed, though he agreed to a request from Haig on 19 September that the heads of the two leading divisions of XI Corps should be within four to six miles of the start line on the morning of the attack. The use of XI Corps, instead of more seasoned units, as the general reserve was, however, open to criticism. Of its three divisions, the Guards Division contained experienced battalions but had only recently been constituted as a formation; the 21st and 24th Divisions – both Kitchener units – had been in France barely three weeks and had seen no front line service at all.

2

1 *Scottish troops marching through a French village on their way to take part in the British attack at Loos in September 1915.*
IWM: Q 60739

2 *View of a ruined street in the mining village of Loos, soon after its capture by the 15th (Scottish) Division. The distinctive twin pylons of the pithead winding gear – known to the British troops as 'Tower Bridge' – can be seen in the right centre of the picture.*
IWM: Q 28986

1

3

3 *A German trench damaged by British artillery fire, near Loos, 28 September 1915.*
IWM: Q 28972

At 5.15am on 25 September, after a four-day bombardment, Haig gave the order for the gas to be released, despite uncertainties about the wind direction. The first British gas attack of the war began at 5.50am, and forty minutes later the assaulting infantry divisions climbed out of their trenches. The gas was largely a failure on the left and in the centre, drifting back across the British trenches in several places. All the same, the 9th (Scottish) Division, in its first major battle, captured the formidable defences of the Hohenzollern Redoubt, Fosse 8 and the Dump, breaking into the German second position near Haisnes. Farther south, the 15th (Scottish) Division took Loos village. During the morning the Germans even started to make preparations to evacuate the area behind the front, but the French Tenth Army, attacking some six hours behind the British, was too late to take advantage of the situation and Vimy Ridge remained frustratingly beyond its grasp.

Sir John French received Haig's request for the reserves at 8.45am and freed the 21st and 24th Divisions by 9.30. Slow transmission of movement orders, and

congestion on the approach roads – partly the fault of Haig's First Army staff – delayed their arrival at the front until well into the afternoon. The two raw divisions were then compelled to advance at night, across an unfamiliar and debris-strewn battlefield, for an attack without effective artillery support against the intact barbed wire of the German second position at 11am on 26 September. Enfiladed from both flanks, the attack, not surprisingly, ended in a disorganised retirement and even the Guards, initially deployed to

4

4 British soldiers returning from the line after taking part in the Battle of Loos. Note the converted London buses being used for Army transport purposes.
IWM: Q 60740

5 The British attack on the Hohenzollern Redoubt in progress on 13 October 1915. A cloud of smoke and gas can be seen in the centre and left of the picture, while bursting shells are visible in the centre and on the right. The British trenches and approaches can be traced by the lines of excavated chalk. The pithead gear of Fosse 8 may just be discerned behind the bursting shrapnel in the centre.
IWM: Q 29001

1

stiffen the line, were unable to take the hotly-contested Hill 70 to the east of Loos. German counterattacks soon recaptured many of the British gains, including the Hohenzollern Redoubt. The French, in trying to avoid a repetition of May, this time kept *their* reserves too far forward and they suffered badly from German shelling. Despite these losses, the French at last captured Souchez on 26 September. The Germans retained the crest of Vimy Ridge but the French also seized an important knoll (later known as 'The Pimple') at its northern end, holding it for nearly five months. Another British attack against the Hohenzollern Redoubt on 13 October succeeded only in securing its western face.

The autumn fighting in Artois generated yet more grim statistics. British casualties were over 50,000. The French lost some 48,000 and the total German losses on both the French and British fronts were about 56,000. For the British there had been a few encouraging signs early in the battle, notably the performance of the two Scottish New Army divisions. Sir John French certainly bears much of the responsibility for holding on to the reserves too long and keeping them too far back. Conversely, once they had been transferred to First Army control, their tactical handling by Haig and his staff had been less than distinguished. The BEF and its commanders still had a great deal to learn.

CHANGE OF COMMAND

The failures of 1915 may have shaken French faith in the infallibility of their offensive doctrine, but not all Allied illusions had been dispelled. Their generals were now well aware that protracted operations would be required to achieve the truly decisive victory, although no one had a clear idea how long the task would take. The experience of the past year showed that careful preparation, heavy bombardments and violent infantry assaults together usually ensured that attacking troops could break into and capture the enemy front line trenches. The second part of the problem – exploiting the success – remained largely unsolved. As the German defences on the Western Front became deeper and stronger, the Allied commanders recognised the principles, but had still to master the techniques, of mounting a series of assaults on successive positions, each calling for fresh bombardments and reserves. Furthermore, while the essence of attrition had also been grasped, many soldiers tried too often to combine it with a breakthrough. A breakthrough attempt was justified if there were real strategic objectives behind the enemy front being attacked; attrition was best employed where the ground itself was not of primary importance to the attacker but could be used to lure in and destroy the maximum number of enemy troops. The distinction was not fully understood by many of the most senior Allied commanders, who continued to be preoccupied with the capture of particular objectives rather than planning limited battles to kill Germans.

1 *French soldiers in a trench on Vimy Ridge in October 1915.*
IWM: Q 49224

2 *Field-Marshal Sir Douglas Haig, the Commander-in-Chief of the British Expeditionary Force from December 1915 until the end of the war. He actually held the rank of General when he took over from Sir John French, and was promoted to Field-Marshal in December 1916. His period of command is still the subject of much historical controversy. He has been widely criticised for his conduct of the costly battles of attrition on the Somme in 1916 and at Arras and Ypres in 1917, but he displayed considerable tenacity during the German attacks of March-April 1918 and, between August and November that year, defeated the main body of the German Army in the greatest succession of victories in the British Army's history.*
IWM: Q 23659

2

CHANGE OF COMMAND

1 *A French dugout in the Ravin de Souchez, scene of bitter fighting throughout the 1915 battles in Artois. The troops in this picture, taken in October 1915, belong to the 68th Infantry Regiment.*
IWM: Q 49296

2 *Men of the 2nd Battalion, Scots Guards, repairing the sandbag revetting of a British front line breastwork-type trench in the Laventie sector, December 1915.*
IWM: Q 17402

In the German and French armies in 1915 there were some tactical developments, largely initiated at a junior level, which pointed the way forward to a more flexible role for the infantry. By the end of the year the Germans were organising and training special squad-sized assault detachments, or 'storm troops'. In contrast to the columns and skirmish lines of 1914, these small squads moved independently across No Man's Land to deal with enemy strongpoints and machine gun nests, taking with them their own trench mortars, flamethrowers and assault cannon for immediate fire support. Grenades became the chief weapon of individual members of the assault detachment and carbines were carried instead of rifles. In France similar ideas were expressed by Captain André Laffargue, an infantry officer whose pamphlet *The Attack in Trench Warfare* came to Foch's notice. The British were still grappling with the unfamiliar problems of handling large masses of citizen soldiers and currently lagged behind in such tactical thinking. However, the notable increases in munitions output and the introduction of the Mills grenade and Stokes mortar during the year indicated that they would soon be winning the war of *matériel* on which so much else hinged.

The controversy over the conduct of the Battle of Loos led to Sir John French's removal and General Sir Douglas Haig's appointment as Commander-in-Chief of the BEF on 19 December 1915. Opinions differ as to how far Haig actually resorted to intrigue to get rid of his superior, with whom he had become progressively disenchanted since Mons. Certainly Haig did not hesitate to make his criticisms of French known in influential circles. Haig's recommendations also helped to secure the appointment of Lieutenant-General Sir William Robertson as Chief of the Imperial General Staff (CIGS) on 23 December. As a condition of taking office Robertson insisted that the CIGS should henceforth be the Cabinet's sole adviser on operations. With the painful decision to evacuate Gallipoli already

1

2

3

taken, these two appointments signalled the ascendancy of the Western Front in British strategic orientation at the end of 1915.

In the search for a more unified strategy, the Inter-Allied Military Conference at Chantilly from 6 to 8 December decided that the ability of the Central Powers to switch forces quickly from theatre to theatre on interior lines of communication could be reduced in 1916 if the Allies delivered simultaneous offensives on the Western, Eastern and Italian Fronts, employing only minimum forces in secondary theatres. At the end of December, Joffre wrote to Haig suggesting that the principal Franco-British attack of 1916 might take place astride the River Somme. On 23 January 1916 he also proposed that, before the general offensive, the BEF should seek to exhaust German reserves in 'wearing-out fights' in April and May. Haig regarded the 'wearing-out fight' as a vital preliminary phase of the main battle and not as a separate operation. Determined to avoid dissipating the strength of the expanding but under-trained BEF in premature attacks, he resisted this aspect of Joffre's proposals. At the same time, he accepted the broader implications of Britain's subordinate position in the military alliance and, despite his own preference for a Flanders offensive, agreed with Joffre, at a meeting on 14 February, that the BEF would participate in a combined offensive on the Somme on or about 1 July 1916.

3 *General (later Field-Marshal) Sir William Robertson, Chief of the Imperial General Staff from December 1915 to February 1918. The British government's principal advisor on military operations during that period, he generally supported Haig's view that the war could only be won by defeating the Germans in France and Belgium. His opposition to alternative strategies brought him into conflict with Lloyd George, particularly after the latter became Prime Minister in December 1916. However, Robertson was not uncritical of Haig's conduct of operations on the Western Front and shared the concern of some politicians about the mounting casualty rates in 1916 and 1917. Robertson, who had enlisted as a trooper in the 16th Lancers in 1877, was the first British field-marshal to rise from the ranks.*
IWM: Q 69626

TRENCH LIFE

Even in the quietest of sectors, when no big battles or trench raids were in progress, units in the front line suffered a daily drain of casualties from artillery, trench mortar and sniper fire. Death was a constant companion in the trenches. A foolhardy novice, ignoring all warnings from old hands and driven by curiosity to take a peek over the parapet, might die with a sniper's bullet in his brain on his first day in the line. Equally, men with many months of active service behind them could be buried in a dugout or blown to pieces by a random shell. While some succumbed, mentally or physically, to the unrelenting stress of trench warfare, the majority endured, busying themselves with the never-ending tasks which provided fleeting distractions from morbid thoughts and helped to make life in the line marginally more tolerable.

For most British front-line infantrymen during a tour of trench duty, the daily routine began just before dawn with the morning 'stand to', when everybody clambered onto the fire step to guard against an early attack by the enemy. This was often a curtain-raiser for the ritualised aggression of the 'morning hate', as both sides relieved the tension of the night hours with bursts of small-arms and machine-gun fire or token shelling to re-emphasise their presence. As soon as it was light a tot of rum might be issued, and rifles were then cleaned and inspected. An unofficial truce, tacitly accepted on either side of No Man's Land, customarily settled over the lines while breakfast was being cooked.

1 *Men of the 2nd Australian Division manning the fire step in a front line trench at Croix du Bac, near Armentières, on 18 May 1916.*
IWM: Q 580

2 *Two members of the 42nd Canadian Infantry Battalion (Royal Highlanders of Canada) cleaning a Lewis gun in a reserve trench. The daily inspection and maintenance of weapons was a vital part of trench routine.*
IWM: CO 2196A

3

3 *Duckboards being carried over a trench in the British support line near Cambrai at night in January 1917.*
IWM: Q 6420

4

4 *A pump being used to drain a front line trench occupied by the 11th (Service) Battalion, The Lancashire Fusiliers, near Ploegsteert Wood in January 1917.*
IWM: Q 4653

DAILY LIFE IN THE TRENCHES

1 *Men of the 15th (Service) Battalion (1st London Welsh), The Royal Welsh Fusiliers, filling sandbags in a trench at Fleurbaix on 28 December 1917.*
IWM: Q 8372

2 *Territorials of the York and Lancaster Regiment taking coils of barbed wire up to the front line trenches held by the 62nd Division in the Oppy-Gavrelle sector near Arras, January 1918.*
IWM: Q 8436

3 *Captain W.H. Wynne-Finch, Adjutant of the 2nd Battalion, Scots Guards, asleep in a trench near Vermelles, in the Loos sector, in the autumn of 1915.*
IWM: Q 17383

1

2

3

4

4 *Men of the Border Regiment resting in 'funk holes' in the front line near Thiepval Wood in August 1916, during the Battle of the Somme.*
IWM: Q 872

Then, after an inspection by the company or platoon commander, the NCOs would assign men to a multitude of 'domestic' chores, such as draining and repairing the trenches, replacing duckboards, digging latrines and filling sandbags. Those who had temporarily escaped sentry duty or fatigues would pass the time preparing their midday and evening meals, reading and writing letters, and simply trying to snatch precious moments of extra sleep – perhaps the greatest luxury of all in the front line.

As evening approached the trenches once more sprang to life, since many of the tasks connected with supply and maintenance could only be performed in comparative safety at night. Dusk saw a repeat of the morning 'stand to', following which groups of soldiers would be detailed for sentry duty, each soldier spending up to two hours on the fire step. Others would be sent back to the rear to collect rations and water; go out into No Man's Land to patrol and man listening posts in shell holes and forward saps; or carry out much-needed repairs to the parapet or defensive barbed wire.

The relief of front line units was also invariably conducted under cover of darkness, except in the direst emergencies. Besides their own weapons and equipment, troops moving up into the line were frequently weighed down with assorted trench stores, including shovels, picks, duckboards, corrugated iron sheets, rolls of barbed wire and screw pickets. It could take a relieving battalion several exhausting and exasperating hours to wend their way through soggy and damaged communication trenches in the gloom. The journey would not be made any easier by the fact that the enemy was almost certain to put down machine gun and artillery fire on junctions and crossroads to inflict further losses.

FRONT LINE WEAPONS

Allied and German infantrymen alike were armed with bolt-action, magazine-fed, high velocity repeating rifles. Standard weapons in service on the Western Front during the First World War included the British .303-inch SMLE (Short Magazine Lee-Enfield) Mark III or Mark III*, the German 7.92mm Mauser-designed Gewehr 98, and the French 8mm Lebel Model 86/93 or Berthier 07/15 rifles. Trained professional soldiers, such as the men of the original British Expeditionary Force, were capable of firing fifteen aimed rounds a minute with the SMLE. In the hands of the average infantryman, the maximum effective range of these weapons was about 500 yards.

Most front line battalions eventually contained a number of specialist snipers and observers. When the unit came into the line they would position themselves in concealed posts along the battalion front or perhaps operate from shell holes in No Man's Land. The soldiers concerned frequently worked in pairs. One man would actually shoot at the enemy, using a rifle with a telescopic sight, while his companion looked through binoculars or a telescope to try to spot targets and estimate ranges. Snipers often wore camouflaged clothing, and sometimes fired through steel loopholes, which were either fitted into the trench parapet or were carried around with them. It was customary for British snipers to go with their own battalions when the unit was transferred to a different sector. German snipers, on the other hand, tended to stay in the same part of the line for months on end. This enabled them to obtain more detailed knowledge of the local terrain and trenches and so achieve greater efficiency than their British counterparts.

1

2

Infantrymen were also armed with bayonets. The British Pattern 1907 sword bayonet, with a blade length of seventeen inches, and the German Model 98/05, which had a blade fourteen inches long, were intended for both cutting and thrusting, whereas the French Model 1886 epée bayonet – nicknamed 'Rosalie' – had a thin, twenty-inch cruciform blade and was designed primarily as a thrusting weapon. Despite the emphasis placed on the bayonet in tactical doctrine and training manuals, particularly by the French Army, its use in combat appears to have been much less common than anticipated. British statistics suggest that under 0.5 per cent of wounds resulted from bayonets, though admittedly it is not recorded how many immediate deaths they caused. However, other edged weapons, such as fighting knives, were often carried on trench raids, together with improvised clubs and coshes.

Machine guns, with a cyclic rate of fire of between 450 and 600 rounds per minute, each provided firepower equivalent to that of forty to sixty ordinary riflemen. The major armies went to war in 1914 with a proportion of two machine guns per battalion. As the war went on the numbers inevitably increased, as did demands for lighter models than the belt-fed British Maxim or Vickers guns, or the German MG 08. In May 1915 British General Headquarters in France asked for four of the light, magazine-fed Lewis guns for each infantry battalion in addition to the four Maxims or Vickers by then already laid down, and at the end of 1915 War Office estimates of machine gun requirements were based on an establishment of sixteen for every battalion. In October that year the Machine Gun Corps was formed, to enable the heavier Vickers guns to be concentrated in order to improve their tactical handling. Thereafter, the Lewis gun became the standard machine gun of the BEF's infantry battalions which, by the spring of 1918, had 32 of these weapons each. The Machine Gun Corps itself initially

1 *Men of the 1/6th Battalion, West Yorkshire Regiment, with a 3-inch Stokes mortar in an emplacement near the front line at Cambrin on 6 February 1918.*
IWM: Q 8461

3

4

5

2 *The crew of a German MG 08 machine gun in action on the Western Front.*
IWM Q 87923

3 *A Lewis gunner of the 1/7th Battalion, The King's (Liverpool Regiment) cleaning his weapon in the line at Givenchy on 15 March 1918.*
IWM: Q 10738

4 *A Vickers machine gun traversing German trenches at night in the Cambrai sector, 4 June 1918.*
IWM: Q 6969

5 *A German 25cm heavy minenwerfer being loaded.*
IWM Q 23710

1 *Bombers of the 1st Battalion, Scots Guards, priming Mills grenades in Big Willie Trench, near Loos, in October 1915. 'Big Willie' ran southeast from the German defensive stronghold known as the Hohenzollern Redoubt. Four-and-a-half-million Mills grenades were produced during the last quarter of 1915 alone, and over fifty million had been manufactured by the end of the war.*
IWM: Q 17390

comprised infantry machine gun companies, cavalry machine gun companies and motor machine gun batteries. In 1918 machine gun battalions were organised by grouping together three or four companies. One such battalion, with up to 64 Vickers guns, was allocated to every infantry division. German infantry, including the assault detachments and storm troops, also made increasing use of the Model 08/15 and Bergmann light machine guns from 1916 onwards. As the war entered its final year, some German infantry companies on the Western Front had as many as six 08/15s each. The machine gun was certainly one of the dominant weapons of the First World War. On countless occasions, even a limited number of them proved capable of paralysing attacks by thousands of troops and of inflicting terrible losses. In this sense they contributed significantly to the stagnation of trench warfare but, as a defensive weapon, they could be, and *were*, overcome with the right tactics – as the events of 1918 demonstrated – and the casualties they caused never approached the scale of those resulting from artillery fire.

Trench mortars fired explosive bombs which, besides providing support for the infantry in both an offensive and a defensive role, were employed to demolish enemy trenches, machine gun posts, dugouts and barbed wire. Since they were usually sited in or near the support line, the daily work of the trench mortar batteries was closely associated with the activities of the infantry. However, their presence was not always welcomed by front line troops, as mortar bombardments invariably provoked an instantaneous response in kind from the enemy. Some of the earliest improvised mortars produced by British units in France were fashioned from iron water pipes and fired primitive projectiles made out of jam tins. Spring guns and catapults were similarly used to hurl rudimentary bombs at the opposing trenches. Yet, by mid-1916, the BEF had been issued with standardised light, medium and heavy mortars. Medium and heavy mortars served with divisional artillery and were operated by gunners, while light mortars worked mainly with infantry brigades, being fired by specially trained infantrymen.

The outstanding British light mortar was the Stokes 3-inch model. Developed in 1915, its great advantage was its simplicity. It consisted of a steel tube, not unlike a length of drainpipe. When a projectile was dropped down the tube, a percussion cap in the base of the bomb was fired on impact with a striker fitted in the base of the barrel. This method of loading gave great rapidity of fire – between twenty and thirty rounds a minute – and enabled the crew to keep several bombs in the air at a time. After March 1917 a new system of propellant charges stretched its range from 430 yards to around 825 yards. In the latter stages of the war a British division on the Western Front normally had three light trench mortar batteries, each with eight mortars, and three medium batteries and one heavy battery, each with four mortars.

The Germans, too, were equipped with light, medium and heavy *Minenwerfer*, and with large numbers of the smaller *Granatenwerfer* or bomb throwers. The German 25cm heavy mortar, when firing a projectile weighing more than 200lbs, with an explosive charge of 103.6lbs, was able to hit targets up to 515 yards away and create a room-sized crater. Even so, these projectiles could be spotted in flight, giving Allied soldiers time to reduce possible casualties by yelling a warning or blowing a pre-arranged number of blasts on a whistle to let their comrades know where the rounds were likely to fall.

The grenade, or 'bomb' as it was more familiarly known in the First World War, soon became one of the principal weapons in the trenches. It was either thrown by hand, usually at ranges of forty yards or less, or fired from rifles. Grenades were particularly valuable for fighting at close quarters in the trenches themselves, where a rifle's field of fire was severely limited. Most front line battalions therefore included their own specialist group of trained bombers.

Grenades were of two main types, according to their means of ignition and detonation. Percussion grenades exploded on impact, while time bombs

2

2 *A dump of British 2-inch ML trench mortar projectiles in their carrying blocks, at Acheux, in July 1916. These trench mortar bombs were known to British troops as 'toffee apples' or 'plum puddings'.*
IWM Q 1376

3 *Germans manhandling a wheeled 7.6cm light trench mortar.*
IWM: Q 23816

4 *British soldiers with 4-inch Stokes mortar bombs in canvas carriers slung on their backs. The men are resting on light railway trucks at Brielen on 3 August 1917, during the Third Battle of Ypres.*
IWM: Q 5853

3

4

detonated after a delay pre-set by a time fuse. As with trench mortars, British troops were forced at first to make crude grenades from jam tins fitted with short lengths of time fuse. Not surprisingly, such weapons were unreliable and hazardous to use. The emergency types were largely replaced, from the end of 1915, by the Mills bomb, the most successful Allied grenade of the war. A time-fused grenade, it had a cast-iron, barrel-shaped body which was weakened by a series of grooves, causing it to break up into lethal fragments on detonation. Over fifty million Mills bombs had been produced by the end of the war. The principal German type was the *Stielhandgranate* or stick grenade, known to British troops as the 'Potato Masher' because of its shape. Essentially a thin metal cylinder filled with an explosive charge, it was attached to a hollow wooden handle through which ran the fuse. To activate it, the soldier removed a metal cap from the base of the handle and pulled a cord which was thereby exposed. It could be thrown further than the Mills bomb but was less deadly, depending on blast rather than fragmentation for its effect.

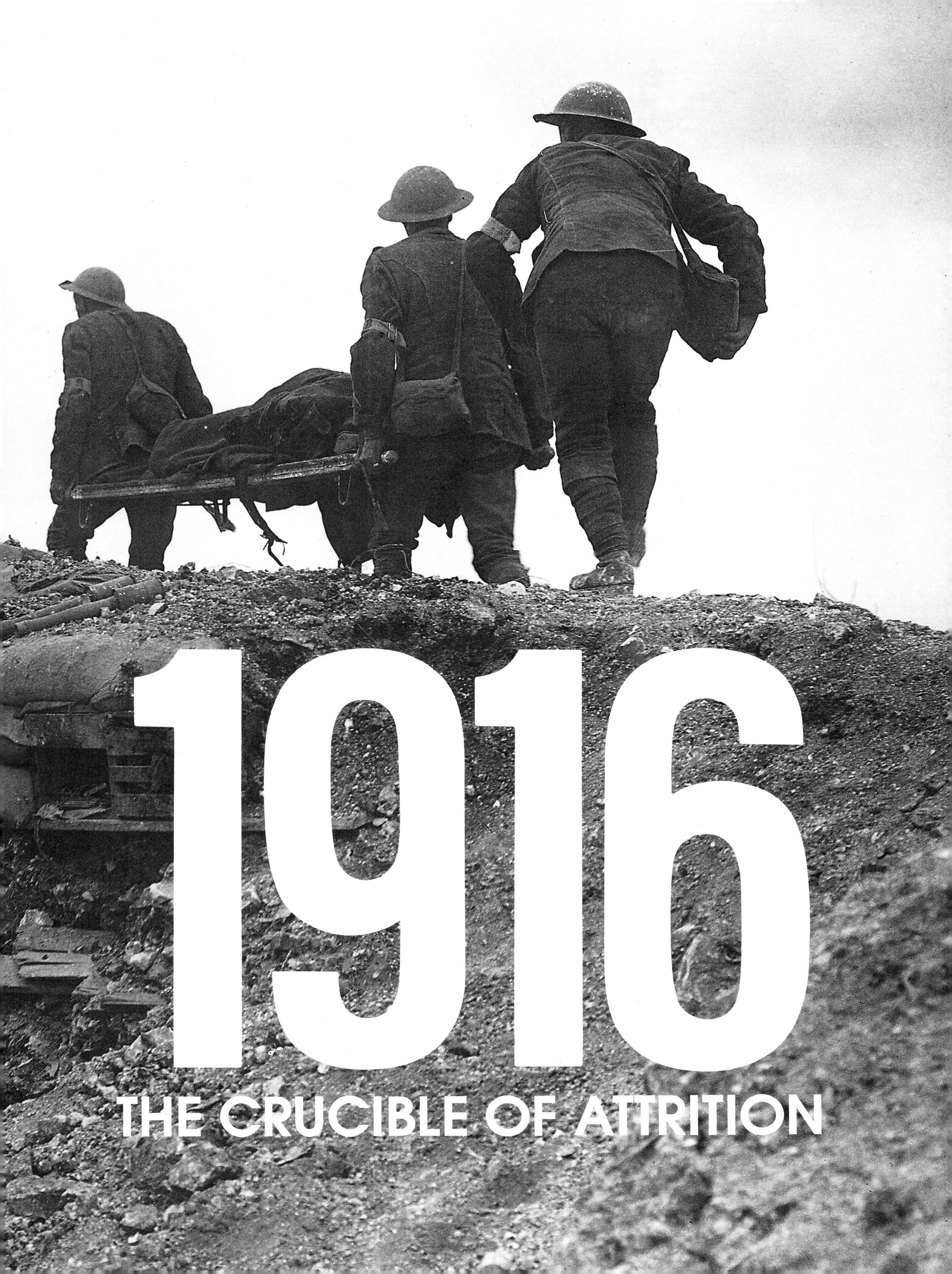

1916
THE CRUCIBLE OF ATTRITION

Previous page: *British stretcher bearers carrying a wounded man over the top of a trench in the ruined village of Thiepval, on the Somme battlefield, in late September 1916.*
IWM: Q 1332

VERDUN: THE PLANNING

The Allied plans for 1916 were forestalled by Falkenhayn. In the absence of major threats to the Central Powers from the east at the close of 1915, he could at last consider an offensive of his own in the west. In December 1915 he recognised that a significant victory was needed in the coming year to counter the growing Allied superiority in men and *matériel*. Describing Britain as Germany's 'arch-enemy', he hoped that the U-boats might be allowed to wage an unrestricted campaign to bring Britain to her knees. A war against neutral shipping might bring an angry United States into the conflict, but there was a good chance Britain would capitulate before American intervention could be made to count. On land, Falkenhayn concluded that the most effective policy would be to persuade the French of the futility of further sacrifice, thereby knocking Britain's 'best sword' on the Continent out of her hand.

The lessons of 1915 were enough to deter Falkenhayn from attempting the 'uncertain method of a mass breakthrough' against the French. Instead he intended to launch a limited offensive, picking as an objective a sector which the French would feel

1 *German troops gather round a field kitchen in a French village.*
IWM: Q 56577

2 *A German 30.5cm howitzer being prepared for action.*
IWM: Q 45556

3

3 *Crown Prince Wilhelm of Germany seated at his desk. Born in 1882, he was the eldest son of Kaiser Wilhelm II. As 'Little Willie' he became a favourite target of Allied propagandists and cartoonists. Something of a philanderer in his youth, he appeared ill-suited in character and temperament for high command, but was given the German Fifth Army on the outbreak of war and led it at Verdun in 1916. Although most of the key decisions were taken by his chief of staff, von Knobelsdorf, the Crown Prince showed a shrewder grasp of the realities of the Battle of Verdun than many other senior German soldiers, including Falkenhayn, and by April 1916 he wished to call off the offensive once it was clear that German casualties were rivalling those of the French. Later in 1916 the Crown Prince was appointed to command his own Army Group. In the last two years of the war, Crown Prince Wilhelm's Army Group was involved in all the major operations between the Aisne and the Meuse, as well as taking part in the* Michael *offensive of March 1918.*
IWM: Q 23740

4

4 *The interior of a German headquarters dugout.*
IWM: Q 61026

compelled to defend whatever the cost. 'If they do so', he wrote, 'the forces of France will bleed to death' whether the Germans reached their stated goal or not. While the German infantry would advance to threaten the apparent objective, an unprecedented concentration of artillery would do the main work of execution as successive batches of French reinforcements were sucked into the maelstrom of fire.

For the killing ground Falkenhayn selected Verdun, a fortress-city symbolising French national pride. It had held out for some ten weeks during the Franco-Prussian War and, in 1914, it had again withstood repeated attacks, forming a defensive bulwark and hinge in the centre of the French line. If it had fallen then, the whole of the Allied front might have collapsed. From Falkenhayn's viewpoint, Verdun was an ideal choice for other reasons besides its emotional importance to the French, as it stood in a salient which could be swept by the German artillery from three sides. The Kaiser's backing for his plan would be guaranteed by the fact that the offensive would be carried out by the Fifth Army, under the heir to the throne, Crown Prince Wilhelm. The real decision-maker in the Fifth Army, however, was the Chief of Staff, von Knobelsdorf, who had been specially appointed by the Kaiser. 'Whatever he advises you, you must do', Wilhelm II had told his son.

Virtually surrounded by hills and ridges on both banks of the Meuse, Verdun was also guarded by rings of forts, the strongest and most dominating of which was Fort Douaumont, situated on a 1,200-foot height on the right bank, to the northeast of the city. But the defences were not as solid as they seemed, most of the guns having been removed from the forts to provide additional artillery for Joffre's autumn offensives. Lieutenant-Colonel Emile Driant, a member of the French Chamber of Deputies, incurred Joffre's anger by making Verdun's weaknesses known to his fellow Deputies and, indirectly, to Galliéni, now Minister of War. By a twist of fate, early in 1916 Driant was commanding two battalions of *Chasseurs* in the Bois des Caures, almost in the centre of the German Fifth Army's front of assault.

To this day historians disagree as to whether Falkenhayn intended to take Verdun itself. Some evidence exists to indicate that Falkenhayn meant the Verdun operation to be a controlled diversion that might draw Allied troops from elsewhere and so create openings for the Germans in other sectors. Falkenhayn's decisions to confine the assault to the right bank, to restrict it to nine divisions and to keep the reserves in his own hands, all suggest that the seizure of the city was *not* his main aim. At the same time the Crown Prince was permitted to plan the offensive on the assumption that its objective was 'to capture the fortress of Verdun by precipitate methods'. There was less confusion of purpose over the artillery's role. A massive concentration of 1,220 guns was assembled in great secrecy behind the German front. The weather, however, was impossible to regulate. Blizzards, rain and gales caused the postponement of the attack from 12 to 21 February, giving the French a few precious days during which they brought up two extra divisions as reinforcements.

VERDUN : THE ASSAULT

The battle began at dawn on 21 February, when a 38cm naval gun, twenty miles from Verdun, fired the opening round. Missing its target, a key bridge over the Meuse, the shell burst in the courtyard of the Archbishop's Palace. The weight and ferocity of the subsequent nine-hour bombardment was beyond any previous experience. Along the entire eight-mile front a torrent of fire rained down on the stunned French defenders. In the Bois des Caures, trees were shattered, uprooted and hurled aside like skittles. Over 80,000 shells fell in this small area alone.

The savage bombardment presented the Fifth Army with a rare opportunity. For once on the Western Front, an immediate massed infantry attack would have had a real chance of success, as the guns had destroyed French communications with their front line and blocked the forward movement of reinforcements. Unfortunately for the Germans, their operational planning had erred on the side of caution.

A German infantryman takes cover in a damaged trench beside the corpse of a French soldier.
IWM: Q 23760

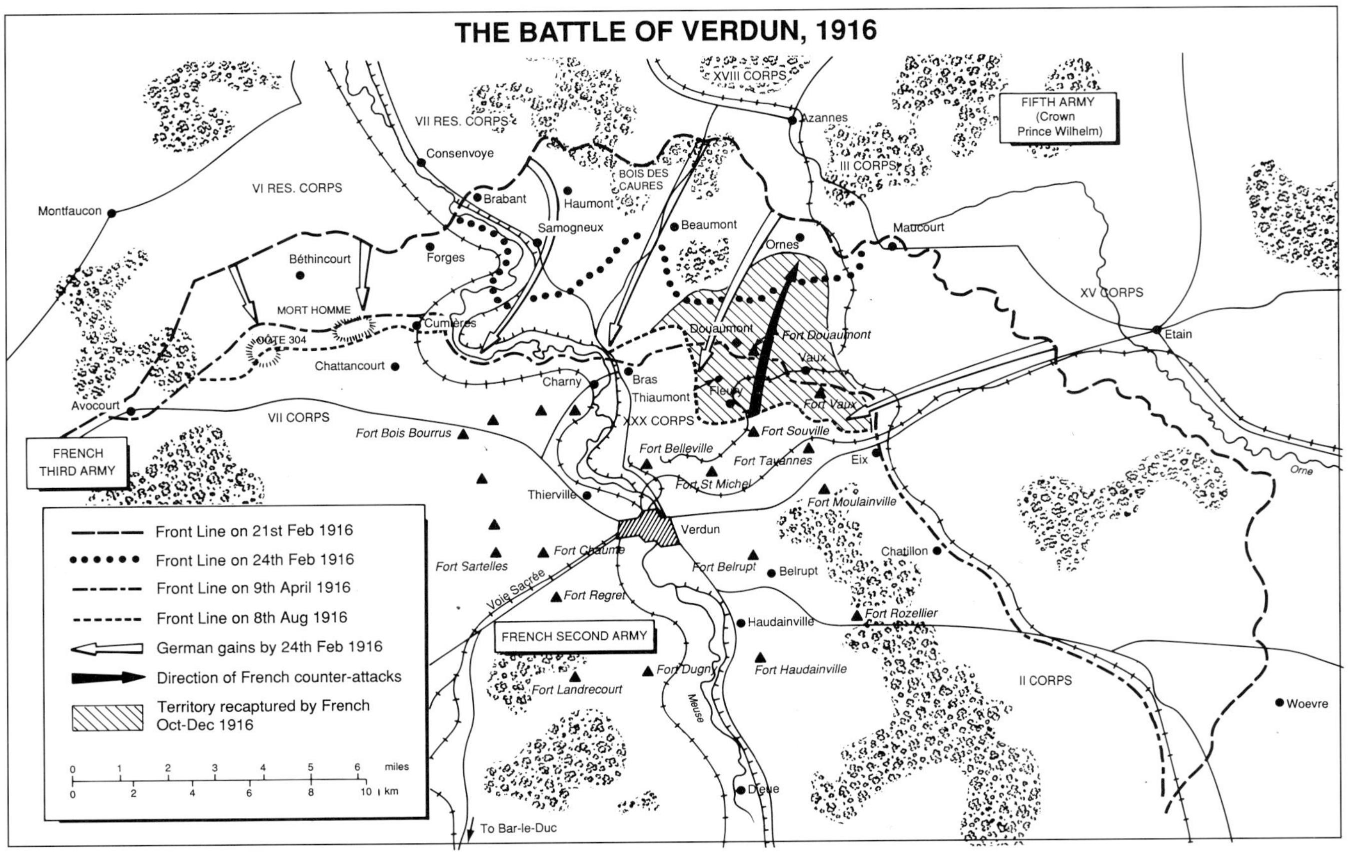

1 *General view of Verdun, looking across the River Meuse. The photograph was taken in November 1916, towards the end of the battle.* *IWM: Q 58315*

It had been decided that on the first day the advance would be restricted to strong fighting patrols, accompanied by flamethrower detachments, which would infiltrate the French front and search for weaknesses. Von Zwehl, commanding the VII Reserve Corps, showed what might have been possible. Contrary to orders, he sent in his storm troops close behind the patrols and captured the Bois d'Haumont in five hours, though because of Driant's intelligent use of strongpoints rather than continuous trench lines in the Bois des Caures, his *Chasseurs* had survived in sufficient numbers to offer stubborn resistance to the German XVIII Corps.

After another brutal bombardment, it was von Zwehl who again set the pace the next day, smashing through a regiment of elderly Territorials on the left of the French 72nd Division at the Bois de Consenvoye before taking the village of Haumont. The success of VII Reserve Corps tore a hole in the French first line and uncovered the flank of the Bois des Caures. Here the gallant Driant was killed in the late afternoon, attempting to pull back to Beaumont with the remnants of his battalions. A substantial portion of the French front line had now caved in, but the Germans had not had things all their own way. Though French losses were horrific, German casualties also rose ominously, especially among their valuable storm troops.

On 23 February the Germans were halted in front of an intermediate line which, having been created on de Castelnau's orders within the past month, did not appear on German maps. The French 51st Division's tenacious defence of Herbebois finally ended that evening but, in general, German progress had been slow during the day. Elements of the 37th African Division were arriving to support the exhausted French units of General Chrétien's XXX Corps, and powerful French artillery was now assembling on the left bank of the Meuse.

Any encouragement the French may have taken from these events was short-lived. Samogneux fell before dawn on 24 February. The 51st and 72nd Divisions had lost nearly two thirds of their combined strength and were at breaking-point. Beaumont was taken by the Germans and in barely three hours the French second position disintegrated. The Moroccan *Tirailleurs* and Algerian Zouaves of the 37th African Division were fed into the battle piecemeal, with no prepared defences to shelter them from the icy weather or the relentless German bombardment. In the critical sector covering Fort Douaumont, the 3rd Zouaves –

Chrétien's last reserves – simply evaporated before the advance of the Brandenburgers of von Lochow's III Corps. By nightfall the French XX Corps, under Balfourier, began to relieve Chrétien's battered units, but it was touch and go whether Balfourier would be able to shore up the crumbling front.

VERDUN: THE FALL OF FORT DOUAUMONT

During the afternoon of 25 February, the 24th Brandenburg Regiment pushed forward into the gap left by the disappearance of the 3rd Zouaves. In their excitement, some detachments went beyond the stated objective and reached Fort Douaumont which, partly due to a recent command and staff mix-up, was garrisoned by fewer than 60 French Territorial gunners under a sergeant-major. Conscious that the fort was strangely silent, a handful of Pioneers, led by a sergeant named Kunze, boldly worked their way through the outer defences into the dry moat. Kunze and two others managed to climb undetected through a gun embrasure into one of the fort's galleries. The structure had not been seriously damaged, despite being pounded by 42cm howitzers, but the reverberations and fumes caused by the enormous shells had driven most of the garrison to seek refuge in the bowels of the fort. Three other small groups of Brandenburgers, each led by an officer, also penetrated the fort independently after Kunze, and by 4.30pm the garrison had surrendered. Verdun's principal defensive bastion had been seized by the Germans at negligible cost.

In Germany, news of the fall of Fort Douaumont was greeted with national rejoicing. In France the shock-waves were instantaneous and far-reaching. The way to Verdun seemed clear and plans were made to evacuate the city. As early as the evening of 24 February, before the capture of Douaumont, De Langle de Cary – commanding the Central Army Group – had proposed a retirement to the heights east and southeast of Verdun. However, at French General Headquarters, the pugnacious de Castelnau persuaded Joffre to bring Pétain's Second Army out of reserve to

2 *Pétain (left) shaking hands with Joffre.*
Hulton-Deutsch Collection: Key AX/ 908576

3 *The battered southeast face of Fort Douaumont, photographed after the battle, in December 1916.*
IWM: Q 58318

hold the left bank of the Meuse. De Castelnau then went to Verdun in person on 25 February. Armed with full powers from Joffre, he at once rejected the idea of a withdrawal, ordered that the right bank should continue to be defended at all costs, and pressed for Pétain's responsibilities to be extended to include that sector. By deciding to stand firm on the right bank, de Castelnau was falling into Falkenhayn's attritional trap, but the abandonment of Verdun would have gone totally against the grain of French doctrine, temperament and national sentiment.

Left to make his own decision, the hard-headed Pétain would probably have opted for controlled withdrawal. By the same token, given his new defensive role at Verdun, there were few French generals better fitted to carry it out. An unambitious and unaffected officer who disliked intrigue and show, Pétain brought two priceless qualities with him to Verdun. Not unlike Plumer in the British Army, he had a good grasp of the nature of modern firepower, and he also commanded the instinctive respect and trust of the front line soldier. His appearance at Verdun had immediate and beneficial effects on French morale. Restoring confidence in the forts so that they could serve as the spine of a new 'Line of Resistance', Pétain played Falkenhayn at his own game by concentrating the French artillery to inflict the maximum casualties on the Germans. In addition, with the rail links to Verdun cut by German long-range guns, Pétain took care to ensure that supplies were maintained along the single secure road to the south, a route which became known as the *Voie Sacrée* (Sacred Way). Four months later, vehicles were travelling up and down this vital artery at the rate of one every fourteen seconds.

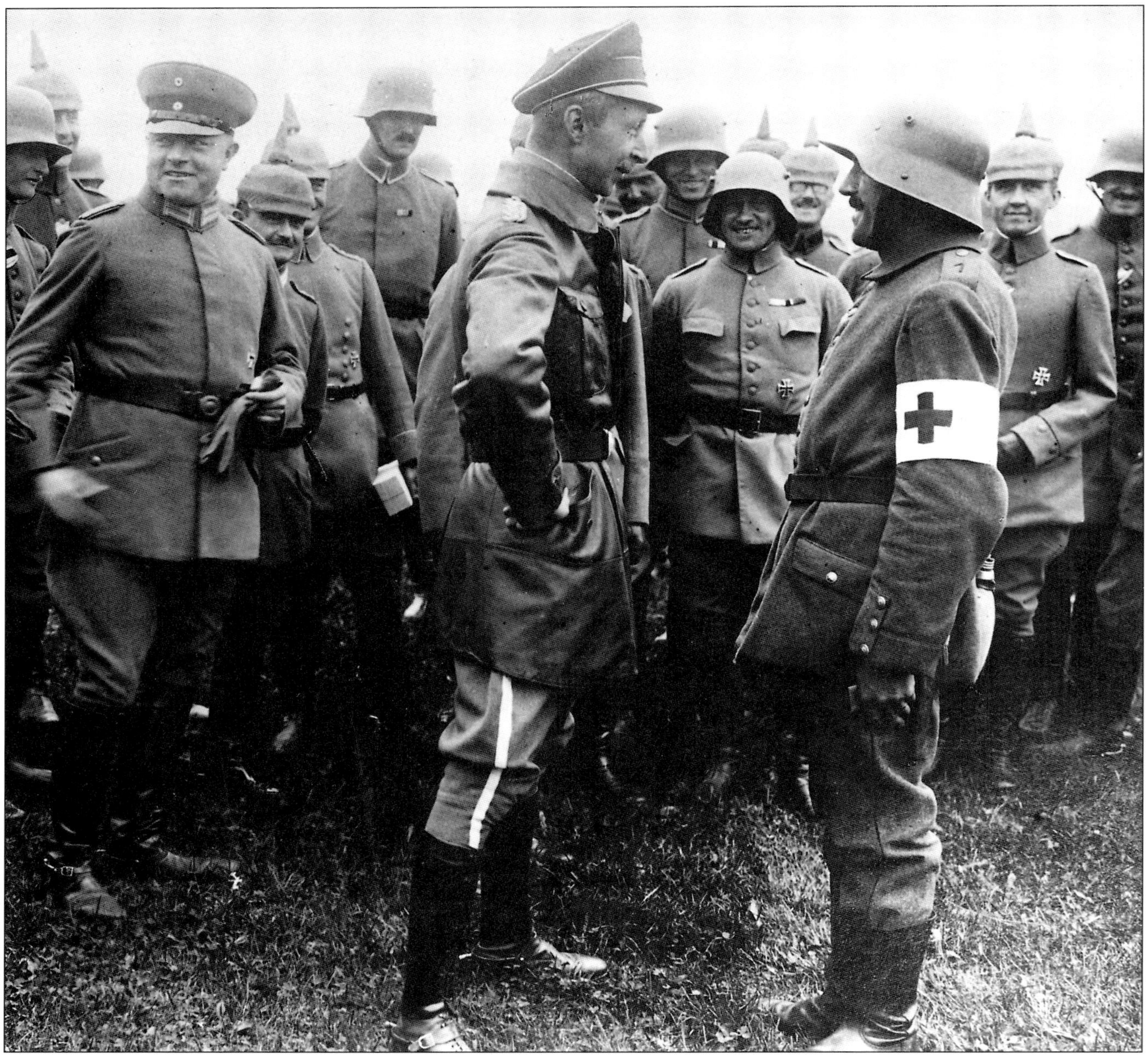

1

1 *Crown Prince Wilhelm, commander of the German Fifth Army, talking to a stretcher bearer during a visit to his troops at the front.*
IWM: Q 23744

2 *General (later Marshal) Henri Philippe Pétain, who skilfully conducted the defence of Verdun in the spring of 1916, concentrating his artillery to increase German losses, reorganising French logistical support and improving the system of reliefs from front line duty. Promoted to head the Central Army Group in April 1916, he became Commander-in-Chief of the French Army in May 1917, and restored its morale after the mutinies precipitated by the failure of the Nivelle offensive. The wisdom of his attempts to institute a policy of defence in depth was borne out by the German offensives of 1918, but his proposal to withdraw southwards, away from the British, at the height of the crisis in March that year resulted in the more aggressive and optimistic Foch being given the task of coordinating Allied operations on the Western Front for the remainder of the war. Pétain was created a Marshal of France in December 1918. In the Second World War he succeeded Reynaud as Prime Minister on 16 June 1940, quickly concluding an armistice with Germany. Having been head of the collaborationist Vichy régime from 1940 to 1944, he was sentenced to death for treason in 1945, although this was subsequently commuted to life imprisonment. He died in 1951.*
IWM: Q 5660

VERDUN: THE SPRING FIGHTING

Even before Pétain's measures made their impact on the battlefield, the German drive was running out of steam. The inability of the Germans to seize the prize within reach stemmed partly from Falkenhayn's miserly allocation of reserves and the Fifth Army's caution in delaying the main infantry assault until the second day. Above all, they now paid the price for restricting the initial attack to the right bank. As they dragged their guns forward over the shell-cratered ground, they were increasingly vulnerable to flanking fire from French artillery massing on the left bank near the Bois Bourrus ridge and behind a long, low hill called *Le Mort Homme* (The Dead Man). At the end of February the Crown Prince and von Knobelsdorf convinced Falkenhayn that the French flanking batteries must be suppressed. Accordingly, troops were made available to extend the offensive to the left bank. A big attack would be launched here on 6 March, with the *Mort Homme* as its main objective, while a renewed effort would be made on the right

2

3

4

bank, against Fort Vaux, soon afterwards. The battle was gathering its own frightening momentum, passing well beyond the 'limited offensive' envisaged by Falkenhayn. Crown Prince Wilhelm saw the danger, advising that the battle should be stopped if German losses began to exceed those of the French. As the next three months revealed, his fears were not without foundation.

In March, despite early successes on the left bank, the Germans failed to take the *Mort Homme*. Each German assault was inevitably followed by a French counterattack, and neither side was granted a moment's respite from the other's awesome artillery fire. By the end of March German casualties numbered 81,607, only 7,000 less than the French. Pétain's institution of the 'Noria' system, whereby units were rotated more rapidly in and out of the line, improved the morale and freshness of the French troops, giving them an edge over the Germans, who were kept at the front for longer periods. The relief of the French Tenth Army around Arras by the BEF also eased French manpower problems. The German Fifth Army's command structure for the battle was simplified, with

3 *French troops about to fire an 86mm Aasen light trench mortar in March 1916.* IWM: Q 69481

4 *General Charles Mangin. His policy of relentless attack was a significant factor in increasing the human cost of the Battle of Verdun, but his successes in the autumn of 1916 led to him being given command of the French Sixth Army. He was removed in the wake of the failure of Nivelle's spring offensive in 1917, later regaining favour under Foch and commanding the French Tenth Army in the counterstroke on the Marne in July 1918. Mangin's vigorous approach to battle was more productive in the changed tactical conditions of 1918, and he performed better than most French generals in the final Allied offensive.* IWM: Q 34781

VERDUN: THE SPRING FIGHTING

1 *A French 105mm gun near Verdun in 1916.*
IWM: Q 69619

General von Mudra being handed responsibility for the right bank and the gifted gunner General von Gallwitz taking charge of the left bank, but German frustration grew in April as the *Mort Homme* and *Côte 304* – a neighbouring height to its west – stayed in French possession.

Falkenhayn, whose character shifted unpredictably between ruthlessness and self-doubt, began to consider the need to 'seek a decision elsewhere'. The Crown Prince had even greater reservations about continuing. Von Knobelsdorf, in contrast, was determined that the battle should go on. He manoeuvred the replacement of the able but pessimistic von Mudra with the combative von Lochow, and exploited his own unique position and influence to win Falkenhayn's support for further attacks. Early in May, after a heavier bombardment than that of 21 February, von Gallwitz dislodged the French from *Côte 304,* and by the end of the month, at terrible cost, the *Mort Homme* was at last wholly in German hands. The conditions had been created for another assault on the right bank, where the front had moved less than a mile since February.

Pétain had waged a skilful defensive battle, slowing German progress to an expensive crawl, yet Joffre was critical of Pétain's reluctance to take the offensive and worried that the 'Noria' system was using up reserves earmarked for the Somme. Joffre eased his own anxieties by promoting Pétain to replace De Langle de Cary in command of the Central Army Group, and by giving the Second Army to General Robert Nivelle, a vigorous disciple of the de Grandmaison school. Nivelle took over the day-to-day conduct of the battle on 1 May, ushering into the spotlight of the Verdun fighting General Charles Mangin, a divisional commander whose penchant for attacks regardless of cost caused some troops to dub him 'the butcher' or 'eater of men'. Instead of heeding Pétain's sound advice to wait until he had sufficient men to strike on a broader front, Mangin, backed by Joffre and Nivelle, threw his 5th Division into a bloody and futile attempt to retake Fort Douaumont on 22-23 May. With attack-minded generals now holding sway on both sides of No Man's Land, it was a portent of the miseries still to come.

VERDUN: SUMMER FURY

The slaughter went on unabated through the summer. Falkenhayn, whose optimism was temporarily restored by gains on the left bank, gave his blessing to Knobelsdorf's plans for a new five-division thrust on the right bank, with the object of capturing Fort Vaux, Fort Souville and the strongpoint known as the *Ouvrage de Thiaumont*, the last significant obstacles before Verdun. Codenamed 'May Cup', the assault began on 1 June. For a week the garrison of Fort Vaux, under Major Sylvain-Eugène Raynal, maintained a magnificent defence, bitterly contesting every inch of the fort's dark underground corridors against German flamethrower, grenade and gas attacks, until unbearable thirst forced them to surrender on 7 June. The following day the Germans briefly took possession of the *Ouvrage de Thiaumont* but lost it again almost at once. In a microcosm of the whole battle, this feature changed hands fourteen times between 8 June and 24 October. More immediately, however, cracks had opened in Pétain's 'Line of Resistance'.

2

3

4

Pétain himself was growing resentful at continuing British inaction on the Somme. Joffre's jealous husbanding of troops for that offensive and Nivelle's unremitting counterattacks at Verdun were squandering the advantages of the 'Noria' system. By 12 June Nivelle had only one fresh brigade in reserve. Fortunately for the French, the Germans, at the crucial moment, once more lacked the manpower to capitalise on the situation. General Brusilov's offensive against the Austrians on 4 June obliged Falkenhayn to send three divisions from the west to the Eastern Front. Undaunted, Knobelsdorf circumvented the Crown Prince's opposition to further attacks and assembled enough men – including the élite Alpine Corps – to strike at Fort Souville, less than two-and-a-half miles from Verdun.

By this stage the Germans, like other armies on the Western Front, were learning how to exploit the rapidly-developing techniques of the 'creeping barrage', which enabled the infantry to advance behind a moving curtain of artillery fire towards their objectives. The Germans were also making increasing use of infiltration tactics, whereby storm troops and specialist assault teams in the leading waves were trained to bypass strongpoints and push deep into enemy positions before attacking them from the flanks or rear. For the attack on Fort Souville on 23 June a surprise tactical ingredient was added – 'Green Cross' shells containing the deadly new phosgene gas. Employing this mainly to silence the French gunners, the Germans captured the village of Fleury, causing Nivelle to issue an Order of the Day which concluded

2 *View of the southwest side of Fort Vaux after the fighting in 1916.*
IWM: Q 58317

3 *General Joffre decorates and congratulates a French private who has distinguished himself in the fighting at Verdun.*
IWM: Q 70069

4 *One of the galleries of Fort Vaux.*
IWM: Q 78064

1 *Kaiser Wilhelm II (centre) studies a map with von Hindenburg (left) and Ludendorff (right). Hindenburg served as Commander-in-Chief of the German armies on the Eastern Front from November 1914 to August 1916, when he became Chief of the General Staff. For the rest of the war he acted mainly as a figurehead, allowing Ludendorff, as First Quartermaster General, to shape much of Germany's military policy. From the autumn of 1916 Ludendorff wielded immense influence over Germany's economy, political life and military operations, but the failure of his 1918 strategy and his uncompromising attitude to Allied peace terms led him to resign in October 1918. After the war Ludendorff's right wing views grew more pronounced and he took part in Hitler's abortive Munich putsch of 1923, though his increasing mental instability caused even the Nazis to break with him. Hindenburg, however, was elected President of Germany in 1925, remaining in office until his death in 1934.*
IWM: Q 23746

with a phrase destined to become one of the most famous in French history: *Ils ne passeront pas!* (They shall not pass!) Pushing forward on too narrow a front with too few reserves, the Germans were stopped short of Fort Souville. Another major crisis had been survived by the French.

The battle had long ago lost its real strategic purpose. Both sides were now fighting principally for national honour. So much blood had been shed at Verdun that no one could easily take the decision to call a halt. Obstinately, Knobelsdorf organised one last attempt against Fort Souville on 11 July. A small group of thirty soldiers actually reached the glacis of the fort and looked down on Verdun, but they were all killed, captured or driven off. This was the closest the Germans got to their goal. With the overall strategic situation transformed by the long-awaited start of the Allied Somme offensive on 1 July, Falkenhayn had already ordered the Fifth Army to 'adopt a defensive attitude' at Verdun. But he had grasped the nettle too late. On 23 August a disillusioned Kaiser finally agreed to the Crown Prince's pleas and transferred Knobelsdorf to the Eastern Front. Four days later Romania entered the war against the Central Powers, incidentally hastening the downfall of Falkenhayn, who had declared this would not happen. On 29 August he was replaced as Chief of the General Staff by Field-Marshal Paul von Hindenburg. The latter was accompanied by his own indispensable Chief of Staff, Erich Ludendorff, the hero of Liège. After two years' absence in the east, Ludendorff was soon to make his authority felt in every sector of the Western Front.

VERDUN: THE COUNTERATTACK

Having helped to mastermind most of Germany's successes on the Eastern Front, Ludendorff knew precisely how important he was to Hindenburg. He rejected the title of 'Second Chief of the General Staff' and insisted on that of 'First Quartermaster General' besides being granted joint responsibility with Hindenburg for all decisions. From now on, under Hindenburg's largely symbolic though sometimes calming leadership, Ludendorff assumed almost dictatorial powers, exerting immense influence over German political life, foreign affairs and the economy, as well as military operations.

Hindenburg and Ludendorff made their initial visit to the Western Front early in September, swiftly effecting a number of fundamental changes in German strategy and tactics. First, on 2 September, a strict defensive strategy was decreed for the Verdun sector. Secondly, they moved away from the rigid linear defence imposed by Falkenhayn who, in July, had ordered that ground must be held at all costs and, if lost, retaken by immediate counterattack. It was now accepted that in some circumstances loss of ground was inevitable. A more flexible zonal defence system was to be adopted, embracing the ideas of officers such as Colonel von Lossberg, Chief of Staff of von Below's First Army. They included siting the key positions on reverse slopes away from direct observation; placing a lightly-held outpost zone in front of the main defence or battle zone; and keeping strong counterattack forces ready to hand outside

the range of shelling. The third crucial step taken by Hindenburg and Ludendorff in September was to initiate the construction of new defensive positions in the rear of the existing lines. These would not only enable the Germans to incorporate the principles of elastic defence in a system of great depth but would also shorten their front and help them to economise on manpower.

Not all of these changes were of immediate help to the weary Fifth Army as it awaited the expected French counter-offensive at Verdun. Under the watchful eye of Pétain, who made sure there were enough men and guns to strike on a broad front, the French attack was planned in detail by Nivelle and would be executed by Mangin, now in command of the critical sector on the right bank. Among more than 650 artillery pieces available to the French were two 40cm railway guns of great range, accuracy and penetrating power, which would be employed against Fort Douaumont. Nivelle gave a pivotal role to the creeping barrage, of which he was one of the earliest and foremost exponents. Moving its fire forward 100 yards every four minutes, the artillery supporting the infantry would be more concerned with the suppression of enemy troops than the destruction of specific targets.

The French tactics proved irresistible when their first counterstroke was launched on 24 October. On

2 *Senegalese troops about to board a train at a French railway station on their way to the front in June 1916.*
IWM: Q 78086

3 *French troops at Fort Douaumont firing a captured German MG 08 machine gun.*
IWM: Q 69971

3

that day, Fleury and the *Ouvrage de Thiaumont* were quickly taken, and the symbolic prize of Fort Douaumont recaptured by Moroccan troops. Fort Vaux passed back into French hands on 2 November. Within a few more days the French recovered much of the ground they had lost between February and July. A further savage attack on 15 December took the French lines two miles beyond Fort Douaumont, though the Germans retained the *Mort Homme*.

So the terrible battle of attrition finished. Total French casualties at Verdun were around 377,000 while the Germans lost about 337,000 men. The French Army had come through major crises in February and June and had saved Verdun, but nobody had gained any apparent strategic advantage from the bloodletting, certainly not the Germans. Falkenhayn's fatal irresolution and failure to match the means to the end had merely resulted in the German Army being 'bled white' along with the French. Neither Army ever fully recovered from the hell of Verdun before the end of the war.

1 *A crowd of volunteers waiting to enlist at the Central London Recruiting Depot in Great Scotland Yard, Whitehall, in August 1914.*
IWM: Q 81797

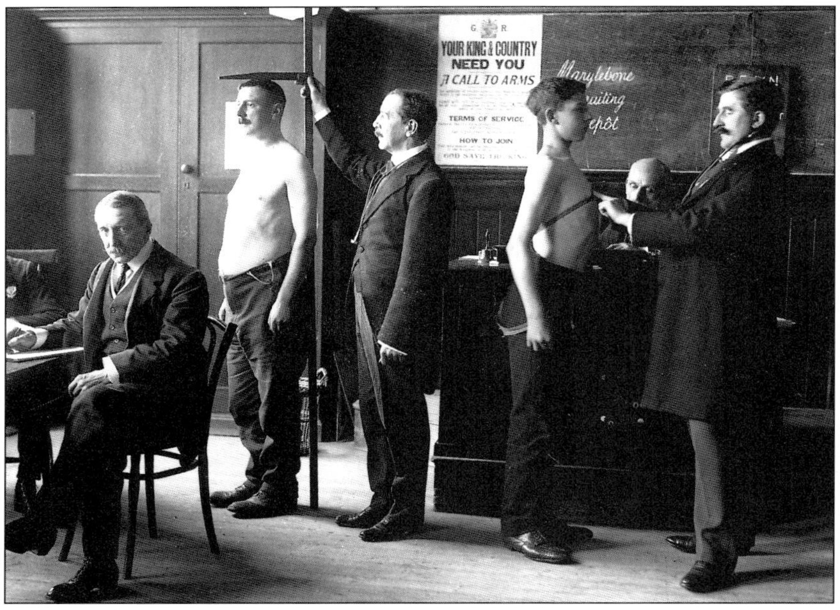

2 *The height and chest measurements of volunteers for the British Army being checked at a recruiting office in Marylebone, London, early in the First World War.*
Hulton-Deutsch Collection: CP 21-11

3 *Members of the University and Public Schools' Brigade boarding London buses in Hyde Park before leaving for training at Epsom in Surrey, September 1914.*
IWM: Q 53268

4 *Recruits of the Lincolnshire Regiment at rifle drill in September 1914. Most are still wearing their civilian clothes. The rapid expansion of the British Army in the autumn of 1914 caused acute shortages of uniforms, weapons and equipment for units training at home. Few battalions were armed as well as this photograph suggests until they had been in existence for several weeks or even months.*
IWM: Q 53286

THE BRITISH EXPEDITIONARY FORCE IN 1916

By June 1916 the BEF numbered well over one million men, including contingents from Australia, Canada, India, New Zealand and South Africa. It could now field fifty-eight divisions, organised into four armies. Apart from the increase in its front-line strength, there had been a corresponding growth in its staff, base depots, medical, veterinary and supply services, lines of communication troops and the Royal Flying Corps. According to historian Correlli Barnett, it was 'the largest, most complicated and most comprehensive single organisation ever evolved by the British nation'.

The creation of this mass citizen army was the result of a gigantic act of improvisation in Britain and her Dominions in the months after the outbreak of war. Drawn as never before from all levels of society, with many well-educated recruits serving in its ranks, it contained the flower of British and Imperial manhood. The steady decline in voluntary recruiting returns from the late autumn of 1914 forced Britain to break with tradition and introduce conscription for single men in January 1916, and extend it to married men in May that year. The effects of this, however, had yet to be felt in the BEF which, in June 1916, was still unique among the major armies in that it was composed of volunteers.

A number of those who had enlisted in response to Kitchener's appeals for recruits had helped to fill the gaps in the old pre-war Regular and Territorial units which had suffered heavy casualties in 1914 and 1915, but the majority were serving in the divisions of the five 'New Armies' raised from scratch, at Kitchener's instigation, after August 1914. Of the 247 infantry battalions which were selected to attack, or act as immediate reserves, at the start of the Somme offensive, 141, or over half, were New Army units. Though brimming with confidence and patriotic enthusiasm, comparatively few of the New Army formations on the Western Front had fought in a large-scale battle. On the other hand, the New Zealand Division and the four Australian divisions that arrived in France between March and June had a good nucleus of men who had gained combat experience in the tough school of Gallipoli.

The character of the BEF in 1916 was perhaps best exemplified by the 'Pals' battalions of the New Armies. Raised by civilian recruiting committees, mainly in the industrial towns and cities of northern England, the Pals battalions were largely made up of friends, workmates or men with a common social or geographical background, who were encouraged to enlist together by the promise that they would be allowed to serve and fight together. The unofficial titles of these units reflected their origins. For example, the 31st Division included the Leeds Pals, the 1st and 2nd Bradford Pals, the 1st and 2nd Barnsley Pals, the Hull Commercials, Hull Sportsmen and Hull Tradesmen, the Accrington Pals and the Sheffield City Battalion. The 36th (Ulster) Division was formed primarily from the units of the Protestant Ulster Volunteer Force, first raised to fight Home Rule, and contained five battalions from Belfast alone. Since the Territorial Force had, until 1916, also recruited from relatively narrow geographical areas, the BEF on the eve of the Somme embodied a high proportion of formations which were closely identified with particular communities at home.

5

5 *Field-Marshal Lord Kitchener, the Secretary of State for War, leaving the War Office on 2 June 1916 to address Members of Parliament. Three days later he was dead. Having accepted an invitation to head a military mission to Russia, he sailed in the cruiser HMS* Hampshire *from Scapa Flow on 5 June, and was drowned when the ship struck a mine off the Orkneys that evening. Kitchener may be described as the architect of the greatly expanded British Army that fought on the Somme in 1916.*
IWM: Q 56658

6

6 *New recruits of the 12th (Service) Battalion, York and Lancaster Regiment – the Sheffield City Battalion – drilling at Bramall Lane football ground in September 1914. The battalion took part in the 31st Division's attack on Serre on 1 July 1916.*
IWM: HU 37016

PATROLS AND RAIDS

PATROLS & RAIDS

When darkness descended over the trenches, patrols would be sent out into No Man's Land. Normally comprising an officer or NCO and a handful of men, these patrols were primarily intended to obtain information about the strength and general readiness of the enemy opposite, including the state of his parapet and barbed wire. The men in the patrol would creep stealthily forward to get as close to the enemy front line as possible, probing for weaknesses in his defences and listening for sounds which might provide clues as to his activities. Anyone exposed by the sudden light of a flare tried to stay absolutely still, and prayed that they would not be spotted. If rival parties met in No Man's Land a short, brisk fight would often ensue, although it was not unknown for each side to turn a blind eye to the presence of the other.

The facts brought back by such patrols were necessary to the high command for the planning of raids and large-scale attacks. Trench raids were much more substantial affairs than patrols, and were mounted with the deliberate purpose of getting into the enemy positions. They were usually carefully prepared and rehearsed and were supported by trench mortar and artillery bombardments, often in the form of a 'box barrage' around the threatened sector to delay the arrival of enemy reserves. As well as seizing prisoners to gain intelligence, the attackers would seek to destroy enemy dugouts and machine-gun posts. Raids organised by brigades and divisions could be highly elaborate operations, resembling minor offensives, with assault, cover and support parties and specialist sub-groups for bombing, wire-cutting and trench blocking.

In the BEF during 1915, raiding, though encouraged by GHQ, tended to be initiated at the lower levels of command and was determined by local conditions. Haig, however, viewed the trench raid as an essential element of a wider policy of attrition. From the start of 1916, therefore, raiding was carried out on a more regular and systematic basis under increasingly centralised control from GHQ. The Canadians helped to pioneer many of the techniques of trench raiding. The Australians, too, with their qualities of enterprise and bushcraft, established a fearsome reputation for what they euphemistically called 'peaceful penetration'. By mid-1918 their aggressive patrolling and raiding gave them a clear psychological and tactical advantage over their opponents. But if GHQ saw raids and patrols as a means of dominating No Man's Land and maintaining an offensive spirit among their troops, trench raids were unpopular with most front-line soldiers, many of whom felt that they simply resulted in unnecessary casualties for no real tactical or territorial gain.

1

2

3

4

1 *A raiding party of the 1/8th (Irish) Battalion, The King's (Liverpool Regiment), at Wailly, near Arras, on 18 April 1916. Some of the men are wearing helmets captured in a raid on the German trenches the previous night. More than 40 officers and men were involved in the raid. Second Lieutenant E.F. Baxter, the only officer killed during the operation, was posthumously awarded the Victoria Cross.*
IWM: Q 510

2 *British infantrymen wearing snow suits for camouflage as they clamber out of a trench at the start of a night patrol near Cambrai on 12 January 1917.*
IWM: Q 6423

3 *Men of a Territorial battalion of the York and Lancaster Regiment in camouflaged clothing shortly before setting out on a trench raid in the Oppy-Gavrelle sector, near Arras, on 12 January 1918.*
IWM: Q23580

4 *A daylight patrol of the 1/6th Battalion, The Seaforth Highlanders, clearing dugouts in a captured German trench near Greenland Hill, northeast of Roeux, during the Battle of the Scarpe, 29 August 1918. The troops fired and threw grenades into the dugouts to dislodge any German survivors.*
IWM: Q 7012

THE SOMME: PLANS AND PREPARATIONS

The principal reason for choosing the Somme front in Picardy as the location of the Franco-British offensive of 1916 was that the sector marked the junction of the French and British armies on the Western Front. There were no obvious strategic objectives, such as vital road or rail centres, close behind the German lines and, as the sector had hitherto been quiet, the Germans here had been able to build defences of immense strength in the chalky terrain, with fortified villages and dugouts up to forty feet deep. By late June the situation at Verdun had further undermined the original thinking regarding a joint attack astride the Somme. The French contribution to the initial assault was now limited to eleven divisions and, for the first time, the British were to play the main part in an Allied offensive on the Western Front, easing the pressure on the French Army.

1

1 Lieutenant-General Sir Henry Rawlinson, commander of the British Fourth Army throughout the Battle of the Somme. He is pictured here outside the headquarters of the Fourth Army at the Chateau de Querrieu, a few miles northeast of Amiens on the Amiens-Albert road. Rawlinson was responsible for several of the basic flaws in the planning for the initial British attack on the Somme. He absorbed the lessons of the offensive well, however, and in 1918 proved an outstanding tactician when the Fourth Army was given a spearhead role in the final Allied drive to victory.
IWM: Q 4031

2

2 A British 9.2-inch rail-mounted gun bombarding German positions on the Somme in the summer of 1916. The gun seen in this photograph was the only one of its particular type and calibre out of 467 heavy guns and howitzers behind the Fourth Army's front on the Somme at the end of June 1916.
IWM: Q 98

3

3 One of the platoons of 'D' Company of the 7th (Service) Battalion, the Bedfordshire Regiment, passing through a French village on its way to the line, just before the opening of the Somme offensive. The battalion formed part of the 54th Infantry Brigade of Major-General Maxse's 18th Division, and was involved in the attack on the Pommiers Redoubt near Montauban on 1 July 1916. The battalion lost two officers and 79 other ranks killed, and 13 officers and 212 other ranks wounded, out of a total of 321 casualties which it suffered in this action. Nine other men died of their wounds and six went missing. The officer seen here at the head of his men is the platoon commander, Lieutenant Douglas Keep. He was killed the following year.
IWM: Q 79478

Haig intended that, on the opening day, the British Fourth Army (formed under Rawlinson on 1 March) should overrun the German front line defences from Serre to Montauban, as well as the German second position on the ridge from Pozières to the Ancre and on the slopes in front of Miraumont. On the northern flank the 46th (North Midland) and 56th (London) Divisions were to pinch out the German salient at Gommecourt in a diversionary attack. To their right, VIII Corps (31st, 4th and 29th Divisions) would strike between Serre and Beaumont Hamel, while across the Ancre, the 36th (Ulster) and 32nd Divisions of X Corps attempted to take the formidable defences of the Thiepval plateau, including the Schwaben and Leipzig Redoubts. In the centre, III Corps (8th and 34th Divisions) was to attack Ovillers and La Boisselle on either side of the Albert-Bapaume road. XV Corps (21st, 17th and 7th Divisions) would assault Fricourt and Mametz, and on the extreme right, next to the French, the 18th and 30th Divisions (XIII Corps) were to capture Montauban. The French Sixth Army, north and south of the Somme itself, was to support the

British thrust by aiming for the German second position between Maurepas and Flaucourt, opposite Péronne. If the British assault proved successful, Haig then hoped to break through the second position on the high ground between Ginchy and Pozières. In the longer term the seizure of the German third position in front of Le Sars and Flers would threaten Bapaume and clear the path for the Reserve Army, under Gough, to advance northward and roll up the German lines towards Arras.

The absence of an immediate strategic target behind the German front need not have mattered had there not also been a divergence of views between Haig and Rawlinson concerning the underlying concept of the operations. Once again, as at Loos, Haig visualised a breakthrough, whereas the more pessimistic Rawlinson preferred a 'bite and hold' approach, in which the troops would consolidate each trench line gained and smash the inevitable counterattacks while the artillery prepared the way for the next step. To Rawlinson the primary objective was not ground but 'to kill as many Germans as

4 *Major-General H de B de Lisle, commander of the British 29th Division, addressing troops of the 1st Battalion, The Lancashire Fusiliers, at Mailly-Maillet on 29 June 1916, shortly before the start of the Battle of the Somme.*
IWM: Q 738

5 *A dump of empty 18-pounder shell cases, just part of the total fired by the field artillery of one British division in the bombardment of Fricourt before the attack of 1 July 1916.*
IWM: Q 113

possible with the least loss to ourselves'. In practice he tried to adhere to the spirit of Haig's general directive yet, since Haig left the detailed preparations for the attack to him, and because the basic differences of approach were never properly discussed or reconciled, the final assault plan was full of wrong assumptions and inherent contradictions. The lack of firm tactical guidance from GHQ also extended downwards from Rawlinson to his corps commanders. On the one hand, Rawlinson – doubting the capacity of the New Army divisions to master subtle tactics – dictated that the infantry should go forward steadily in successive waves of long, close-formed lines; in other respects he allowed subordinates a fair amount of latitude in shaping their individual artillery plans or in tackling the problem of crossing No Man's Land, an unfortunate consequence being that over-rigid battle tactics were imposed in some corps sectors.

1

2

1 and 2 *The Church of Notre Dame de Brebières in Albert, a familiar sight to British soldiers behind the Somme front in 1916. The tower was surmounted by a golden figure of the Virgin Mary holding aloft the Infant Jesus. The statue had been knocked over at a precarious angle by a shell in 1915, but had not fallen to the ground and had been secured by French engineers. The legend grew that if the statue did fall, then the war would end. It was, in fact, brought to earth in the spring of 1918 when Albert fell to the Germans. The town was recaptured by the British 18th Division on 22 August 1918. The church has since been restored.*
IWM: Q 1399 and CO 872

3

3 *The explosion of the huge mine under the Hawthorn Redoubt near Beaumont Hamel at 7.20am – ten minutes before zero hour – on 1 July 1916. The mine, containing 40,000lbs of ammonal, had been laid by the 252nd Tunnelling Company, Royal Engineers, and caused a crater 130 feet across by 58 feet deep. Although the Redoubt was destroyed, together with three sections of the defending company from the 119th Reserve Regiment, the attack on Beaumont Hamel was a costly failure.*
IWM: Q 754

4

4 *British troops, visible as black dots against the white of the excavated chalk, attacking German trenches near Mametz on 1 July 1916.*
IWM: Q 86

5

5 *The 103rd (Tyneside Irish) Brigade, part of the 34th Division, advance from the Tara-Usna Line to attack La Boisselle on the morning of 1 July 1916. Just behind them, in a trench, another wave can be seen waiting to go 'over the top'. The 34th Division, with 6,380 casualties, suffered heavier losses than any other division on 1 July.*
IWM: Q 53

The main drawback was that the technical means were inadequate, and the methods inappropriate, to meet the peculiar set of tactical conditions then prevailing on the Somme, where the Germans held most of the advantages. This applied especially to the week-long preliminary bombardment by 1,537 guns. The slow rate of advance by the infantry across No Man's Land was considered unimportant as the artillery was expected to have pulverised the defences. The infantry attack, it was predicted, would truly be a 'walk-over'. In fact, the guns were spread too thinly along the front; they included only 467 'heavies'; too much reliance was placed on shrapnel rather than the more effective high-explosive to cut wire and destroy German trenches, and many of the shells were 'duds'. Perhaps mercifully, all this was unknown to the majority of the British troops who watched and listened to the seemingly mighty bombardment as the hour of assault drew ever nearer.

THE SOMME: THE BLOODIEST DAY

Zero hour for the Somme offensive was 7.30am on Saturday, 1 July 1916. Larks could be heard singing as the British barrage lifted from the German front line and the infantry moved forward in their long lines. As in all big, set-piece trench assaults, the key to success lay in winning the 'race to the parapet', the infantry's first task being to progress through the enemy's barbed wire and into the front trenches before the Germans emerged from their deep dugouts to open fire with their machine guns. In most places on that hot July morning, the attacking divisions lost the race. For once, Rawlinson had underestimated the difficulties of capturing the German front line. Owing to the British artillery's general failure to deal with the wire and reach the dugouts, many defenders survived the bombardment and were able to cut down the attacking infantrymen in rows as they advanced at their

1 *German dead in a shell hole between Carnoy and Montauban on the southernmost sector of the British Fourth Army's front of assault at the start of the Somme offensive.*
IWM: Q 65442

2 *A roll call for the 1st Lancashire Fusiliers in a reserve trench near Beaumont Hamel after the attack on 1 July 1916. The battalion suffered 483 casualties on that day, including 8 officers and 156 other ranks killed.*
IWM: Q 734

1

2

deliberate pace across No Man's Land. British counter-battery work, too, had mostly been poor, so German guns which had previously remained silent and unlocated now added to the carnage,

Even the detonation of enormous mines under the German trenches at Hawthorn Redoubt, on the VIII Corps front, and at La Boisselle, where the 34th Division attacked, did not lead to success. Indeed, the decision by VIII Corps to lift the barrage when the Hawthorn Redoubt mine was blown at 7.20am gave the Germans there an extra ten minutes to recover and man the parapet. On other corps sectors, inflexible and unrealistic fire plans meant that the artillery barrage, lifting from objective to objective according to a rigid schedule, often got too far ahead of the struggling infantry and could not be recalled. The only substantial British successes on this first day were in the south, where the 18th and 30th Divisions, helped by the French heavy artillery on their right, took all their objectives, including Montauban, and the 7th Division captured Mametz village. Significantly, troops of the 18th Division, commanded by the perceptive Major-General Ivor Maxse, were moved out into No Man's Land, closer to the German trenches, before zero hour and then attacked under a creeping barrage. The 7th Division at Mametz similarly employed a form of creeping barrage. The impressive progress of the French Sixth Army on 1 July was partly due to its preponderance of heavy artillery, but the French had profited from their experiences at Verdun and advanced in small groups instead of lines. Elsewhere no tangible gains were achieved. The men of the 36th (Ulster) Division, some of whom had also

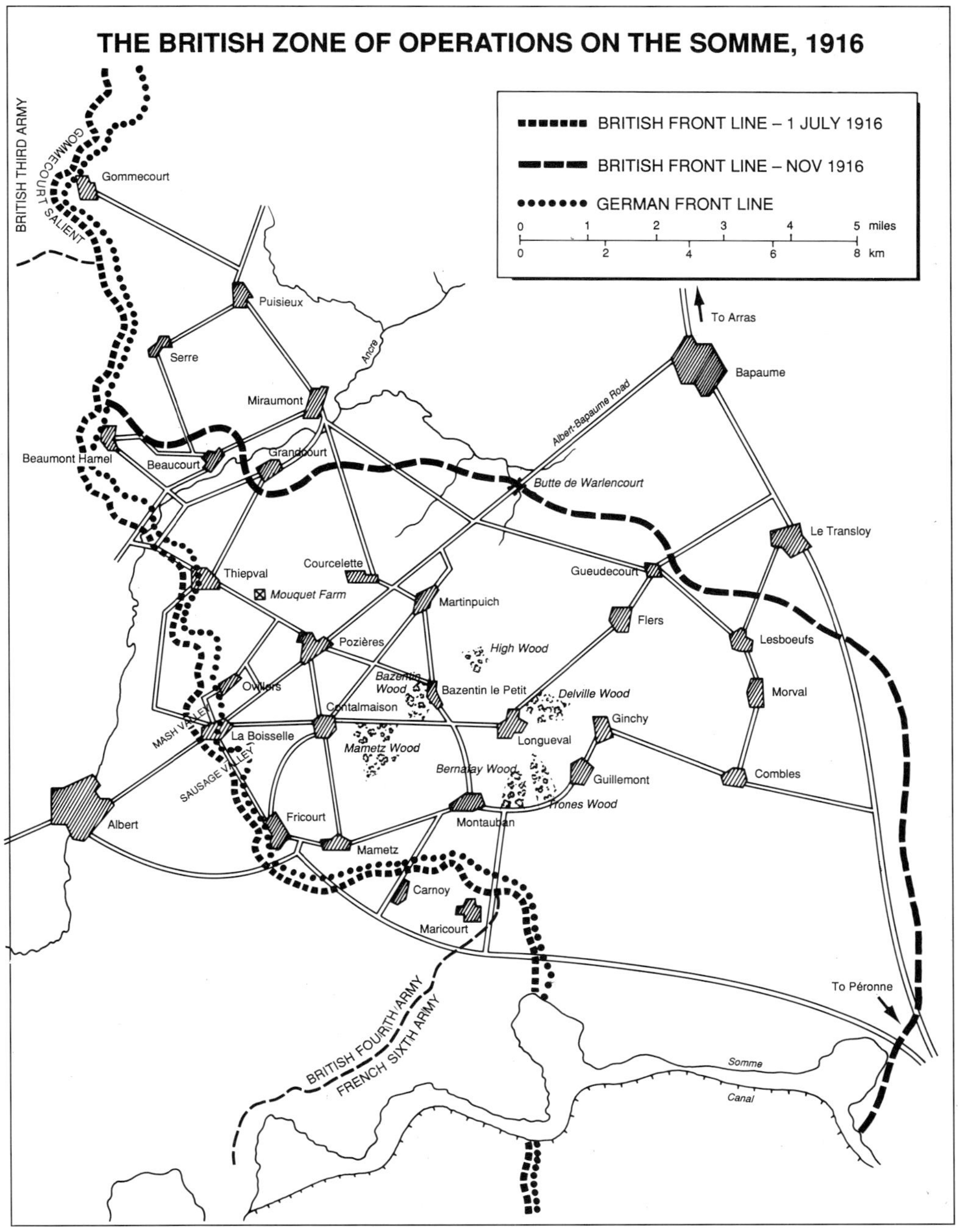

3

assembled in No Man's Land prior to the assault, attacked with great dash and gallantry at Thiepval and captured the Schwaben Redoubt, though they were forced to withdraw by nightfall because of the hold-ups on their flanks. At Gommecourt, the Territorials of the 56th (London) Division took their objectives, but were likewise compelled to retire when the neighbouring 46th Division failed.

The limited gain on the right – about three-and-a-half miles wide and a mile deep – cost the British the staggering total of 57,470 officers and men, of whom 19,240 were killed and 35,493 wounded. These were the biggest losses ever suffered by the British Army in a single day. At La Boisselle, the 34th Division, which contained four Tyneside Scottish and four Tyneside Irish battalions, suffered 6,380 casualties. Thirty-two infantry battalions, including the 1st Newfoundland Regiment, lost over 500 men, or more than fifty per cent of their battle strength. Throughout Britain in the days that followed, the delivery of telegrams heralded countless individual tragedies and the drawn blinds in

3 *A wounded man being brought in across the sunken road at Beaumont Hamel after the assault on 1 July.*
IWM: Q 753

1 *The steps leading down to a huge German underground shelter at the northern corner of Bernafay Wood, near Montauban, on 3 July 1916, following its capture by the 9th (Scottish) Division. The photograph gives a good idea of the depth and size of many of the German dugouts on the Somme.*
IWM: Q 4307

2 *The shattered remains of Delville Wood, near Longueval, the scene of bitter fighting in July and August 1916. The photograph was taken in September that year, less than a month after the wood had finally been cleared of Germans.*
IWM: Q 1156

the homes of the bereaved became all too familiar. The slaughter of Britain's citizen soldiers on the Somme was a major psychological shock and is still planted deep in the nation's collective folk memory. After 1 July the highly localised volunteer Army of 1916 began to lose its distinctive character. Replacements no longer always came from a unit's parent regiment and, within a few months, conscripts were filling the gaps in the ranks.

THE SOMME: SLOGGING MATCH

The first day of the Somme offensive was the nadir of the BEF's fortunes. The British had other bad days during the war, particularly in March and April of 1918, but none matched the scale and intensity of the tragedy experienced on 1 July 1916. With the struggle at Verdun having reached its 132nd day, there was no question of calling off the Somme battle which, in the end, would itself continue for a further four-and-a-half months. As July wore on, Haig began to think less of an immediate breakthrough and to regard the fighting more as a 'wearing-out' battle preparatory to the next decisive blow, probably in mid-September. Meanwhile, on 3 July, following Falkenhayn's order that not one foot of ground should be yielded, General Fritz von Below, then commanding the German Second Army, similarly decreed that the will to stand firm 'must be impressed on every man in the Army' and that 'the enemy should have to carve his way over heaps of corpses'. These policies set the pattern of incessant British attacks and equally determined German counterattacks which, as John Terraine points out, represented the true texture of the Battle of the Somme.

In the first three weeks, Gough's Reserve Army gradually took over responsibility for the northern half of the battlefield, until its boundary with Rawlinson's Fourth Army ran just to the right of the Albert-Bapaume road. Against the wishes of Joffre, who wanted him to renew the assault in the tough central sector between Pozières and Thiepval, Haig decided to exploit the earlier success on the right. From 2 to 13 July, therefore, the focus of operations was on Rawlinson's front as the Fourth Army strove to capture Trones Wood, Mametz Wood and Contalmaison to cover the flanks of a planned attack on the German second position. Although Haig had serious doubts about the methods chosen, Rawlinson and the men of the New Armies showed something of their real abilities on 14 July when, after a tricky night assembly in No Man's Land, a 6,000-yard stretch of the German second position between Longueval and Bazentin le Petit was taken at one bound in a dawn attack. Considering the horrors of a fortnight before it was a dazzling and daring feat, yet it was not quite

3

3 *The 20th Deccan Horse in Carnoy valley on 14 July 1916, shortly before their unsuccessful attack at High Wood. The 20th Deccan Horse and the 7th Dragoon Guards together suffered 102 casualties and lost 130 horses in the action.*
IWM: Q 821

4

enough. Longueval fell by the end of the month, but not neighbouring Delville Wood where, in a bitter contest amid shattered trees and tangled undergrowth, the South African Brigade suffered over 2,300 casualties out of 3,153 officers and men from 14 to 21 July. The aptly-nicknamed 'Devil's Wood' was not finally cleared until 27 August. A few hundred yards to the northwest, High Wood was apparently empty of Germans on the morning of 14 July. The commander of the British 7th Division was prevented from taking advantage of this opportunity by Lieutenant-General Horne of XV Corps, who wished to leave the operation to the 2nd Indian Cavalry Division. By the time its squadrons had arrived in the early evening the chance was gone. It took another two months for the British to secure complete possession of High Wood.

From 23 July the Reserve Army was engaged in a hard struggle for Pozières on the Albert-Bapaume

4 *Australians loading a 9.45-inch trench mortar in the Chalk Pit, south of Pozières, in August 1916. The projectile fired by this type of mortar was popularly known among the soldiers as a 'Flying Pig'.*
IWM: Q 4092

1 *British gunners, stripped to the waist, load an 18-pounder field gun in the Carnoy valley, near Montauban, on 30 July 1916.*
IWM: Q 4065

2 *British support troops move up across the battlefield under fire to take part in the attack on Ginchy, 9 September 1916. Ginchy, which lay between Delville Wood and Combles, was captured from Bavarian troops by the 16th (Irish) Division, part of the XIV Corps, on that day.* IWM: Q 1302

road. Pozières offered not only splendid observation over the surrounding countryside, but also an alternative approach into the rear of the Thiepval defences. In this sector the Australian divisions of the I Anzac Corps amply demonstrated their fine fighting prowess, taking the village and the fortified remains of the windmill on the crest of the ridge beyond its eastern end by 5 August. Attempts to advance northwest from the tip of a cramped salient towards Mouquet Farm and Thiepval attracted concentrated German artillery fire and caused the Australians, who suffered losses of 23,000 in five weeks, to criticise Gough's narrow-front tactics. Coming so soon after a calamitous subsidiary attack, involving the 5th Australian Division, at Fromelles on 19-20 July, the Pozières operations eroded Australian faith in British generalship. On the southern flank, as the French inched towards Péronne, Rawlinson tried to assist the progress of General Fayolle's Sixth Army by capturing Guillemont and Ginchy, but neither fell until early September.

Not all the suffering was on one side. Falkenhayn's decision to order a 'strict defensive' at Verdun on 11 July was one sign that the effects of the British offensive were being felt. Throughout July and August Falkenhayn's insistence on unyielding defence placed the German divisions on the Somme under increasing strain. Their strength began to diminish alarmingly; there was less time for rest and training, and the quality of reinforcements declined. Fresh German troops arriving on the Somme were quickly depressed by the obvious Allied material superiority. The officers and men of the BEF could, however, be excused for failing to discern these trends. To them the Germans were still extremely stubborn and skilful opponents.

THE SOMME: DEBUT OF THE TANK

The nature of the fighting on the Somme altered somewhat from mid-July to mid-September, taking on the character of semi-open warfare rather than siege-type operations. The Germans were no longer always occupying continuous trenches and instead often held irregular lines of loosely-connected shell holes. As the battle went on, and particularly after Hindenburg and Ludendorff came to power on 29 August, the

1

2

4

3

forward German positions were held more thinly, with greater emphasis being placed on defence in depth. Although the creeping barrage was now much more extensively employed, there was also a need for the British infantry to modify their linear 'wave' tactics and pay more heed to the possibilities of fighting their way forward in smaller bodies with their own support weapons, like the storm troops and assault detachments currently being developed by the Germans. While British infantry companies and platoons should have been becoming more self-reliant in firepower and aiming to infiltrate between strongpoints rather than assaulting them frontally, there was still an unfortunate tendency to rely largely on heavy bombardments and rigid artillery programmes which were, in fact, unsuitable for attacks on separated groups of enemy fire positions. In addition, the changed conditions of the 'wearing-out' battle were not immediately appreciated by some divisional commanders and staffs who were called upon to organise what they saw as wasteful 'line straightening' operations to secure elbow room or better jumping-off positions for the next major offensive effort. Others accepted 'line straightening' as a necessary evil in a war dominated by artillery, so that a simple, and therefore accurate, barrage line could be established for subsequent assaults.

3 *A Mark I tank crossing a British trench as it moves forward to participate in the fight for Thiepval in late September 1916. The large wheels at the rear of the tank were intended to help its steering and trench-crossing ability. However, they were found to be ineffective and easily damaged, so were dropped in November 1916.*
IWM: Q 2486

4 *A 'C' Company Mark I tank (C.19 – 'Clan Leslie') in Chimpanzee Valley on 15 September 1916, the day that tanks went into action for the first time at Flers and Courcelette on the Somme. Note the anti-grenade net on top of the tank, and also the machine's early camouflage pattern. This model is a 'Male' tank, carrying two 6-pounder guns.*
IWM: Q 5572

1

2

1 *Waves of British infantry advancing to support the attack by XIV Corps at Morval on 25 September 1916.*
IWM: Q 1309

2 *A British soldier's grave in a shell hole near Combles, marked by an inverted rifle driven into the ground.*
IWM: Q 4316

With members of the War Committee at home beginning to question whether the gains on the Somme were commensurate with the casualties, Haig was under pressure to produce good results from his planned mid-September offensive. Misled – not for the last time – by exaggerated reports from Brigadier-General Charteris, his Chief of Intelligence at GHQ, concerning the supposed near-exhaustion of the enemy, Haig was optimistic of achieving the desired breakthrough. The forthcoming push, against the German third position, would involve a reversion to the big set-piece assault, but now Haig was able to unveil a new weapon – the tank. Conceived by Lieutenant-Colonel Ernest Swinton in 1914 as a tracked armoured vehicle capable of surmounting barbed wire obstacles, crossing trenches and destroying machine guns, the tank had been developed – with the active encouragement of Winston Churchill – under the wing of the Admiralty Landships Committee. Two variants of the Mark I Tank, designed by William Tritton and by Lieutenant W.G. Wilson of the Royal Naval Air Service, were sent to France in late August 1916 : the 'Male' version, armed with two 6-pounder guns for attacks on strongpoints, and the 'Female' variant, carrying four Vickers machine guns for trench-clearing and dealing with close-quarter rushes by enemy infantry. Swinton had advised against using tanks in 'driblets' but Haig wanted to employ them to tackle separate strongpoints that might delay the infantry advance, and therefore distributed them evenly along the line instead of launching them together in a concentrated body. The actual breakthrough would, he hoped, be brought about by the artillery and infantry, the density of guns being double that of 1 July. Rawlinson, whose Fourth Army had the main role, proposed attacking in stages on three successive nights. This time Haig overrode him, forcing Rawlinson to adopt a bolder approach.

The objectives of the attack, which took place on 15 September, included the capture of the German third position at Flers and the subsequent seizure of

Gueudecourt, Lesboeufs and Morval. On Rawlinson's left, the Canadian Corps of Gough's Reserve Army was to take Courcelette. Of the 49 tanks available to support the infantry on the morning of the assault, only 36 arrived at their starting points. Helped forward by a creeping barrage, they caused some alarm among the German defenders. Four of the tanks assigned to the 41st Division reached Flers and one entered the main street, while the others engaged strongpoints and machine gun posts on the village's eastern outskirts. Flers duly fell to XV Corps and the Canadians took Courcelette but, although High Wood and Martinpuich were also secured, the advance on 15 September was limited to about 2,500 yards on a front of less than three miles. The Germans held on to Morval and Lesboeufs for another ten days, and Gueudecourt and Combles were not captured until 26 September. The offensive stalled as the breakthrough once more eluded Haig.

3

3 *A twelve-horse team and men hauling on ropes are needed to move a British 60-pounder gun into a fresh position near Bazentin le Petit on the Somme in October 1916.*
IWM: Q 4364

THE SOMME: GRIM HARVEST

Criticisms have often been levelled at Haig for committing the tanks prematurely in September 1916, and for using them in 'driblets' rather than in mass formation. There is, perhaps, some substance to the latter charge although, given the small numbers, slow speed (less than 4 mph) and mechanical unreliability of the Mark I tanks, it might have been an equal or bigger mistake to risk them all in one narrow sector of the front before their capabilities were better known. One should remember that Haig firmly believed in the prospects of a breakthrough and that, on the same day, simultaneous Allied offensives were in progress in the French sector to the south, on the Italian Front and in Transylvania. He can therefore be excused for thinking that another chance to use tanks might never occur. Even if it did, there was no guarantee either that their existence could be kept secret much longer, or that such *untried* weapons would be any more successful if their debut was delayed until they could be employed on a larger scale.

It is harder to explain why Haig persisted with the Somme offensive after mid-September. The principal reason appears to have been that he was genuinely convinced the Germans would ultimately collapse, provided that he maintained the pressure on them. On 26 September the Reserve Army began an attack on the Thiepval ridge from the Schwaben Redoubt to Courcelette. Mouquet Farm fell to the British 11th Division and Thiepval to the 18th Division on the opening day, but it was 14 October before the 39th

THE SOMME: GRIM HARVEST

1 *German barbed wire at Beaucourt sur Ancre, a village to the east of Beaumont Hamel, in November 1916.*
IWM: Q 4593

2 *Wooden sleighs, used for the transportation of wounded over muddy ground, at Le Sars in October 1916.*
IWM: Q 1495

3 *Pack horses struggling through mud and water near Thiepval to take 18-pounder shells up to forward battery positions during the fighting on the Ancre, November 1916.*
IWM: Q 65389

4 *A wounded soldier at a dressing station in Aveluy Wood shows a comrade his damaged steel helmet, which has had a piece blown out of it. The photograph was taken on 13 November 1916, on the opening day of the British attack astride the River Ancre.*
IWM: Q 4510

1

2

3

Division cleared the surviving defenders from the hated Schwaben Redoubt. To the right, or east, the Canadians became involved in a desperate struggle for Regina Trench which lasted until 10 November. In the meantime, between 1 and 20 October, the Fourth Army was crawling painfully towards Le Transloy, capturing Le Sars on 7 October. During October rain turned the battlefield into a quagmire, which some soldiers thought was as bad as that at Ypres a year later. The final phase of the offensive took place on the Ancre from 13 to 19 November. Despite the dreadful conditions and repeated postponements, this operation went ahead, partly because of the favourable impression which a late advance would create at the imminent inter-Allied conference at Chantilly. Gough's Fifth Army – as the Reserve Army was now known – attacked astride the River Ancre, north of Thiepval, to reduce the German salient between Serre and the Albert-Bapaume road. Although the 51st (Highland) Division took Beaumont Hamel and the 63rd (Royal Naval) Division captured Beaucourt, the village of Serre – an objective on 1 July – remained in German

4

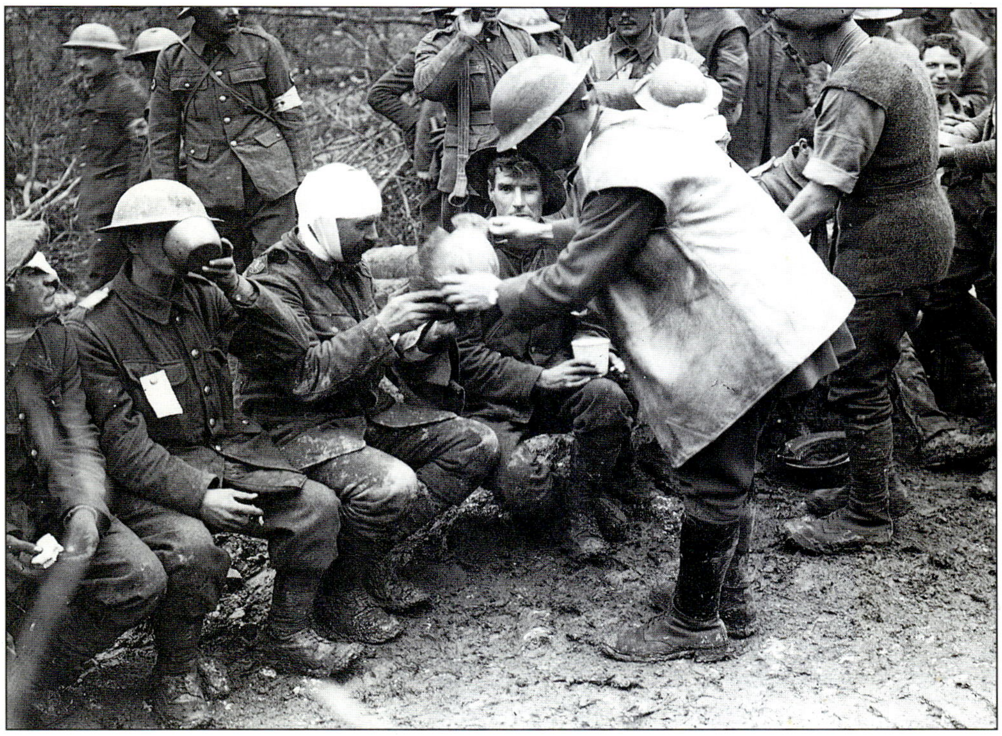

hands when the offensive ended. Overall, since 1 July, the BEF had seized a strip of territory approximately 6 miles deep by 20 miles wide, yet was still 3 miles from Bapaume.

For Britain and the Dominions, the cost of the offensive was an appalling total of 419,654 casualties, while the French lost 204,253. Estimates of German casualties vary widely between 450,000 and 680,000. What is certain is that the continuous British attacks forced the Germans to modify their strategy on the Western Front, a Hindenburg memorandum of 21 September 1916 declaring that the Somme front was all-important and must have first call on available units. There were also signs of improved tactical thinking at divisional level in the BEF, with commanders like Stephens of the 5th Division and Maxse of the 18th Division beginning to advocate the abandonment of long lines or 'waves' in attack, and to urge the increased use of Lewis light machine guns so that infantry platoons might become more self-supporting in an advance. As Britain's citizen army learnt its trade, the Imperial German Army was undoubtedly being weakened. The shrewd Crown Prince Rupprecht of Bavaria remarked that what was left of the 'old first-class, peace-trained German infantry had been expended on the battlefield' and Ludendorff himself conceded that the Army 'had been fought to a standstill and was utterly worn out'.

1

1 *A wounded British soldier being brought in during the attack on the Ancre, 13 November 1916.*
IWM: Q 4538

2

2 *A working party, clad in waterproof capes and thigh-length trench waders, waiting for orders in the rain at St Pierre Divion in November 1916, during the last phase of the British Somme offensive.*
IWM: Q 4602

WAR OF THE GUNS

Artillery dominated the battlefields of the First World War, causing more terrible injuries and a bigger death toll than any other type of weapon. Of all wounds suffered by British soldiers during the conflict, 58 per cent were inflicted by shells and trench mortar projectiles, whereas slightly less than 39 per cent were from machine gun and rifle bullets.

Expecting a short war of movement, the armies of 1914 were well equipped with mobile, quick-firing field guns. However, the advent of trench warfare – itself the product of the defensive capabilities of modern firepower – also underlined the importance of howitzers which, with their higher trajectory, could lob shells over breastworks and parapets into enemy

1

positions. Each side similarly began to depend more and more upon high-explosive rounds to destroy the other's strongpoints and barbed wire. These factors soon led to a rise in the proportion of medium and heavy artillery pieces in the opposing armies. As the trench systems became stronger and deeper, artillery bombardments before big offensives lasted longer and increased in weight and intensity, so negating any attempt at surprise in the attack. In addition, the enormous numbers of shells fired in such bombardments created landscapes of craters and mud, making it doubly difficult to send reinforcements and guns forward rapidly enough to exploit local successes.

In the second half of the war, considerable improvements and refinements in artillery techniques helped to resolve the tactical dilemma which the guns themselves had engendered. The 'creeping' or 'rolling' barrage, which provided a moving screen of shells in front of advancing troops, was adopted as a standard feature of attacks in 1916, with more emphasis being placed on the suppression or neutralisation of hostile

2

batteries rather than just their physical destruction. In 1917 the British introduced the instantaneous '106' percussion fuse, which made it possible to cut barbed wire efficiently without cratering the ground. Other techniques which came of age that year included the accurate location of enemy batteries by means of sound-ranging and flash-spotting; the extensive use of topographical survey work and detailed battlefield maps prepared with the aid of air photography, and 'calibration', whereby the idiosyncracies of each individual gun – such as muzzle velocity and barrel wear – were taken into account when drawing up a fire programme. All these advances facilitated the development of 'predicted' fire, which eradicated the need for the registration of targets by preliminary shooting. As the German artillery expert, Colonel

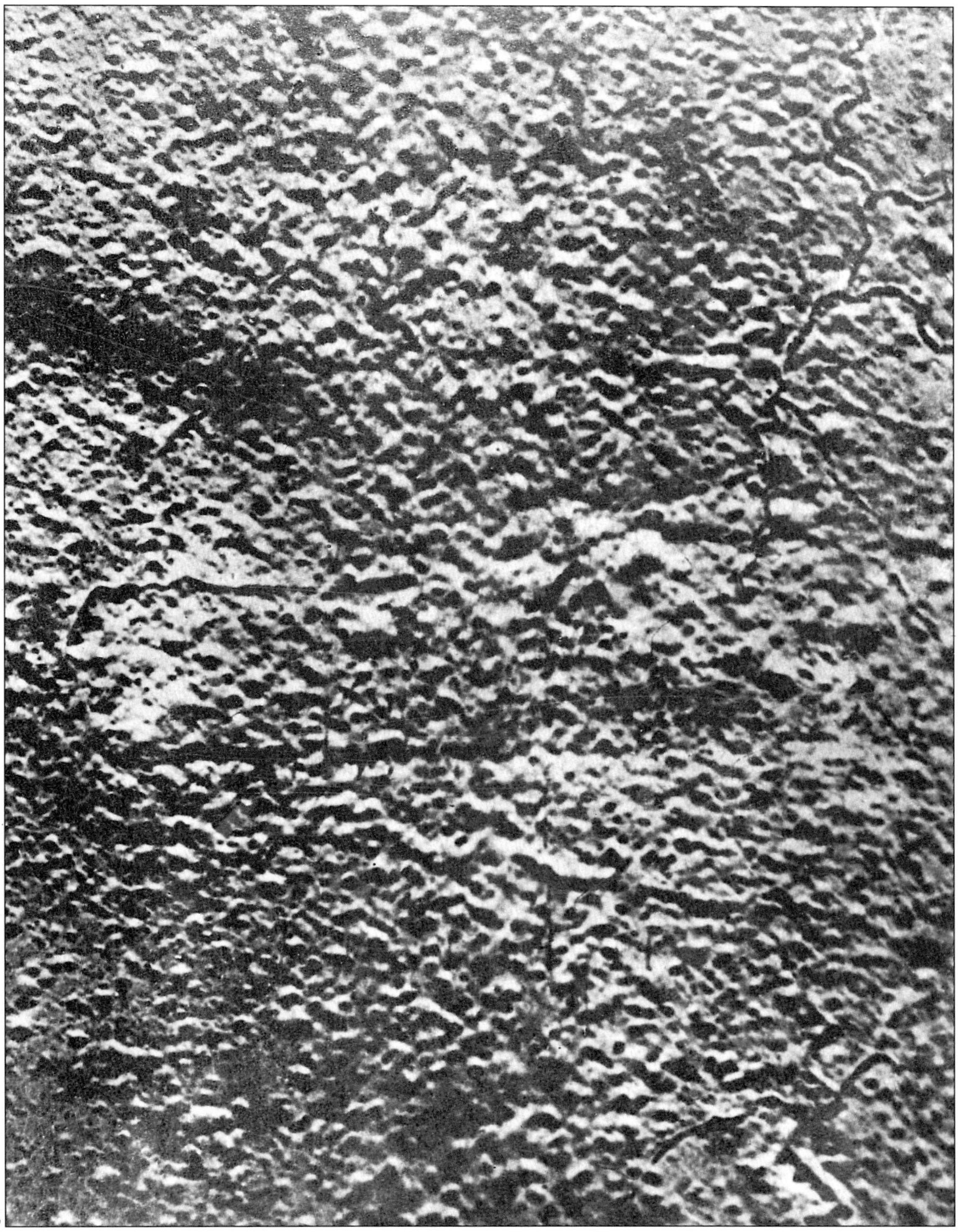
3

1 *British Forward Observation Officers use the shattered trees of High Wood as cover while spotting targets for the artillery during the Battle of the Transloy Ridges on the Somme in October 1916.*
IWM: Q 4372

2 and 3 *The destructive power of First World War artillery is illustrated by these two aerial photographs, which show Mouquet Farm, near Thiepval, as it appeared before and after the bombardment of 1916.*
IWM: Q 27637 and Q 27639

4 *8-inch howitzers of the 39th Siege Battery, Royal Garrison Artillery, firing in the Fricourt-Mametz Valley in August 1916, during the Battle of the Somme.*
IWM: Q 5817

5 *A German 15cm howitzer about to fire at a target near Cambrai.*
IWM: Q 23810

4

5

1 *Shells piled behind the 8-inch Mark VI howitzers of the 54th Australian Siege Battery near the Ypres-Comines Canal during the Third Battle of Ypres, in 1917.*
IWM: E (AUS) 4606

Georg Bruchmüller, demonstrated at Riga on the Eastern Front in September 1917, followed by the British at Cambrai in November, surprise and precision could be achieved at the same time to unlock the trench stalemate.

Bruchmüller's methods, which were employed with devastating effect in the German offensives of March to July 1918, involved the use of predicted shooting and creeping barrages in a carefully-orchestrated and massive hurricane bombardment lasting only some three to five hours. During this time the German gunners would mix high-explosive, gas and smoke shells and shift their fire back and forth within the defensive zone and beyond. Besides smashing strongpoints and neutralising batteries, the bombardment also usually caused the maximum disruption to Allied roads and communications, enabling German storm troops to infiltrate the defences and progress many miles. In the final Allied offensives of 1918, British and Dominion gunners displayed equal or greater skills, combining with tanks, armoured cars and ground-attack aircraft, as well as the infantry, in properly integrated teams which restored genuine movement to the battlefield.

2 *Moving a German 77mm field gun across the battlefield in 1918.*
IWM Q 54404

3 *A battery of German 77mm field guns engaging the British IX Corps from the ruins of a village near Fismes during the German offensive on the Aisne at the end of May 1918.*
IWM: Q 55319

2

3

COMMUNICATIONS

COMMUNICATIONS

In 1914 the opposing armies relied largely upon visual signals and telegraph links for their communications in the field, but the coming of trench warfare soon revealed the weaknesses of these methods. The size of the armies involved, the destructive power of modern artillery and the rapid development of aerial reconnaissance all placed an immense strain upon the equipment and techniques of the day and, throughout the war, the problems of communication in the forward areas were never wholly overcome.

Visual signalling by flags, shutters, lamps and heliographs was slow and unsatisfactory in battle, when shell bursts and smoke could obscure messages and signallers might well be exposed to enemy fire. Carrier pigeons and dogs were also employed to deliver messages, but could only work in one direction. On the other hand, pyrotechnic devices, such as signal flares and rockets, were used extensively by all armies, particularly at night.

By the end of 1915 wireless was indispensable to air co-operation with the artillery in the registering of targets and the fall of shot yet, in other respects, its value in land fighting was limited until the last year of the war. In the BEF compact and portable wireless sets were not available to front line units in anything

1 *A soldier of the Royal Engineers with a messenger dog in France on 28 August 1918. This photograph clearly shows the tin cylinder in which the messages were carried, attached to the dog's collar.*
IWM: Q 9276

2 *Men of the Royal Garrison Artillery using a daylight signal lamp in a shell hole in front of Fricourt Wood in September 1916. The lamp was bright enough to enable signallers to flash messages in Morse code during daylight hours.*
IWM: Q 4131

like adequate numbers before the latter half of 1917. Theoretically, the BF (British Field) Trench Set, issued in 1916, could be carried by three men, but under battlefield conditions it actually needed six more to help move the set and its heavy accumulators. In addition, its conspicuously tall aerial made it too vulnerable for employment forward of advanced brigade headquarters. The Loop Set, in contrast, was genuinely portable and its transmitting aerial – only three feet square – could be supported by a bayonet stuck in the ground. Its drawbacks were unreliability and a range of barely 2,000 yards. CW (Continuous Wave) Sets were successfully tested in 1917, their

3 *Cables being buried in the XV Corps sector on the Somme front.*
IWM: Q 27131

4 *Releasing a carrier pigeon from a trench, May 1917.*
IWM: CO 1414

5 *A trench wireless station in the British 12th Division sector, near Pozières, in August 1916, during the Battle of the Somme.*
IWM: Q 7230

1

1 *Australian signallers laying cable at Westhoek in the Ypres Salient on 26 September 1917.*
IWM: E(AUS)798

2 *A signaller of the Royal Engineers operating a wireless set in a dugout on the Western Front.*
IWM: Q 27120

2

subsequent role being mainly with the gunners, providing essential links between observation posts and batteries.

The general disruption of British communications during the German March offensive of 1918 led to an immediate increase in the use of wireless at every level from GHQ down to battalion headquarters. In spite of interference from other stations, some divisions dealt with up to 120 wireless messages a day at this time. In the final Allied offensives, British divisions had four Trench sets and infantry brigades had five Loop sets each, while further Loop sets were given to some infantry battalions and artillery batteries. However, when security considerations were paramount, many officers were reluctant to send messages by wireless because of the delays which ciphering entailed and, even if sufficient sets were available, front line units were not always able to move them forward quickly because no extra transport was forthcoming. Thus, in the days before 'walkie-talkies' and efficient radio telephony, wireless continued to be regarded merely as a possible back-up to line telegraphy.

The line telegraph and the field telephone remained the principal means of communication in the battle zone. Their main shortcoming was that the miles of cable on which they depended were too easily broken by artillery fire. Originally cables were laid along the floor of trenches or fixed to the trench walls. From 1915 onwards they were buried, ultimately to a standard depth of six feet, and they were sheathed in brass, lead or steel for added protection against shells or trench traffic. Nevertheless, they could still be damaged by heavy bombardments and breaks in cables were difficult and dangerous to trace in the midst of battle. The dual problems of burying and repairing cables were greatly magnified in the muddy conditions prevailing in low-lying Flanders, especially the Ypres Salient.

Because of the complexity of the cable systems during the static phase of trench warfare, a small local advance or retirement was enough to disrupt the entire network in that sector. When a large-scale offensive was in progress, headquarters staffs frequently lost direct contact with forward units, rendering it impossible for them to maintain immediate tactical control of the battle. All too often units had to fall back on runners, usually at a high cost in casualties.

With the adoption by the Germans of more elastic, defence in depth tactics from late 1916, both sides had to move a significant part of their artillery whenever one of the defence zones was overrun. Consequently there were lengthier respites from heavy bombardments after assaults, and more chance of pushing buried cables forward quickly into captured territory. The restoration of mobile operations on the Western Front in 1918 forced the armies to shake off their siege warfare habits and learn to make do with far less elaborate systems. Apart from the pauses when assaults on major positions like the Hindenburg Line were being prepared, or during the battles themselves, the need to bury cables was much reduced, since the dangers of any particular sector being subjected to a prolonged bombardment had now also considerably diminished. But, to the end, runners and despatch riders were still required when other systems broke down.

3

3 *A signals exchange manned by Royal Engineers in a captured German dugout beneath Fricourt Chateau, on the Somme front, in September 1916.*
IWM: Q 1396

4

4 *Royal Garrison Artillery telephonists at work in a dugout within 500 yards of the German lines near Langemarck on 21 August 1917, during the Third Battle of Ypres.*
IWM: Q 2750

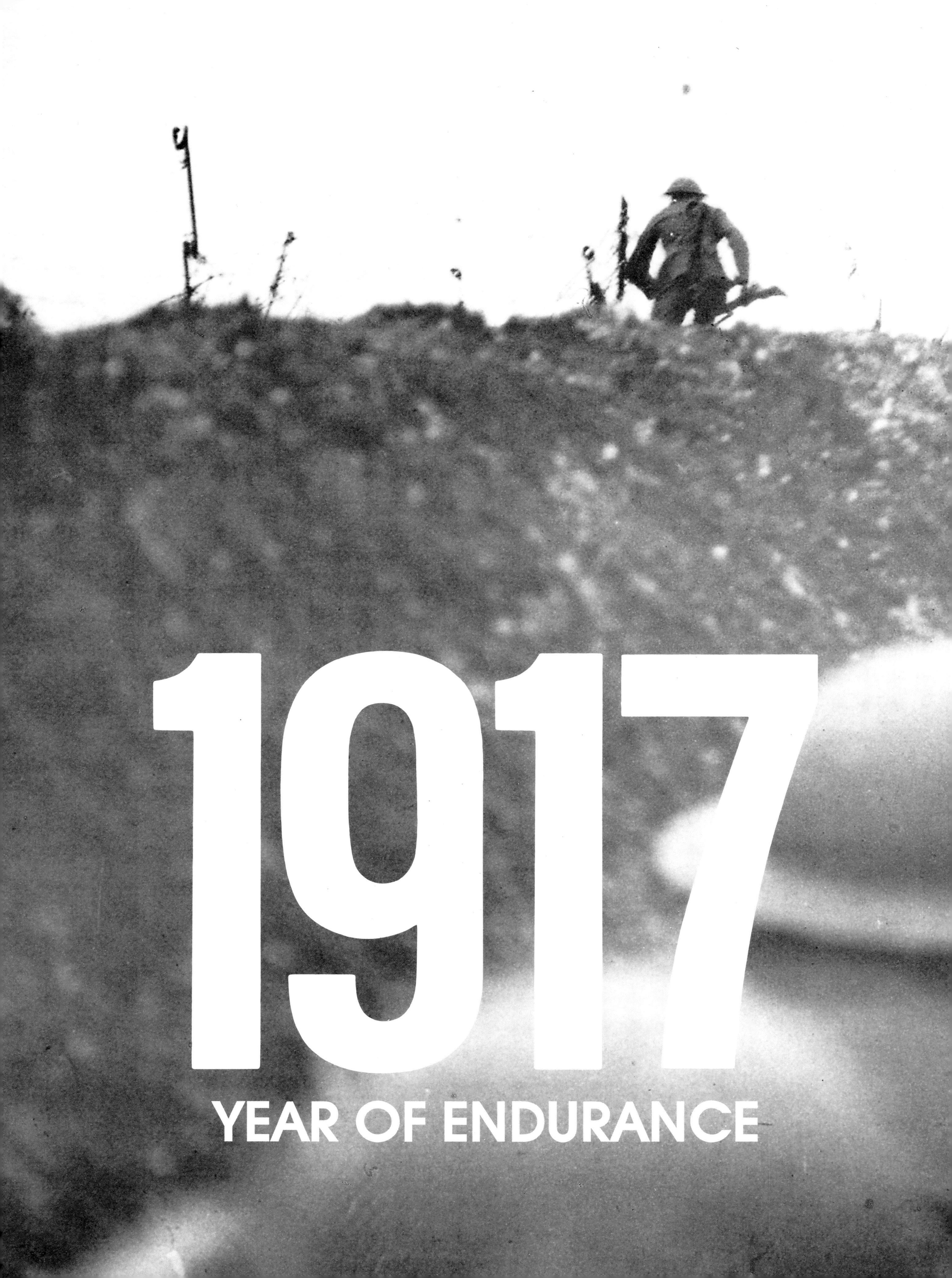

1917
YEAR OF ENDURANCE

Previous page: *Soldiers of the 10th Battalion, The Cameronians (Scottish Rifles), climbing out of a forward sap during a raid on German trenches near Arras on 24 March 1917. Soon after this picture was taken some of the raiders were killed by British shells which fell short of their target. The raid also failed to secure any information about the identity of the German units opposite.*
IWM: Q 5100

NIVELLE AND THE PROMISE OF VICTORY

As the Somme battle drew to a muddy close, the Allied conference at Chantilly in November 1916 reaffirmed that France and Belgium would remain the principal theatre of operations for 1917. Joffre and Haig had already agreed that, in their next joint offensive, they would attack simultaneously on a broad front – the French between the Oise and the Somme and the BEF from Bapaume to Vimy Ridge. If conditions permitted, the offensive would begin on or around 1 February. Subsidiary attacks would take place in Upper Alsace and on the Aisne. With encouragement from the War Committee and Admiralty at home, Haig secured Joffre's agreement to include, in the Allied plans for 1917, his long-cherished idea for an offensive in Flanders. This would probably be in the form of an advance from Ypres to clear the Belgian coast and would be launched in the summer, some time after the other operations.

Changes of political and military leadership on both sides of the Channel in December 1916 overturned these plans. In Britain, Lloyd George succeeded

1 *Herbert Asquith (later Earl of Oxford and Asquith), British Prime Minister from April 1908. His Liberal administration took Britain into the war in 1914, but he was forced to form a coalition Cabinet in May 1915 following the 'Shells Scandal' and also the resignation of Admiral Fisher, the First Sea Lord, over the handling of the Dardanelles campaign. Asquith's balanced, moderate style of Cabinet government became markedly less effective as the demands of the war grew and he gave way to the dynamic Lloyd George in December 1916.*
IWM: Q 80726

2 *Haig and Joffre in animated conversation with Lloyd George at the British XIV Corps headquarters at Méaulte on 12 September 1916, three days before the attack at Flers-Courcelette, when tanks were used for the first time. On the left of the group is the Socialist Deputy Albert Thomas, then the French Under Secretary for Munitions.*
IWM: Q 1177

3 *General Robert Nivelle. An artillery officer with an English mother, Nivelle had distinguished himself at the Marne in 1914, when he brought his guns into action quickly to engage the Germans at short range. His counterstrokes as commander of the French Second Army at Verdun made him extremely popular, and he succeeded Joffre as Commander-in-Chief in December 1916. However, the disappointing results of his offensive in the spring of 1917 led to mutinies in the French Army and to his own replacement by Pétain on 15 May.*
HULTON-DEUTSCH COLLECTION

3

4

Asquith as Prime Minister on 7 December. Horrified by the cost of the Somme and determined to find a strategic alternative to the Western Front, Lloyd George was highly critical of Haig and Robertson but insufficiently sure of his own political power base to dismiss them. However, he soon had an unexpected opportunity to undermine their authority, albeit by an indirect route. Allied failures and casualties in 1916, particularly at Verdun, resulted in mounting complaints about Joffre in the French Chamber of Deputies. To preserve his own government, Aristide Briand, the French Prime Minister, steered Joffre into retirement during the latter half of December, though the fallen hero was created a Marshal of France by way of compensation. Elevated into his place was General Nivelle, the new French hero after his recent victories at Verdun.

Bristling with self-confidence, Nivelle was certain that in the scientific handling of artillery he had found the formula for success on the Western Front. A saturation bombardment, followed by a creeping barrage of considerable depth and by violent infantry assaults, would enable his troops to penetrate the German defences and reach the enemy's gun line at one bound, achieving a decisive breakthrough or 'rupture' within forty-eight hours. In Nivelle's plans, French and British forces would undertake preliminary attacks between the Oise and Arras to pin down German reserves, while the French would deliver the main blow on the Aisne, with a 'mass of manoeuvre' of some twenty-seven French divisions ready to exploit the anticipated breach. Impressed at first by Nivelle's 'straightforward and soldierly' bearing, Haig – who was promoted to Field-Marshal on 27 December – gave the scheme his general support, if not without misgivings. The BEF had been relegated to a subsidiary role in the offensive and was required to take over another twenty miles of front, as far as the Amiens-Roye road, to free French divisions for the 'mass of manoeuvre'. Haig's chief concern was the fate of his proposed Flanders offensive. He made it known that he would fully cooperate in Nivelle's grand design only as long as it did not jeopardise the operations to clear the Belgian coast.

The Allied political leaders, sickened by months of attrition, succumbed to the charm and eloquence of the plausible Nivelle, and allowed themselves to be seduced by his promise of a rapid breakthrough. Even Lloyd George, the arch 'Easterner', was willing to look favourably on this latest plan for yet another big western offensive. If it failed, his own arguments for an alternative strategy would be strengthened; if it succeeded, he could take his share of the credit for backing new methods. No less attractive was the prospect of using the offensive, and Nivelle's growing exasperation with Haig, as an excuse to reduce the influence of his generals. At a conference in Calais on 26-27 February 1917, convened partly to discuss the

4 *David Lloyd George (later Earl Lloyd-George of Dwyfor). Chancellor of the Exchequer at the outbreak of war, he became Minister of Munitions in May 1915, greatly increasing Britain's subsequent output of guns and shells before serving as Secretary of State for War from July to December 1916. He then succeeded Asquith as Prime Minister, holding that office until 1922. A vigorous war leader, who set up a more streamlined War Cabinet, he was anxious to find strategic options other than the Western Front and was suspicious of the generals, yet stopped short of removing Haig from command.*
IWM: HU 53323

1

2

1 *British troops in a captured German trench at Serre in March 1917. The Germans had held on to the village of Serre throughout the British offensive on the Somme in 1916. It was here that the British 31st Division, largely composed of Pals battalions from the north of England, had suffered 3,599 casualties on 1 July 1916. Serre was occupied by troops of the 7th, 9th and 62nd Divisions on 25 February 1917 in the preliminary stages of the German withdrawal to the Hindenburg Line.*
IWM: Q 1787

2 *British cyclist troops are welcomed by the remaining inhabitants of the French village of Vraignes, which had been abandoned by the Germans as they withdrew to their new positions in March 1917.*
IWM: Q 1881

serious inadequacies of the railways behind the British sectors of the front, Lloyd George conspired with the French in an attempt to make Haig permanently subordinate to Nivelle, leaving the former with responsibility for little more than personnel and discipline in the BEF. Protests from an enraged Robertson, and then pressure from the King and the War Cabinet, eventually forced Lloyd George to dilute the Calais proposals rather than risk a political crisis. Haig was only to be subordinate to Nivelle for the period of the planned offensive, and the BEF would retain its separate identity. Despite the compromise, the incident intensified the mutual mistrust and antagonism between the Prime Minister and his senior soldiers, and scarcely improved the spirit of cooperation between the British and French armies on the Western Front.

3

3 *A railway station and sidings being blown up by the Germans during their retreat to the Hindenburg Line in the spring of 1917.*
IWM: Q 57515

THE GERMAN WITHDRAWAL TO THE HINDENBURG LINE

In Germany, too, differences between political and military leaders came to a head early in 1917. The Chancellor, Bethmann-Hollweg, favoured a reasonable negotiated peace, whereas Hindenburg and Ludendorff stood for total commitment to ultimate victory. The previous autumn, at the High Command's instigation, Germany had adopted the 'Hindenburg Programme' to increase munitions output, also passing an Auxiliary Service Law to mobilise the country's human resources in a more effective way. Tentative peace feelers from both sides at the turn of the year had come to naught. Public opinion in Britain, France and Germany – though much less jingoistic after the blood-letting of 1916 – would not allow such sacrifice to be betrayed by anything short of outright triumph, and neither the Allies nor the Central Powers were willing to relinquish their principal war aims. In Germany's case these included, for example, holding Liège or maintaining political, economic and military influence over Belgium. Yet the outlook for Germany in 1917 was gloomy. With the Allied naval blockade beginning to cause real hardship at home, Ludendorff knew that the war of manpower and *matériel* was being lost and that the chances of a decisive success on land during the year were slim. He believed Germany's best hope of victory was to cause Britain's collapse by resuming unrestricted submarine warfare. There was clearly a danger that the United States, sorely provoked by the U-boat campaigns of 1915 and 1916, would finally declare war on Germany, but Ludendorff calculated that the submarines would produce the desired result before America could bring her full

THE GERMAN WITHDRAWAL TO THE HINDENBURG LINE

military potential into play. His views prevailed, and the Kaiser decreed that unrestricted submarine operations should commence on 1 February. For the foreseeable future, Germany would stand on the defensive in France and Belgium.

This policy was facilitated by progress in the construction of the fresh positions which were being built 25 miles behind the present front, and which embodied the new doctrine of elastic defence in depth. The most important stretch built since September 1916 ran from the neighbourhood of Arras, through St Quentin, to a point between Laffaux and Vailly, east of Soissons. Called the *Siegfried Stellung* by the Germans, it was known to the British as the Hindenburg Line, though in reality it was not so much a line as a series of defensive zones. The 'outpost zone', 600 yards deep, included sentry posts and also concrete dugouts housing small squads of storm troops for immediate local counterattacks to slow the impetus of an advance. Next came the main 'battle zone', extending back some 2,500 yards and containing the first and second trench lines as well as a network of concrete machine gun emplacements. Stationed close behind the second trench line were the leading battalions of counterattack divisions. Later, third and fourth zones would be added, bringing the whole system to a depth of 6,000-8,000 yards. The trenches themselves were protected by formidable belts of barbed wire, with some laid out in zigzag patterns to permit machine guns to sweep the angles. An outlying spur of the Hindenburg Line, called the *Wotan Stellung*, ran northward from Quéant, near Bullecourt, to Drocourt, ten miles northeast of Arras.

1

1 *Support troops of the Australian 30th Battalion pose for the camera amid wrecked buildings on the Cambrai road in Bapaume on 17 March 1917, the day on which the town was entered by the 5th Australian Division.*
IWM: E(AUS) 361

2

2 *Men of the 48th (South Midland) Division in Péronne, entered by the 1/8th Battalion of the Royal Warwickshire Regiment early on 18 March 1917. Like other towns and villages evacuated by the Germans in their withdrawal to the Hindenburg Line, Péronne was badly damaged.*
IWM: Q 4963

When it came to the point, Ludendorff hesitated to order withdrawal to the Hindenburg Line, fearing that the rearward movement might demoralise German civilians and soldiers alike. He was induced to go ahead by Crown Prince Rupprecht, the Army Group commander in whose sector the Hindenburg Line mostly lay. Harried on the Ancre by Gough's Fifth Army, Crown Prince Rupprecht and von Kuhl, his Chief of Staff, told Ludendorff that the troops were worn out and in no condition to fight another battle such as the Somme. The necessary authorisation for the retirement was therefore given on 4 February. The actual scheme for the withdrawal, aptly codenamed *Alberich* after the malicious dwarf of the *Niebelung* Saga, required Rupprecht to implement a 'scorched earth' policy. Rupprecht was disgusted by the methods and extent of the proposed destruction, and was only narrowly dissuaded from resigning his command, but the *Alberich* programme, including the deliberate devastation, duly began on 9 February. In the area being abandoned, roads and railways were blown up, towns and villages razed, trees felled and wells polluted. While mothers, children and old people were left behind, over 125,000 French civilians were evacuated to work elsewhere. The main withdrawal started on 16 March and was largely completed within three or four days. By quitting the Noyon salient, and the smaller salient at Bapaume, the Germans had shortened their front by 25 miles, freed up to fourteen divisions, and disrupted Allied plans. The withdrawal was organised with great efficiency by Rupprecht and

3

4

3 *A view of the ruined village of Athies, showing the crater caused by a mine detonated by the Germans in an effort to slow down the British pursuit to the Hindenburg Line. Athies was taken by the British in April 1917.*
IWM: Q 1941

4 *The ruined Hotel de Ville in the Grand Place at Péronne in March 1917. The large notice left by the Germans bears the legend:* Nicht ärgern, nur wundern! *(Don't be angry, just wonder!)*
IWM: Q 4965

von Kuhl yet, even allowing for the difficulties of moving forward quickly over a devastated area after the worst winter of the war, the Allied pursuit was over-cautious. The French Northern Army Group's preparations for its subsidiary part in the spring offensive were well advanced and its commander – Franchet d'Esperey, who had succeeded Foch in December – sought permission on 4 March for a surprise attack at the earliest possible moment. Nivelle refused to modify the general lines of his own plan of operations and the best chance of dislocating the German retreat went begging.

TRANSPORT & SUPPLY

The expansion of her forces across the Channel created unprecedented supply and transport problems for Britain. The size of the British Expeditionary Force, including its Dominion contingents, increased from around 270,000 in December 1914 to over 2,000,000 officers and men by the beginning of August 1917.

It was fortunate for the BEF that its principal source of supply, the United Kingdom, was sufficiently close to ensure a non-stop flow of material to the British sectors of the Western Front. Another factor in its favour was that it could utilise modern ports which, in turn, were able to handle and store the enormous quantities of ammunition, food and diverse items needed to meet its almost insatiable demands. Moreover, because it was deployed near the Channel ports and in a relatively industrialised region of France and Flanders, the BEF's lines of communication were short, normally static and well served by roads, railways and inland waterways.

The maintenance of roads, especially those immediately behind the battle zone, was an ever-present headache which grew worse in winter or during the period of a major offensive. The steady build-up of the BEF also placed a tremendous strain on the remaining French railway system, and, from early 1917, the British were gradually obliged to accept responsibility for the construction, running and upkeep of all the railways, roads and canals in their area. By February that year more than 500 British locomotives were operating on some 1,000 miles of British-administered track.

The clearing houses for the BEF's supplies were the huge Base Supply Depots at Boulogne, Calais, Dieppe, Havre and Rouen. These included warehouses, bakeries and cold storage facilities. From the Base Supply Depots items were sent in bulk by rail to

1

2

1 *Shells being unloaded from a light railway train at Brielen, 3 August 1917, during the Third Battle of Ypres. The camouflage nets visible in the background are helping to conceal the gun positions from aerial observation by the Germans.*
IWM: Q 5855

2 *Pack horses taking up ammunition to British artillery positions near Aveluy Wood in the autumn of 1916, during the later stages of the Battle of the Somme. The shells are being carried in the cylindrical baskets slung from the saddle of each horse.*
IWM: Q 1468

3

4

3 *Stacks of rations at the Base Supply Depot at Rouen in January 1917.*
IWM: Q 1766

4 *British soldiers boarding converted London double-decker buses in Arras in May 1917 before going back to a rear area for rest. Over 1,300 London buses were used on the Western Front, where they played an invaluable role in the movement of troops from one sector to another. Each bus could transport twenty-five fully-equipped infantrymen.*
IWM: Q 5238

TRANSPORT AND SUPPLY

1 *A congested road at Fricourt on the Somme front in October 1916. Apart from the column of infantry, staff cars, lorries, horse-drawn and mule-drawn transport and a motor ambulance can all be seen. Pioneers are engaged on road-widening work to the right of the infantry column.*
IWM: Q 5794

2 *A column of British motor lorries on the Contay-Amiens road during the Battle of the Somme in September 1916. Towards the left of the picture a group of German prisoners can be seen repairing the road.*
IWM: Q 1084

3 *A supply train steams into a railhead at Frechencourt in France in March 1917. Lorries of a divisional supply column are parked nearby, waiting to be loaded.*
IWM: Q 4819

advanced supply depots and regulating stations where the trucks were sorted out – and reloaded in the case of groceries – according to divisional requirements. They were then moved on in complete 'section pack trains' to the different divisional railheads. Here they were packed into lorries of the divisional supply columns and conveyed to 'refilling points' before being transported by horse-drawn wagons to the regimental dumps in the rear of the communication trenches. Horses, mules and light railways were often used to take ammunition up to the forward battery positions but, for the infantry, items usually had to be carried by hand into the front line – the most arduous and dangerous part of the entire chain of supply.

4 *Barges carrying British troops on the Dunkirk-Furnes Canal in Belgium on 4 August 1917. A column of lorries is on the road running alongside the Canal.*
IWM: Q 3875

4

5

1 *A British military band attracts a sizeable audience of soldiers as it plays in the Grand Place in Arras in April 1917.*
IWM: Q 6407

2 *These light railway trucks, photographed at 'Oxford Circus' on the outskirts of Arras in April 1917, were used for the removal of the spoil from the underground tunnels and workings which were excavated or extended during the preparations for the battle. One of the tractor units which pulled the trucks can be seen on the right of the picture.*
IWM: Q 5093

3 *British armoured cars beside ruined buildings in a street in Arras in April 1917.*
IWM: Q 5164

ARRAS: THE PRELUDE

As Nivelle was unwilling to reshape his strategy, the BEF's role in the spring offensive remained a subsidiary one. By means of a powerful blow on a fourteen-mile front at Arras, the British were to draw German reserves away from the French push on the Aisne. The British Third Army, under General Allenby, was to attack east of Arras, piercing the Hindenburg Line on its right and the older German defences facing its centre and left. The Third Army was then required to take the Hindenburg Line from the flank and rear while advancing on Cambrai. Covering Allenby to the north was General Sir Henry Horne's First Army, including the splendid Canadian Corps, which was to assault Vimy Ridge. In all, over 2,800 guns and 48 tanks were available to support the initial attack.

It was to Allenby's south, on the Fifth Army's sector, that the German withdrawal most affected the British plan. The Bapaume salient, an original objective, had disappeared and, given the problems of bringing up heavy artillery over the devastated zone, Gough was only able to help Allenby by attacking the Hindenburg Line at Bullecourt, near its junction with the *Wotan Stellung* or Drocourt-Quéant Switch. His limited assault was to be made a day or so after that of the First and Third Armies, which was scheduled for 8 April. The German retirement also sabotaged the French Northern Army Group's proposed thrust between the Oise and the Somme, reducing it to a minor attack at St Quentin. Consequently, there was now a sixty-mile stretch from Bullecourt to the Aisne where Allied pressure would be almost non-existent, thus magnifying the importance of the Arras-Vimy operations in pinning down enemy reserves.

Tactically, Arras was a transitional battle for the BEF. Allenby's artillery commander, Major-General Holland, recommended a short, two-day preliminary bombardment. This was turned down by Haig, who wanted to ensure that the German wire was cut and the defenders subjected to the maximum strain. A four-day bombardment was adopted and extended by twenty-four hours when the main BEF attack was postponed – partly at the request of the French – until 9 April. The few tanks at Haig's disposal were split between various Corps in groups of 16 or less. But if the long bombardment and piecemeal deployment of tanks were reminiscent of the Somme, there were

4

4 *Lieutenant-General the Hon. Sir Julian Byng, who commanded the Canadian Corps in the attack on Vimy Ridge on 9 April 1917. In June of that year he succeeded Allenby as commander of the British Third Army, leading it not only at Cambrai in November 1917, but also throughout the major defensive and offensive operations of 1918. He served as Governor-General of Canada from 1921 to 1926 and became Viscount Byng of Vimy in 1928. He was created a Field-Marshal in 1932, a rare distinction for a retired officer.*
IWM: CO 1370

5 *Soldiers fixing scaling ladders in a trench near Arras on 8 April 1917, the day before the start of the British part of the Allied spring offensive.*
IWM: Q 6229

5

distinct improvements in several areas. Ammunition was more plentiful and reliable; the ratio of one gun to every 10-12 yards of front compared favourably with the one gun to every 20 yards of July 1916; the creeping barrage was better understood and applied; the introduction of the instantaneous '106' fuse – though not yet issued on a large scale – greatly increased the artillery's effectiveness in cutting barbed wire without cratering the ground; considerable progress had been made in the location of enemy batteries by flash-spotting and sound-ranging, and indiscriminate general bombardments gave way to careful target selection. Machine gun barrages over the heads of the advancing infantry also became common. Typical of the more meticulous staff work was the use made of the extensive network of tunnels, caves and cellars beneath Arras to shelter troops and bring them fresh to the front lines. At Vimy Ridge miles of subways were dug in the chalk for the same purpose.

1 *British infantrymen climb out of a freshly-dug assembly trench as their attack wave receives the order to advance on 9 April 1917.*
IWM: Q 5118

2 *The scene on newly-won ground near Feuchy crossroads in April 1917, during the early stages of the Battle of Arras. British infantry coming out of action pass a line of 18-pounder field guns. A Mark II tank is moving forward in the background. Note the corrugated iron used to provide cover for temporary bivouacs in an abandoned communication trench.*
IWM: Q 5183

3 *German soldiers surrendering as Canadian support waves advance across Vimy Ridge on 9 April 1917.*
IWM: CO 1155

THE BATTLE OF ARRAS: FALSE DAWN

The value of these preparations was soon evident when the attack began, in sleet and snow squalls, on Easter Monday, 9 April. Even on the Third Army's difficult right flank, VII Corps took the fortified village of Neuville Vitasse and gained lodgements in the front trench of the Hindenburg Line. North of Telegraph Hill, where the Hindenburg Line ended, VI Corps advanced over two miles on average; the 12th and 15th Divisions sweeping down the eastern slope of Observation Ridge in an exhilarating charge to capture German guns in the open in Battery Valley. On the left, XVII Corps advanced a remarkable three-and-a-half miles towards Fampoux – the deepest penetration on the Western Front in a single day since the advent of trench warfare in 1914.

Impressive as these achievements were, they were overshadowed by those of Lieutenant-General Sir Julian Byng's Canadian Corps at Vimy Ridge. Here the 1st and 2nd Canadian Divisions on the right quickly seized their main objectives. In the centre the 3rd Division had similar success, though it experienced problems on its left flank, where the 4th Division was unable to take the ridge's highest point – Hill 145 – until evening. Another feature on the left, the 'Pimple', was retained by the Germans for three more days, but by then the Canadians were securely established along the crest, overlooking the almost untouched countryside of the Douai plain. The storming of Vimy Ridge, at a cost of 11,000 casualties, was among the

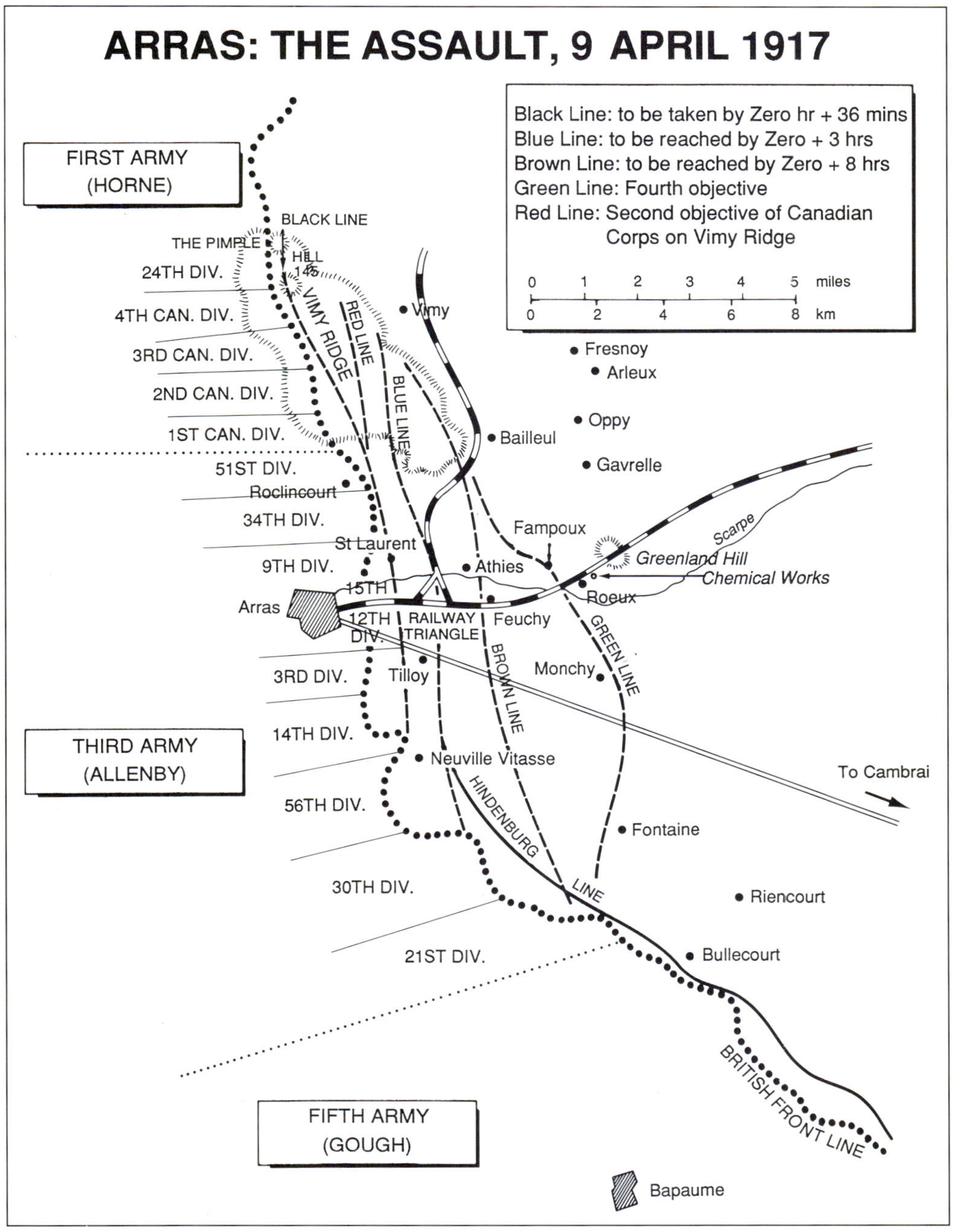

1

2

outstanding operations of the war, not only giving the BEF an invaluable anchor point in the crisis of March 1918 but also fostering Canada's emerging spirit of nationhood.

Up to 11 April the Third Army alone captured 7,000 prisoners and 112 guns, suffering only 8,238 casualties. The contrast with 1 July 1916 could hardly have been more marked. However, the pattern of success did not extend to Bullecourt. Gough unwisely accepted a last-minute proposal from a junior officer that tanks should breach the German wire for the infantry without prior rehearsals or an accompanying barrage. After a false start on 10 April, this ill-conceived and improvised operation went ahead, basically unaltered, the next day. Some of the tanks failed to reach the start line on time and the others either broke down or were hit. As a result, men of the 4th Australian Division found themselves attacking the Hindenburg Line with no supporting barrage and with the German wire almost intact. Against all the odds, the Australians got as far as the second line of German trenches. Despite repeated requests, direct artillery support was denied them because of misleading reports about the progress of the tanks. In the end the survivors were forced to fall back. Of the attacking formations, the 4th Australian Brigade lost 2,258 officers and men out of 3,000 involved, and Australian trust in British generals was again badly shaken.

The German Sixth Army, under Colonel-General von Falkenhausen, contributed to its own reverses in the first days of the battle. The new system of flexible defence had not been properly employed, the forward zones being overmanned and the counterattack divisions being kept too far back to intervene until twelve to twenty-four hours had elapsed. Von Lossberg was brought in as Chief of Staff of the Sixth Army to reorganise the defence. The British 37th Division took the dominating village of Monchy le Preux on 11 April, but the advance was slowing down as German reserves arrived to plug the gaps. Once more the BEF experienced the familiar problems of battlefield communications and of moving artillery over broken ground to deal with the German rear positions, while infantry commanders, junior officers and other ranks were still unable to adapt quickly enough to semi-open warfare once the set-piece assault phase was over. On 11 April Allenby's orders stressed that 'risks must be freely taken' when pursuing 'a defeated enemy'; on 12 April they merely stated that pressure on the Germans must continue to prevent them from consolidating. Under other circumstances it might have been a good moment to stop the offensive. Haig's hands were tied, however, by his commitments to Nivelle.

THE NIVELLE OFFENSIVE

It was cold comfort to Haig to know that Nivelle had been beset by troubles for the past month. Briand's government fell on 20 March and Ribot, the new French premier, placed the Ministry of War in the hands of Painlevé, who was antipathetic to the Commander-in-Chief. The German retirement had practically negated the French Northern Army Group's part in the coming offensive. True, the withdrawal freed French divisions and heavy artillery as well as

1 The Douai plain as seen from the crest of Vimy Ridge following its capture by the Canadian Corps in April 1917. The picture clearly illustrates the enormous advantages of observation which the successful storming of Vimy Ridge gave to the BEF in this sector.
IWM: CO 1352

3

4

2 British troops occupying a German trench in the Tilloy-les-Mofflaines sector, southeast of Arras, a day or two after its capture. The British 3rd Division attacked in this area on 9 April 1917.
IWM: Q 5144

3 Dead horses on the outskirts of Monchy le Preux. The British 3rd Cavalry Division helped the 37th Division to secure Monchy on 11 April, but suffered severely from German artillery and machine gun fire in the process. This was the first significant mounted action by the BEF's cavalry since the operations at High Wood in July 1916. The photograph was taken on 30 May 1917, the battlefield still being littered with dead animals several weeks after the attack.
IWM: Q 3091

4 A captured German medical orderly attends to one of his badly-wounded comrades who has just been carried in by other German prisoners, on a ground sheet slung from a pole, 10 April 1917.
IWM: Q 5127

German, but Nivelle's overall margin of superiority in the critical sector diminished. The physical transformation of the German positions was even more worrying to the French Army Group commanders, particularly Micheler, whose recently-created Reserve Army Group was to effect and exploit the breakthrough on the Aisne. What had been a comparatively weak system was now much stronger and deeper, raising doubts as to whether the breakthrough could be achieved with the desired speed. Nivelle decided to extend the front of attack to the right by calling on the left wing of Pétain's Central Army Group to capture the Moronvilliers heights, east of Reims. In other respects he stuck steadfastly to his existing plan and methods.

Micheler made sure his doubts reached the Prime Minister and a Council of War was convened, in President Poincaré's presence, on 6 April – the day the United States declared war on Germany. At the meeting Pétain and Micheler both forecast that it would be difficult to get beyond the German second position. Painlevé, noting that no relief could be expected from Russia following the Revolution in March, thought that there was a case for deferring major offensive operations until the Americans could join in. There was also a general feeling that Nivelle's attack should be stopped if it did not break the German front or if losses were severe. Faced with this chorus of doubts and disapproval, Nivelle offered to resign. Their bluff called, the politicians quickly assured him of their total confidence and he did not press the matter. Even so, the episode was a disturbing prologue to the offensive. There was more grim news when Nivelle learned that detailed plans for the assault were missing after a local German attack south of the Aisne on 4 April. The Germans clearly knew what was coming yet Nivelle again refused to alter his arrangements.

At least the front-line infantrymen were still in good spirits. Emboldened by Nivelle's optimistic declarations and supported by 3,810 guns, the *poilus* of the French Fifth and Sixth Armies displayed their traditional courage and *élan* when they finally went

1

1 *Germans in a dugout in Champagne in the spring of 1917. Someone has written 'Happy Easter' on the door.*
IWM: Q 61040

2

2 *A German sentry and troops at rest outside a shelter in a reserve trench near Reims in July 1917.*
IWM: Q 56578

3 *A German 21cm howitzer being loaded in the Champagne sector of the Western Front.*
IWM: Q 54419

4 *A French St Chamond tank at Condé sur Aisne on 3 May 1917, two days before the type's operational debut. It had a crew of nine and was armed with a 75mm gun and four Hotchkiss machine guns. The St Chamond's electrical transmission system made it relatively easy to handle. However, it suffered from unreliability and was too 'nose-heavy' to achieve good cross-country performance.*
IWM: Q 69623

5 *French Schneider tanks moving forward to take part in the April 1917 offensive near Reims. The Schneider tank carried a short 75mm gun, two Hotchkiss machine guns and a crew of six, but had a limited trench-crossing ability which reduced its effectiveness in the battlefield conditions of 1917.*
IWM: Q 56400

into the assault on a 25-mile front on 16 April. As the forward positions were lightly held in the new German defence system, much of the effect of the fourteen-day preliminary bombardment had been wasted, and there were too few howitzers to penetrate all the ravines, quarries and tunnels dotting the region. Thus, in many places the French overran the first line only to encounter masses of machine guns in an intact German second position. Losses were heavy and, despite the use of 128 tanks by Mazel's Fifth Army, the sole success of any significance was a three-mile advance near Juvincourt, north of the Aisne. Indeed, the initial attack had achieved far less than the British 'diversionary' assault at Arras a week before.

On 17 April Nivelle tried to exploit the Fifth Army's gains in the right centre but, ironically, the most encouraging developments were on the left, where pressure from Mangin's Sixth Army prompted the Germans to withdraw some four miles, abandoning the important Braye-Condé-Laffaux triangle along with many guns and large stocks of ammunition. Meanwhile, Pétain launched his subsidiary offensive in Champagne, the Fourth Army under General Anthoine seizing several key heights in the first three days. By 20 April, along the whole front, the French had taken 20,000 prisoners and 147 guns. Set against the Allied offensives of 1915-16 these were good results, but the German front on the Aisne had not been decisively ruptured. The colossal expenditure of ammunition by the French created a serious shell shortage, and a breakdown in medical services caused depressing delays in evacuating the wounded from the battle zone. Reality fell a long way short of Nivelle's bombastic predictions.

By 21 April Nivelle's authority was slipping away. Duchêne's Tenth Army was brought into line between the Fifth and Sixth Armies but, at Micheler's suggestion, Nivelle dropped his grand design in favour of limited operations to reduce the threat to Reims and secure the whole of the Chemin des Dames Ridge. From now on every order and decision was scrutinised by the government. When, on 29 April, Pétain was appointed Chief of the General Staff with extended powers that made him the French government's principal military counsellor, the writing was on the wall for Nivelle. Somehow the French Army found the strength and will for a further series of attacks on 4 and 5 May. Mangin had lost his command to General Maistre two days before yet, remarkably, the Sixth Army gouged a hole in the German salient near Laffaux and captured the German defences along a two-and-a-half-mile front on the Chemin des Dames. The Tenth Army took the prized Californie plateau at the eastern end of the ridge. None of this could save Nivelle. French losses for the whole offensive reached 187,000 as against 163,000 on the German side. If these were not abnormally high by First World War standards, they were bad enough for an Army and people whose hopes had been falsely raised. On 15 May, as signs of mutiny became increasingly apparent in the French Army, Nivelle was removed from the post of Commander-in-Chief and replaced by the pragmatic Pétain, while Foch – whose star was again ascending after a temporary eclipse – was made Chief of the General Staff.

PROLONGING THE AGONY

The disappointing start to the French offensive made the prolongation of the BEF's operations at Arras all the more necessary to divert German attention from the Aisne. Haig wisely ordered a pause to organise another coordinated, large-scale attack, which opened on 23 April. This time the objectives were modest. Aware that there was no possibility of surprise, and anticipating attrition rather than deep penetration, Haig and the respective Army commanders agreed on an assault by nine British and Canadian divisions of the Third and First Armies on a nine-mile front against the line Gavrelle-Roeux-Guemappe-Fontaine les Croisilles. Under von Lossberg's guidance, the German Sixth Army had quickly learned the principles of flexible, zonal defence and the German artillery, mastered a fortnight before, was now more numerous, less accurately located, and often beyond the range of the British 'heavies', which were still having difficulties moving forward across a sodden and broken battlefield. Inability to improvise was also causing British staff work to deteriorate. In several places the tired attacking divisions were therefore supported only by feeble and scrappy barrages as they advanced north and south of the Scarp against awesome machine gun and artillery fire. For the infantry, the fighting was some of the toughest of the war, a 'soldiers' battle' typified by the fierce struggle for the fortified village of Roeux and the nearby Chemical Works. Gains were patchy, but after two days the British had captured

1

1 *British stretcher bearers at a dressing station glance round as the Germans shell Monchy le Preux on 24 April 1917. British field guns can be seen in action in the open beyond the dressing station.*
IWM: Q 6293

2 *A ditched British tank by the side of the Fampoux road during the Battle of Arras, April 1917.*
IWM: Q 6434

Gavrelle and Guémappe along with two miles of German defences east of the Roeux-Gavrelle road.

During the last week of Apnl Haig grew increasingly uneasy about Nivelle's offensive. Haig was willing to continue at Arras to prevent the Germans from taking the initiative, though as the U-boat campaign approached its height and the days passed by, he also became more and more anxious to clear the Belgian ports at the earliest opportunity. Hoping to distract German attention from Flanders as well as the Aisne, to wear out enemy reserves and to establish a good defensive line east of Arras, he ordered another big attack for 3 May. However, with the Flanders offensive firmly in mind, he declined to bring in fresh divisions. Hence many of the British units in action on 3 May were either depleted and exhausted or were composed largely of inexperienced conscripts. On the First Army's front, the Canadians again distinguished themselves by taking Fresnoy. Elsewhere success was negligible, except at Bullecourt, in Gough's sector, where the Australians gained a precarious foothold. The decision to extend the Bullecourt lodgement resulted in a

1

2
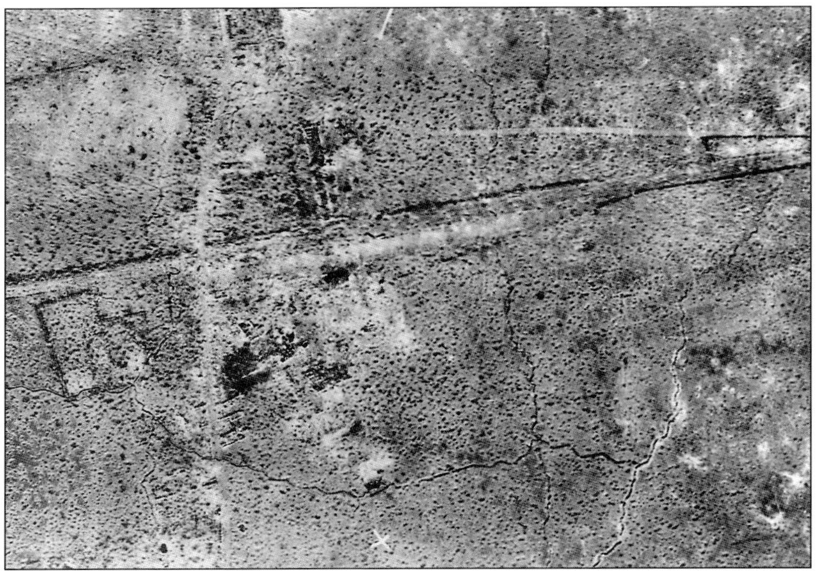

1 and 2 *Aerial photographs of the Chemical Works at Roeux before and after the Battle of Arras. The collection of sheds, warehouses and chimney stacks which made up this former dye factory had been fortified by the Germans. The Chemical Works was also connected by tunnels to a big concrete blockhouse hidden among the outbuildings of a nearby chateau. It therefore constituted one of the toughest defensive positions in the Arras sector. The Chemical Works was finally taken by the British 4th Division on 11 May.*
IWM: Q 47846

3

3 *An officer of the Australian 22nd Machine Gun Company looks out across No Man's Land near Bullecourt on 23 April 1917, in an effort to spot any movement in the gaps made by the artillery in the German wire in front of the Hindenburg Line.*
IWM: E(AUS) 604

4 *Wounded British prisoners being marched to a German dressing station after the British 31st Division's attack at Oppy Wood on 3 May 1917. The division suffered approximately 1,900 casualties in this action.*
IWM: Q 23675

bloody, 14-day battle for the village, involving six British and Australian divisions. By the time this murderous local action ended with the clearing of the village on 17 May, the stench from the unburied dead of both sides was appalling. To the north, the Germans recaptured Fresnoy, but Roeux and the Chemical Works at last came into British possession between 11 and 14 May.

Up to the fall of Bullecourt, the BEF suffered 159,000 casualties at Arras in 39 days – the highest daily casualty rate for any major British offensive in the First World War. The battle had not fulfilled its early promise yet no one could accuse Haig and the BEF of failing to meet their obligations to the French, even at the cost of using up men, material and time, which would all be sorely needed in Flanders later in the year. At least Haig was finally free of his subordination to Nivelle. Allenby, however, was to leave the Western Front in June. His relations with Haig were strained and, having come under criticism for his handling of the latter stages of the Arras battle, he was transferred to Palestine to command the Egyptian Expeditionary Force.

5 *Sentries of the 8th Australian Battalion in a trench in part of the Hindenburg Line captured during the fighting for Bullecourt in May 1917. The nearest standing figure is Lieutenant W.D. Joynt, who won the Victoria Cross near Péronne in August 1918.*
IWM: E(AUS) 439

THE BEF'S MEDICAL SERVICES

MEDICAL SERVICES

The First World War made greater demands on the medical services of all the nations involved than any previous conflict. The size of the armies, the scale and intensity of the fighting, and the power of modern weapons all combined to produce unprecedented numbers of casualties. The British Expeditionary Force in France and Flanders alone suffered 2,690,054 battle casualties during the war. Of these, 677,515 officers and other ranks were killed, died of their wounds or went missing, while a further 1,837,613 received non-fatal wounds.

Just over 12 per cent of the total number of British soldiers who served on the Western Front were killed or died, and nearly 38 per cent were wounded. This meant that half of all the British soldiers who crossed to France could expect to become casualties, some more than once, and about one in eight would be killed. The infantry had by far the heaviest losses. In the great offensives of 1916 and 1917, 88 per cent of all British casualties were suffered by infantry units, the next highest proportion being in the Royal Artillery, which incurred 6 per cent of the total. Non-battle casualties, resulting from sickness or accidental injury, were even higher. In the BEF these added up to 3,528,468 cases among officers and other ranks, of whom 32,098 died, from causes ranging from meningitis to pneumonia and frostbite.

The expansion of the British Army after August 1914, and the huge casualties on the fighting fronts, led inevitably to a corresponding increase in the size of the Royal Army Medical Corps, which grew from less than 20,000 all ranks, including Territorials, in August 1914, to over 140,000 by November 1918.

For British and Dominion troops in France, a chain of medical facilities extended back from the trenches to the coast. The first links in the chain were the regimental stretcher bearers, whose task it was to collect the seriously wounded from No Man's Land, often under fire, and take them to the regimental aid post. Each British infantry battalion had 16 stretcher bearers on its strength, although this number was invariably doubled to 32 before a big offensive. At the regimental aid post, usually located in a cellar or dugout in the support or reserve lines, the battalion medical officer and his orderlies would diagnose the wounds, give injections and apply or change dressings,

1

1 *Wounded being evacuated from the battlefield under shellfire at Ginchy on 9 September 1916, during the Battle of the Somme.* *IWM: Q 1303*

2 *British stretcher bearers attend a wounded man in a trench near Beaumont Hamel on 1 July, 1916.* *IWM: Q 739*

2

THE BEF'S MEDICAL SERVICES

only performing surgery in the most urgent cases. From the aid post, first the stretcher bearers, and then the horse-drawn and motor ambulance vehicles of the three field ambulance units in each division, carried those who were unable to walk along a series of relay and collecting posts to the advanced and main dressing stations. Here, too, the priorities of the medical teams were the temporary treatment and classification of wounds but, again, amputations and other emergency operations were undertaken if necessary.

After the dressing stations the wounded were transferred to the casualty clearing stations, where most of the initial surgical treatment was actually carried out. There was roughly one casualty clearing station for every British division in France and Belgium. They were sited seven miles or more behind the front lines, ideally with railway sidings close at hand. By 1917 each casualty clearing station could accommodate 1,000 patients at a time. Those who had survived thus far, but required lengthier treatment or convalescence, were sent on by ambulance train or barge to a base hospital on the coast or evacuated to England. The effectiveness of these medical facilities may be judged by the fact that around 80 per cent of the wounded British soldiers who passed through the system eventually returned to some form of duty. The French medical services, in comparison, were less well organised and equipped, and the French Army had the highest proportion of deaths to wounded on the Western Front. The German system, though efficient, suffered acutely from lack of basic supplies as the Allied naval blockade tightened. In the spring of

1 *The scene in an Australian advanced dressing station near Ypres on 20 September 1917. On that day the 1st and 2nd Australian Divisions of the I Anzac Corps were involved in the Battle of the Menin Road Ridge, part of the Third Battle of Ypres.*
IWM: E(AUS) 715

2 *Stretcher cases awaiting evacuation by motor ambulance outside an advanced dressing station at Blangy, 14 April 1917, during the Battle of Arras.*
IWM: Q 6195

1

2

3 *Canadian wounded being placed in a horse-drawn ambulance at an advanced dressing station on the Western Front in June 1916.*
IWM: CO 96

4 *A badly wounded soldier undergoing surgery in the operating theatre of No.10 Casualty Clearing Station in July 1916.*
IWM: CO 382

5 *Wounded British soldiers are lifted aboard an ambulance train in a railway siding near Doullens, France, on 27 April 1918.*
IWM: Q 8752

3

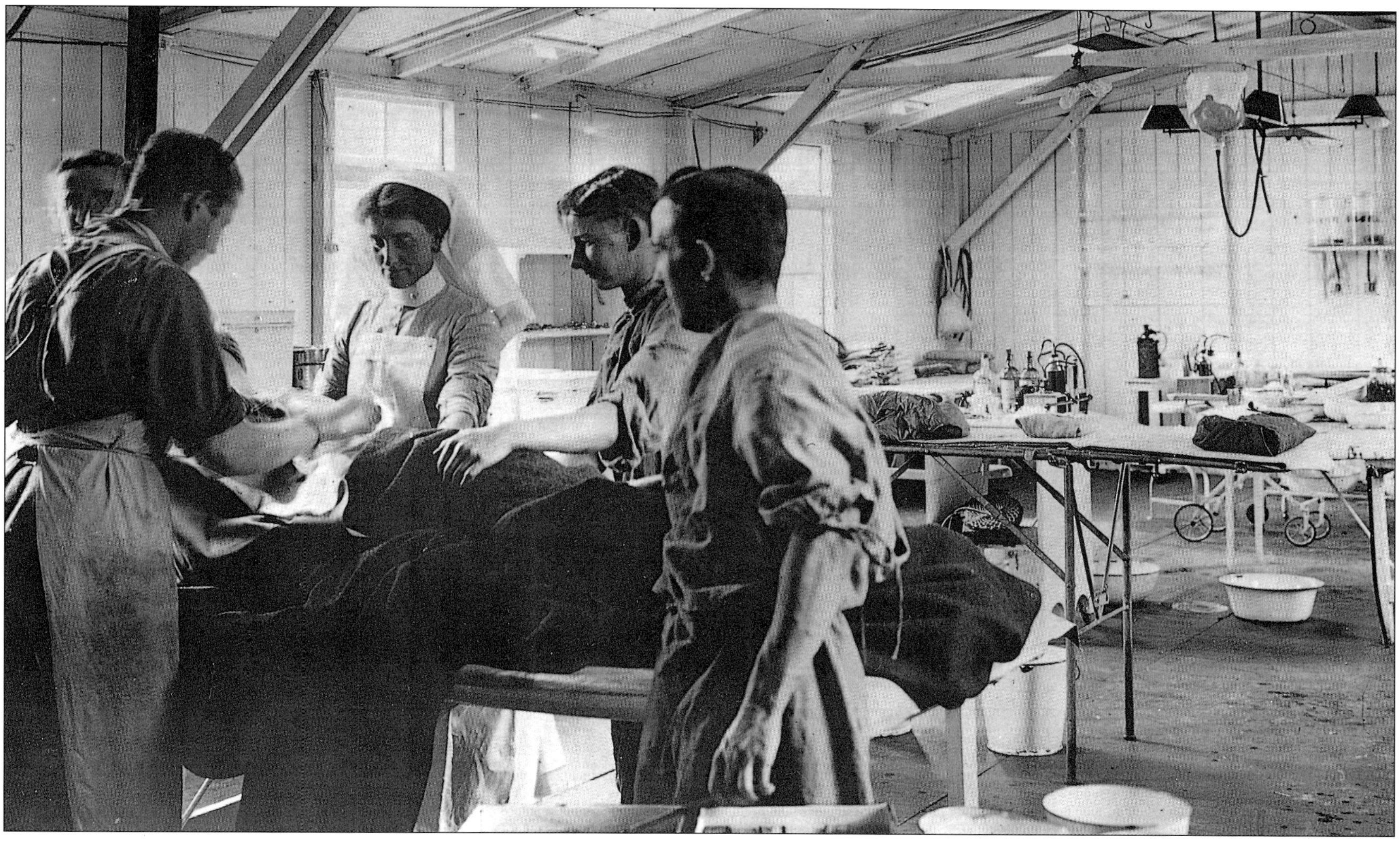

4

5

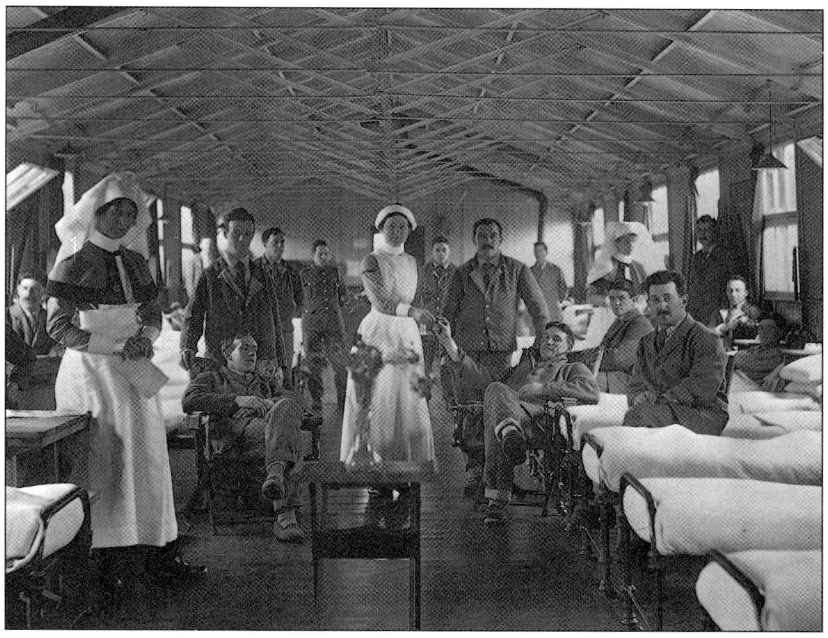

6

1918, German medical officers were reduced to using crepe paper bandages and cellulose paper dressings instead of normal bandages and cotton wool.

At first many military surgeons had little experience to guide them in the treatment of the ghastly and frequently multiple wounds of the type inflicted by modern firepower. In addition, shell fragments and bullets could force heavily contaminated soil or cloth particles deep into a wound, causing a lethal infection known as 'gas gangrene'. Only amputation or the removal of all tissue around the wound had much chance of arresting its insidious progress. Nevertheless, the war years saw a major increase in the practice of blood transfusions and the irrigation of infected wounds by concentrated saline solutions. Considerable impetus was given to the development of plastic surgery, while orthopaedic surgery also made great advances, particularly in the widespread use of splints in the treatment of fractures.

6 *The interior of a ward at No.32 Stationary Hospital at Wimereux, near Calais.*
IWM: Q 8002

1 *Men of the French 313th Infantry Regiment marching along the Montigny road on their way to the trenches in the Marne region on 7 June 1917. Many French units were still prepared to hold the line at this time, though not willing to take part in further offensives.*
IWM: Q 58154

2 *Field-Marshal von Hindenburg (left) with General Fritz von Below, commander of the German First Army, at the latter's headquarters in June 1917.*
IWM: Q 23980

3 *King George V talking to General Pétain at Albert on 12 July 1917. The picture was taken shortly after an Investiture at which the King bestowed upon Pétain the insignia of an honorary Knight Grand Cross of the Order of the Bath.*
IWM: Q 5657

THE FRENCH MUTINIES

The wave of mutinies in the demoralised French Army began on 17 April 1917, when seventeen men of the 108th Infantry Regiment abandoned their posts in the face of the enemy. Between then and 23 October there were 250 recorded cases of collective indiscipline, with the peak being reached in June. All but twelve of these cases occurred in infantry formations, and 68 out of 112 divisions were affected. The acts of indiscipline took various forms, ranging from stone-throwing, window-breaking and the singing of revolutionary songs to incendiarism, mass demonstrations and the refusal by large bodies of men to go back into the line. Many troops were prepared only to hold the trenches, and let it be known that they would not participate in any more fruitless assaults. Neither the extent of the disorders nor their revolutionary character should be exaggerated. Barely one French soldier in every hundred was implicated, and a spontaneous surge of despair after the Nivelle offensive, added to long-standing complaints about conditions at the front as compared with those for industrial workers on high wages, appears to have played a much bigger role than political agitation in kindling the mutinies.

Pétain, the new Commander-in-Chief, gradually restored the health and confidence of the French Army with a blend of discipline and understanding. From a total of over 23,000 sentenced for various crimes, 55 men are known to have been executed. On the other hand, Pétain swiftly tackled the most common grievances of the *poilu*, granting more leave and rest and improving food, accommodation, welfare facilities and medical services. The French Army had recovered sufficiently by late August to carry out a well-organised attack at Verdun which retook the *Mort Homme* and *Côte 304*. In October another attack, at Malmaison, won the French possession of the crest of the Chemin des Dames Ridge. Big offensive operations, however, were ruled out until production of war material had greatly increased and the United States Army had arrived in numbers. 'I am waiting for the Americans and the tanks', Pétain repeatedly asserted. From the early summer of 1917, therefore, the main weight of responsibility for the Allied endeavours on the Western Front was assumed by Haig and the BEF.

4

5

THE MINES OF MESSINES

The plan for the Flanders offensive, as presented by Haig to an Army commanders' conference on 7 May, divided the proposed operations into two stages: an attack on the Messines-Wytschaete Ridge, south of Ypres, on or about 7 June, followed by a 'Northern Operation' some weeks later. In the second phase the BEF would aim to take the Passchendaele-Staden Ridge and the Gheluvelt plateau to the east of Ypres, secure the Roulers-Thourout railway and then clear the Belgian coast with the help of an amphibious landing. The seizure of Messines Ridge was a necessary prelude to this main 'Northern Operation', since it would provide a defensive right flank for the subsequent advance and free the ground south and southwest of Ypres, which was needed to enable troops and artillery to assemble for the attack in the centre and on the left of the Salient. Despite his unrivalled experience and knowledge of the Ypres area, General Sir Herbert Plumer was seen by Haig as being too deliberate to conduct the main attack, so this was entrusted to the forceful Gough. Plumer's Second Army was to undertake the assault on Messines Ridge.

Although 'Daddy' Plumer's florid face, white moustache and portly figure made him look somewhat comic, there were few British generals who had a sounder grasp of the principles of trench warfare or who were more affectionately regarded by their men. Known to be careful to minimise losses, Plumer and his devoted Chief of Staff, Major-General Charles Harington, formed a first-class team. Their scrupulous preparations for the Messines attack included the construction of a huge briefing model of the Ridge. Seventy-two of the new Mark IV tanks were allocated to the Second Army and, for the 2,266 guns available, a systematic barrage and counter-battery programme was drawn up which took special account of the German tactics of deep defence and counterattack. The bombardment was to begin on 21 May, becoming

6

4 *Australian troops near the Scherpenberg studying a large contour model of the Messines sector on 6 June 1917, the day before the start of the successful attack on Messines Ridge.*
IWM: E(AUS)632

5 *The ruined village of Wytschaete, captured by troops of the 16th (Irish) and 36th (Ulster) Divisions, fighting side by side, on the morning of 7 June 1917. This photograph was taken the following day.*
IWM: Q 5460

6 *View across the Douve Valley, showing an artillery bombardment in progress on 8 June 1917, during the Battle of Messines. The shell bursting on the far horizon marks the place where the rebuilt church of Messines stands today.*
IWM: Q 2295

more intense at the end of the month. The most distinctive feature of the Messines operation, however, was the digging of a number of enormous mines under the German front defences on the Ridge. Some of these mines had been started over a year before and one – Kruisstraat No.3 – had a gallery as long as 2,160 feet. The mines were to be blown immediately prior to the infantry assault against the German positions, which bulged eastwards from the ridge in a well-defined salient. In the attack, II Anzac Corps, on the right, was to capture the southern shoulder of the Ridge and Messines village itself; IX Corps was to seize the central sector and Wytschaete village, and X Corps was to take the northern portion.

At 3.10am on 7 June, nineteen of the mines – containing almost one million pounds of high explosive – were detonated, the shock being felt in London. Covered by the smoke-screen of a creeping barrage, the nine attacking divisions quickly overcame the stunned and panic-stricken German survivors in the outpost and forward zones. Thanks also to thorough battle rehearsals, based on lessons from Vimy Ridge, the leading assault groups surrounded or outflanked many of the German machine gun nests and pillboxes, which trained mopping-up parties then helped to clear along with enemy dugouts and other strongpoints. Such tactics again demonstrated how far the battlefield performance of the BEF had improved, at least in the assault phase, during the last twelve months. By 9am, with relatively light casualties, the Second Army was established on the crest of the Ridge. In the afternoon the advance resumed towards the Oosttaverne Line, which ran like a bowstring across the eastern slope of the Ridge, forming the chord of the German salient. The Second Army's losses now started to mount, partly through overcrowding on the Ridge and confusion in the IX Corps and II Anzac Corps sectors, where some units came under fire from their own artillery. The Oosttaverne Line was wholly in Plumer's hands by 11 June and all gains consolidated in another three days, at a total cost of 25,000 casualties. German losses were about 23,000, including 10,000 missing.

Like the storming of Vimy Ridge, the Messines attack was an outstanding success and a model of overall planning and execution. Yet, as at Arras, the British failed to follow up the victory. Both Haig and Plumer recognised the possibility of gaining a foothold on the western end of the Gheluvelt plateau – precisely what the Germans feared most – but Plumer told Haig on 8 June that he would need three days to move his artillery forward, whereupon Haig transferred two of

1 *German trenches in Oosttaverne Wood, taken by the British in the fighting at Messines, June 1917.*
IWM: Q 2304

1

2 

2 *Hauling an 18-pounder field gun out of the clinging mud near Zillebeke, 9 August 1917.*
IWM: Q 6236

3 

3 *One of the most enduring images of the First World War: British stretcher bearers carrying a wounded man through knee-deep mud near Boesinghe on 1 August 1917, during the Battle of Pilckem Ridge.*
IWM: Q 5935

Plumer's corps to the Fifth Army and instructed Gough to prepare the operation. Gough, perhaps remembering his early blunders at Bullecourt, felt that a preliminary attack towards Gheluvelt might only create an exposed minor salient on his right flank. On 14 June he therefore advised against it, preferring a simultaneous assault along his whole front on the first day of the main offensive. Haig agreed to the postponement of the Gheluvelt attack. Once again the Germans were allowed a respite, while the British threw away a fine chance of exploitation.

MISERY IN THE MUD : THE THIRD BATTLE OF YPRES

The British War Cabinet's general approval for Haig's Flanders scheme, though forthcoming as early as 16 May, was given on the stipulation that the French co-operated to the full with similar offensive action. Since then, of course, the French Army's situation had greatly changed and Lloyd George, for one, now entertained considerable doubts about the wisdom of the BEF attacking the Germans virtually single-handed on the Western Front. Haig – misled as ever by the unrealistic reports emanating from Charteris – remained confident that the British could achieve a decisive result in 1917, but he had other reasons for sticking resolutely to his plans. With the French Army in disarray, Russian military power on the verge of collapse and the Americans by no means ready, there was indeed some logic in believing that the Germans might soon recover the whip hand in the west and deal a mortal blow to the shaken French if the BEF relaxed its pressure. Even if his offensive did not realise all its objectives, it would, Haig claimed, at worst subject the Germans to further attrition and so prepare the way for victory in 1918. Thus he and Robertson viewed the projected transfer of forces to Italy as a potentially perilous weakening of Allied strength in France and Belgium. As shipping losses to U-boats were still unacceptably high, Haig's proposal to expel the enemy from the Belgian coast received weighty support from Admiral Jellicoe, the First Sea

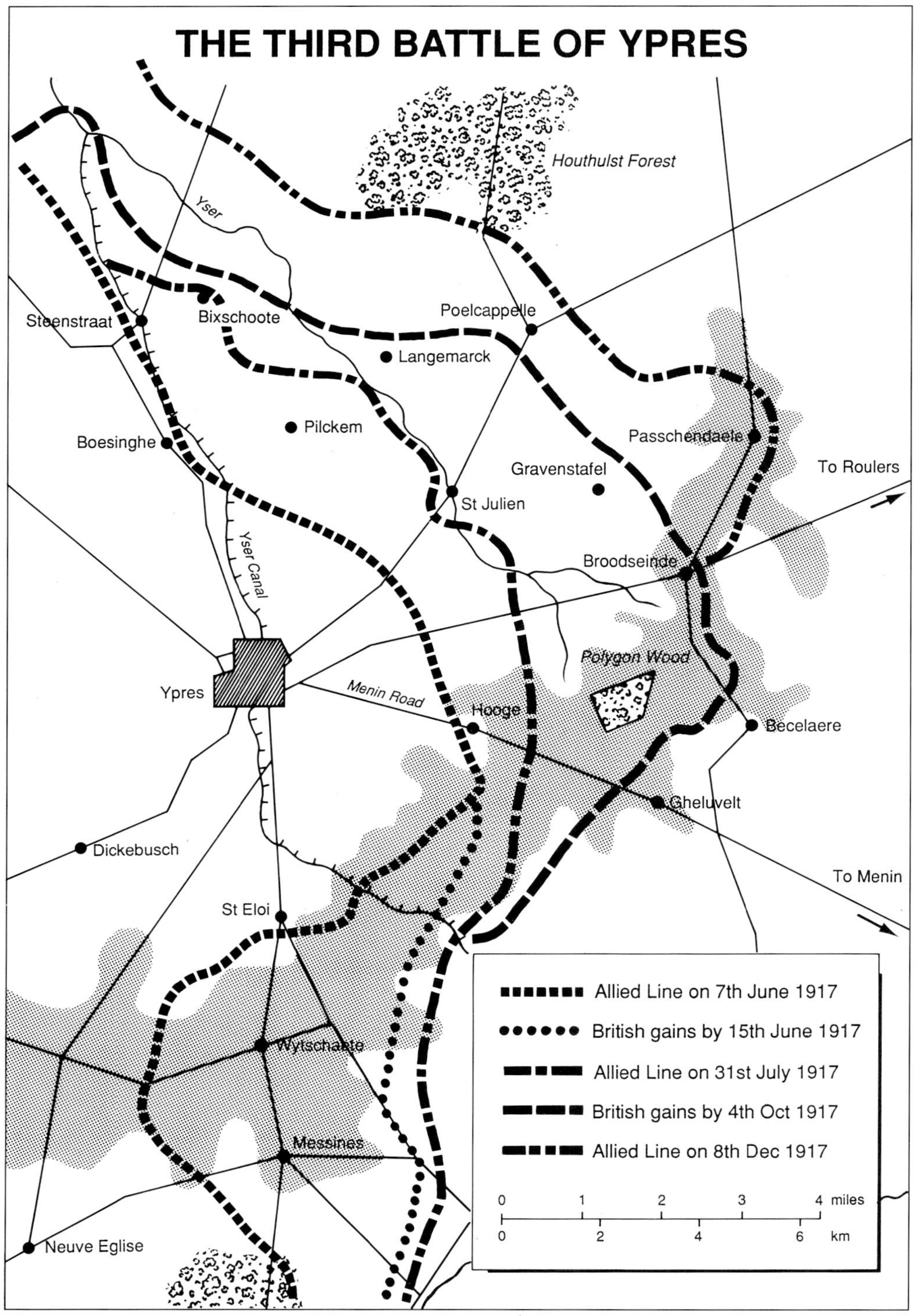

1 *Men of the 13th (Service) Battalion, Durham Light Infantry – part of the British 23rd Division – in a shallow trench before their attack towards Veldhoek on 20 September 1917. By 11am that day, the battalion had taken its main objective, the 'Green Line', situated on the forward slope of the plateau astride the Menin Road. A counter-attack by about 100 Germans during the afternoon was repulsed by Lewis gun and rifle fire. However, the 13th Durham Light Infantry suffered 242 casualties in the operations on 20 September.*
IWM: Q 5969

Lord. Nonetheless, the War Cabinet hesitated to authorise the 'Northern Operation' and it was not until 21 July, three days after the start of the preliminary bombardment, that a belated and grudging go-ahead was forwarded to Haig in writing, with the proviso that the offensive might be terminated if losses exceeded achievements.

It would be wrong to lay the blame for all the difficulties encountered during the Third Battle of Ypres directly at Haig's door. Because the soggy terrain at Ypres precluded the digging of deep trenches, the German Fourth Army, under General Sixt von Arnim, relied more heavily for defence upon a system of fortified farms and ferro-concrete pillboxes behind the thinly-held forward zone. These thick-walled pillboxes, built above ground, were sited so that each could support its neighbour with cross-fire, and most were capable of withstanding the effects of anything up to, or above, an 8-inch howitzer shell. An additional boost to the defenders was the arrival of the ubiquitous von Lossberg as the German Army's new Chief of Staff on 13 June. A pre-emptive German bombardment and attack north of the Yser estuary, in the Nieuport sector, on 10 July severely disrupted preparations for the proposed coastal thrust by the British Fourth Army and the planned amphibious landing was postponed and then dropped. That said, however, it is plain that many of Haig's problems were self-inflicted. He had already made two cardinal mistakes: the first had been to give the principal role in the 'Northern Operation' to Gough, delaying the start of the offensive while the Fifth Army got into position, and the second was his failure to secure the western end of the Gheluvelt plateau prior to the main attack. Haig now exacerbated these errors by permitting Gough to produce an over-ambitious battle plan.

Haig himself, at the end of June, had been thinking in terms of a rapid breakthrough, but had subsequently swung more in favour of proceeding, step by step, in a series of advances of limited depth. As a consequence of Haig's tendency to avoid thrashing such matters out fully with his subordinate commanders, Gough was unfortunately left with the idea that a speedy breakthrough was still required. Accordingly he planned that, on the first day, the Fifth Army should

aim for a deep advance of 6,000 yards, progressing beyond the mass of German field batteries to the enemy's third line. If opposition was light, the troops were to press on to a fourth objective, where Gough expected to have to halt for two or three days to bring up artillery support for an assault, on the fourth day, against the Passchendaele-Staden Ridge. For all his own reservations, Haig again deferred to the commander on the spot and let the Fifth Army's plan stand. He certainly re-emphasised to Gough the crucial importance of seizing the Gheluvelt plateau, yet did

2

3

2 *A stretcher bearer attending to a badly wounded sergeant of the Argyll and Sutherland Highlanders at Clapham Junction, during the Battle of Polygon Wood, on 26 September 1917.*
IWM: Q 6003

3 *'Hell Fire Corner' – arguably the most hazardous spot in the Ypres Salient. Here the Ypres-Roulers railway and the Potijze-Zillebeke road crossed the Menin Road. Because of this, the Germans knew the precise range of the intersection and took full advantage of their knowledge to dislocate British traffic on this important route to the eastern fringe of the Salient. In this photograph, taken on 27 September 1917, camouflage screens can be seen to the left of the Menin Road.*
IWM: E(AUS) 1889

not insist when it became obvious that Gough's initial scheme paid insufficient attention to its capture. In any case, the ground chosen by Haig for the offensive was poor and, being largely under the gaze of German observers, necessitated a long artillery preparation by the British in an effort to silence the German batteries. This involved a reversion to artillery tactics already almost obsolete and which, by destroying the fragile drainage of the area, created conditions that militated against any rapid movement. As at the Somme, the BEF was embarking upon a major offensive with a defective plan and ambiguous objectives.

After the preliminary bombardment by nearly 2,200 guns, nine divisions from the four assaulting corps of Gough's Fifth Army opened the attack at 3.50am on 31 July, accompanied on their right by units of the Second Army and on their left by two divisions from General Anthoine's French First Army between Boesinghe and Steenstraat. Early progress augured well for the offensive. Much of Pilckem Ridge was seized, and the capture of vital observation points both here and at the western end of the Gheluvelt plateau at once denied the Germans advantages they had enjoyed for over two years. The French took Steenstraat and reached Bixschoote, while Plumer's formations secured Hollebeke and the German outpost line west of the Lys. In the key Gheluvelt plateau sector, however, the attack fared badly, with the British II Corps unable to advance far past the German first line. Here only 19 of the 48 fighting tanks allocated to II Corps got into action, and all but one became casualties, many of them being knocked out by a gun mounted inside a gigantic pillbox commanding the Menin Road beyond Hooge. The failure in this sector had the effect of narrowing Gough's attack frontage from 7,000 to 3,500 yards. During the afternoon a persistent drizzle set in – becoming a steady downpour by evening – and German counterattacks pushed the British back in several places. By 2 August the weather had caused the attack to be suspended. Gough's divisions had advanced some 3,000 yards yet were not even half-way to their first day's objectives.

Little further progress was possible that month, the wettest August in Flanders for many years. The Salient was now a sea of mud, and all movement up to the front lines had to be made over slippery plank roads and dangerous duckboard tracks which were prime targets for German gunners. The offensive bogged down in every sense, though there were a few isolated successes. Away to the south, at Lens, the Canadian Corps took Hill 70, pinning down at least five German divisions. In the Ypres Salient the Fifth Army captured Langemarck, but two more efforts to secure the Gheluvelt plateau, characterised by desperate fighting around Inverness Copse and Glencorse Wood near the Menin Road, proved as wasteful and unrewarding as previous attempts. On 25 August Haig did what he should have done in the first place, transferring the leading role in the battle to Plumer and handing over the frontage of II Corps to the Second Army.

As Haig fought off pressure from Lloyd George to stop the offensive, Plumer was granted three weeks to prepare the next blow. The wait was, in many respects, worthwhile. Plumer instituted a new flexible attack

1

1 *Tired and wounded men of the 3rd Australian Division surrounded by bodies of their dead comrades in the Railway Cutting, Broodseinde Ridge, on the Ypres-Roulers line, during the struggle for Passchendaele Ridge. The picture was taken on 12 October 1917.*
IWM: E(AUS) 4644

2

2 *Panoramic view of the battlefield in the Passchendaele Ridge area, showing the state of the ground over which the Canadians had to advance during the final stages of the Third Battle of Ypres. The picture was taken in the 2nd Canadian Division's sector on 14 November 1917.*
IWM: CO 2265

3 *A half-submerged British tank near St Julien on 12 October 1917. The difficulties facing tanks in the Ypres Salient are well illustrated by this photograph.*
IWM: Q 6327

organisation. The assault would be led by lines of skirmishers, with the following infantry deployed loosely in small groups to outflank pillboxes and strongpoints. Each group was trained as a self-contained unit, having its own rifle grenade teams, Mills bombers and Lewis gunners. Mopping-up parties, likewise in small groups, brought up the rear. Fresh infantry reserves were to be close at hand to deal with the anticipated German counterattacks, which would also be hammered by well-planned artillery and machine gun barrages. In the sub-battles of the Menin Road Ridge (20-25 September) and Polygon Wood (26 September-3 October), Plumer's methodical, step-by-step assaults with limited objectives were undoubtedly helped by a spell of dry weather, but a sure sign that they were hurting the enemy was the German decision to abandon their elastic defence tactics in the Salient and hold their forward positions in greater strength, thus rendering themselves even more vulnerable to British artillery. A prominent part was played in these attacks by I Anzac Corps, the Australians being much happier under Plumer than under Gough. They were joined on 4 October by the II Anzac Corps for Plumer's third step, which was

3

1 *'Hyacinth', a tank serving with 'H' Battalion of the Tank Corps, stuck in a German second line trench one mile west of Ribécourt on 20 November 1917. The men in the trench are from the 1st Battalion, The Leicestershire Regiment, part of the British 6th Division.*
IWM: Q 6432

2 *Soldiers of the 1/4th Battalion, The Gordon Highlanders – part of the 51st (Highland) Division – crossing a trench at Ribécourt on 20 November 1917, the first day of the British Cambrai offensive.*
IWM: Q 6278

3 *A tank of 'C' Battalion of the Tank Corps bringing in a captured German 5.9-inch gun to a wood east of Ribécourt, on the Marcoing road, 20 November 1917.*
IWM: Q 6353

4 *British tanks moving forward at Graincourt for the attack on Bourlon Wood, 23 November 1917. On top and at the rear of the nearest tank is an unditching beam. When attached by chains to the tracks, the beam was pulled down beneath the hull, usually enabling the tank to drag itself clear of boggy or difficult ground.*
IWM: Q 6337

intended to take the Broodseinde Ridge and the eastern end of the Gheluvelt plateau. The New Zealanders seized Gravenstafel, and Polygon Wood was finally cleared by the British X Corps to give Plumer another success, but the rain returned, again transforming the Salient into a swamp.

Both Plumer and Gough recommended halting the offensive at this stage. Largely to obtain a firm line on the Passchendaele Ridge for the coming winter, Haig continued for one more month, despite nightmarish conditions in which men drowned in liquid mud. On 6 November the Canadian Corps took Passchendaele village. By then only a mound of rubble, its name has since been popularly applied to the whole Third Battle of Ypres, itself remembered as a potent symbol of the horrors of the First World War. When the offensive did end on 10 November, both sides had incurred approximately 250,000 casualties, terrible enough in all conscience although less than those on the Somme. The BEF had advanced about five miles yet, despite Plumer's praiseworthy operations in September, had attained few of the original strategic objectives. Even the northern tip of the main ridge line was still in German possession.

CAMBRAI : THE MAILED FIST

The grim struggle in the Passchendaele mud did not – as many might have expected – mark the end of the BEF's offensive efforts in 1917. At Cambrai on 20 November the British, for the first time, concentrated

their tanks for a mass attack, using them as a kind of mailed fist instead of deploying them along the front of assault in 'penny packets' for purely local infantry support. The operation was originally conceived by the Tank Corps as a large-scale raid, its primary purpose being not to seize territory but to inflict a sharp tactical defeat on the Germans on ground which, unlike Ypres, was suitable for tanks. Between August and November, however, the scheme was expanded by General Byng and the Third Army staff into a major attack on the Hindenburg Line. Byng and Haig were increasingly attracted by the prospect of restoring the BEF's prestige with a notable victory after the miseries of Third Ypres, and thereby also relieving the pressure on the Italians after their disastrous reverse at Caporetto in the last week of October. The Third Army plan was to break through the Hindenburg system between the Canal de l'Escaut and Canal du Nord, pass cavalry through to isolate Cambrai and take the Sensée crossings while tanks and infantry captured Bourlon Wood, and then clear Cambrai and the area between the various water obstacles. GHQ would decide upon the next step, which would possibly be an advance towards Douai and Valenciennes. The chief problem was that the slogging-match at Ypres and the recent demands for troops to be sent to Italy left the BEF with few reserves for the exploitation of any success at Cambrai. The plan, in short, had become too elaborate for the BEF's existing resources. The situation was aggravated by Byng's intention to employ all his available infantry divisions and tanks in the breakthrough attempt.

To be fair to Byng, there were also some positive features in the Third Army plan. One was the decision to drop the usual long artillery preparation and allow

3

4

the 1,003 guns in support to fire a surprise hurricane bombardment, using the technique of predicted shooting without previous registration. A second interesting aspect was the attack drill – evolved by the Tank Corps and approved by Byng – for tank-infantry cooperation. The 378 fighting tanks, all carrying huge brushwood fascines or bundles to enable them to cross trenches, were to operate in groups of three, with an 'advanced guard' tank moving about 100 yards ahead of two 'main body' tanks in order to suppress enemy fire and protect the following tanks as they led the infantry sections through the wire and over the trench lines. Another 98 tanks either carried supplies, wireless, telephone cable, bridging material or grapnels for pulling away barbed wire. In addition, and building on the lessons of Third Ypres, more use was made of low-flying aircraft to attack enemy batteries and troops.

The initial assault, involving six of Byng's 19 infantry divisions on a six-mile front, began at 6.20am on 20 November. Dramatic gains resulted from the double surprise of a sudden bombardment and tanks appearing *en masse*. The Hindenburg Line and its Support Line were penetrated in most places to a depth of four to five miles, except in the left centre at Flesquières, where the 51st (Highland) Division departed from the prescribed battle drill and lagged too far behind the tanks. The success was such that, in Britain, church bells were rung in celebration. Unhappily for Byng, mechanical breakdowns, and direct hits from German field guns now being employed as anti-tank weapons, quickly reduced the British tank strength. Only 92 tanks were still in action by 23 November. The old difficulty of maintaining the momentum of an advance resurfaced and, with the cavalry's dismal failure to exploit the breach, the battle became basically an infantry fight for Bourlon Ridge, west of Cambrai.

Despite strenuous efforts, the British never entirely secured Bourlon Wood or the adjacent Bourlon village, and were left holding a salient some five miles deep. On 30 November the German Second Army, under General von der Marwitz, delivered a brutal counter-blow against this salient, using a short bombardment with high-explosive, gas and smoke shells as well as large numbers of supporting ground-attack aircraft. Infiltration tactics by storm troops, gradually developed by the Germans during 1916 and 1917, also played a vital role. The arrival of British reinforcements eventually halted German progress, though Byng withdrew to a shorter line in front of Flesquières by 5 December, giving up much of the ground won earlier. Each side had lost over 40,000 more men but, equally, both the British and the Germans had tested tactical methods which at last promised a way out of the trench deadlock.

1917: THE BALANCE SHEET

The year 1917 has often been depicted as one of almost unrelieved misfortune for the Allies on the Western Front. The failure of the Nivelle offensive, the French mutinies, the trudge through the mud at Pilckem Ridge and Passchendaele, and the dashing of bright hopes by the German counterattack at Cambrai, are the aspects emphasised by those who portray the

1 *Lieutenant-General Sir William Birdwood studying a map at his headquarters in 1917. Birdwood had commanded the Australian and New Zealand Army Corps in Gallipoli in 1915. His obvious concern for the men he led made him popular with the Australians, and he was placed at the head of I Anzac Corps when the Australian Imperial Force was expanded in 1916, taking the formation to the Western Front that year. Despite the heavy losses suffered by the Australians in the offensives of 1916 and 1917, Birdwood remained loyal to Haig and Gough and usually avoided criticising his superiors. Haig, however, believed that Birdwood was over-tolerant of the indiscipline of Australian troops and had doubts about his abilities as an operational commander. Nevertheless, the Australian divisions on the Western Front were organised into a single Australian Corps under Birdwood in November 1917. In May 1918 he was given command of the re-formed Fifth Army.*
IWM: E(AUS) 539

2

year in sombre hues. Undeniably it was, from many angles, a bad year for the Allied armies in France and Belgium. By the late autumn there was some evidence of the strain felt by the men of the BEF. Philip Gibbs, the war correspondent, wrote that for the first time 'the British Army lost its spirit of optimism, and there was a sense of deadly depression among the many officers and men with whom I came in touch'. A brief mutiny at Etaples in September was, however, provoked by a notorious training regime and poor accommodation at that particular infantry base camp, and was not indicative of a wholesale collapse of the BEF's morale. The casualty lists of Arras and Third Ypres, and the outcome of Cambrai, added more fuel to the fire of Lloyd George's criticisms of Haig, while news of the capture of Jerusalem in December seemed to strengthen the arguments of the 'Easterners' against those who continued to advocate that priority should be given to the Western Front. Lloyd George was still reluctant to stir up a political crisis by sacking Haig and Robertson outright but, as the year drew to a close, he was seeking ways of reducing their authority by giving them important-sounding but toothless assignments.

Under Pétain the French Army had been carefully nursed back to health since the spring, and had recovered sufficiently to perform well in the limited offensives at Verdun in August and the Chemin des Dames in October, though as a major attacking force it remained an unknown quantity. Certainly Pétain's inclination was to defer large-scale offensive action until the Americans were ready to play a substantial part. At present the build-up of United States troops was agonisingly slow. Only four American divisions had reached France by 1 December. Moreover, the commander of the American Expeditionary Force (AEF), General John Joseph 'Black Jack' Pershing, was under strict instructions not to use his men to reinforce depleted Allied formations, but to keep his units together as a distinct entity. On the other hand, a step towards proper coordination of Allied strategy was taken with the creation of a Supreme War Council at Versailles in November.

The Germans could take some heart from the success of their new artillery and storm-troop tactics at Riga, Caporetto and Cambrai and, bolstered by the transfer of divisions from the Eastern Front after the Bolshevik Revolution in Russia in November, the German forces in the west were retrained accordingly during the winter of 1917-18. But Ludendorff, too, had cause for anxiety. The effects of the Allied blockade were now showing themselves in shortages of horses, fodder, petrol, oil and rubber, all of which threatened to sap the mobility of the German Army in 1918. Ludendorff had been deeply disturbed by reports that a normally reliable division had halted its pursuit of the British at Cambrai on 30 November to loot a captured supply depot.

Viewed from another perspective, the battles of 1917 offered a great deal of encouragement to the BEF. Among its achievements during the year had been the storming of Vimy Ridge and the three-and-a-half-mile advance at Arras on 9 April; the capture of Messines Ridge in June; Plumer's meticulous set-piece assaults at Ypres in September, and the penetration of the Hindenburg Line at Cambrai on 20 November. It is difficult to reconcile the tactical and technical advances which these operations demonstrated with the long-established myth that the BEF was commanded wholly by butchers and bunglers. The year of Passchendaele can also be seen in terms of an upward learning curve for the British Expeditionary Force.

2 The youth and slight physical build of many British conscripts by 1918 is all too apparent in this photograph which was specially taken, for the Adjutant-General's Department, at the infantry base depot at Etaples.
IWM: Q 23584

3

3 A New Zealand soldier examining his shirt for lice in 1917. Also known as 'cooties', 'chats' or 'mickies', lice fed on a man's blood, and each laid up to twelve eggs a day in the seams of his clothing. The irritation they caused frequently resulted in skin disorders and also diseases such as 'trench fever', which gave the victim headaches, a high temperature and back and leg pains. In quiet moments soldiers would crack the lice between their thumbs and fingers, and burn the eggs by moving a candle flame along the seams of their shirts.
IWM: Q 115171

4

4 American soldiers on the deck of their transport ship immediately prior to disembarking at Liverpool in 1918.
IWM: Q 55447

REST AND RECREATION

REST & RECREATION

No soldier stayed in the trenches all the time. The system of rotating units between the front line and reserve areas meant that, even on a tour of duty in the fighting zone, approximately half the strength of a British infantry division would be out on rest or in reserve at any given moment. Periodically the entire division would withdraw twenty miles or more to the rear for a longer rest, enabling it to reorganise and to absorb and train drafts of troops sent out from England. In practice, these spells of 'rest' were rarely, if ever, a time of genuine relaxation for the ordinary soldier. All too often he had to parade for inspections, drill and extra training, or was required to carry equipment and supplies up to dumps near the trenches.

When out of the line soldiers were sometimes housed in hutted camps, or in public buildings in towns like Béthune and Armentières. More frequently, however, they were billeted on the civilian population in villages and farms behind the lines. Although, on the whole, good relations were maintained between the men of the BEF and French and Belgian civilians, there was inevitably some friction. Local inhabitants found cause for complaint in the countless instances of minor damage to property or acts of petty theft perpetrated by the soldiers, while the latter resented being overcharged for food and cigarettes, and were annoyed by the tendency of farmers to remove the handles from pumps and wells to prevent troops from using them.

During their breaks from front line duty, men had the opportunity to visit local *cafés* and *estaminets,* where they could supplement their rations by spending their few francs of pay on a meal of egg and chips and a glass or two of wine or beer. Concert parties and sports – especially team games – were regularly organised to keep them amused and to nourish *esprit de corps*. That soldiers also indulged in less innocent or healthy pursuits is indicated by the fact that, in 1918, the incidence of venereal disease reached an average of thirty-two cases out of every 1,000 men on the ration strength of the forces under Haig. The previous year, twice as many men in the BEF were admitted to hospital with VD as were treated for pneumonia, trench foot and frostbite combined.

Home leave was infrequent for private soldiers. While British officers could look forward to leave every six to eight months, other ranks might receive ten, or at best fourteen, days a year, but many waited as long as eighteen months before being granted a few precious days at home. Most Dominion troops spent their leave in London or visiting relatives elsewhere in Britain.

1

2

1 *A British fatigue party fetching revetting hurdles from a dump near Steenvoordein, April 1918. Such toil was frequently the lot of the infantryman when his battalion was out of the line.*
IWM: Q 10904

2 *New Zealand soldiers waiting to buy stores from a field canteen near the Amiens-Albert road, on the Somme front, in September 1916.*
IWM: Q 1245

3

4

5

3 *Canadian troops billeted in a barn on the Western Front in October 1917. The men are resting on wire beds which have been erected in three tiers to ensure that the barn will accommodate the maximum possible number of soldiers.*
IWM: CO 2076

4 *German troops in their billet in France in July 1917.*
IWM: Q 87910

5 *French and British troops relax together in a Church Army hut at Poperinghe, near Ypres, on 10 May 1918.*
IWM: Q 8801

THE AIR WAR

Since cavalry units were no longer able to carry out their traditional reconnaissance duties because of the trench deadlock, the armies on the Western Front were almost totally reliant upon aircraft to discover what the enemy was doing. Aerial photography soon became essential for gathering accurate information about enemy positions and movements. The air services also spotted targets and reported the fall of shells for the artillery. As aerial observation grew in importance, both sides recognised the need to protect their own reconnaissance machines while destroying those of the enemy. This quickly led to the specialisation of aircraft types and the development of the single-seat fighter. From 1915 the air war over the Western Front was a see-saw struggle, with the opposing air services trying to win supremacy by constantly improving their aircraft, weapons and tactics, yet throughout the war the battle for air superiority revolved around the two-seater observation machines, for it was upon these that the armies depended. Most air fighting, therefore, took place near the trench lines, where the majority of reconnaissance and artillery spotting tasks were performed.

Decisive air combats were rare in the early months of the war. Some airmen carried weapons on patrol, but the aircraft's wings, struts and propeller restricted their field of fire. In 1915 the French fixed steel plates to a propeller in line with the muzzle of a forward-

1 *An observer in the rear cockpit of a German Albatros CV two-seater aiming a belt-fed 7.92mm Parabellum LMG 14 machine gun on a perforated ring mounting.*
IWM: Q 23896

2 *A 'C' type aerial camera fixed to the starboard side of the fuselage of a British BE2c aircraft.*
IWM: Q 33850

the Dutch aircraft designer, to copy the French device and fit it to one of his own monoplanes. Instead, Fokker produced a mechanical synchronising gear which allowed the machine gun to fire only when the propeller blades were clear of the muzzle. The synchronising gear revolutionised air combat, and Fokker monoplanes ruled the skies over the Western Front for several months until the Allies adopted formation tactics and received better aircraft during 1916.

At the end of that year, however, the Germans regained air superiority over France and Belgium, organising special fighter units called *Jagdstaffeln* (hunting sections), with new single-seat aircraft such

3 *Aerial photographs taken over the German lines are made up into a mosaic in a Royal Flying Corps office near Arras on 22 February 1918.*
IWM: Q 8533

3

4

5

4 *An FE2d of No.20 Squadron RFC at Ste Marie-Cappel in 1917. This machine is armed with two free Lewis guns on pillar mountings for use by the observer, while a third fixed Lewis gun is located immediately in front of the pilot. The aircraft is of the 'pusher' type, with the engine behind the pilot. Here Lieutenant W.C. Cambray MC demonstrates how the observer was obliged to stand up in the cockpit to operate the Lewis gun protecting the tail of the aircraft. At such times only the observer's feet were below the rim of the plywood-covered nacelle.*
IWM: Q 69650

5 *A Morane-Saulnier Type N 'Bullet', with steel deflector plates fitted to the propeller in line with the muzzle of the fixed foward-firing machine gun.*
IWM: Q 65882

firing machine gun. These deflected any bullets which struck the propeller, so enabling a pilot to aim an automatic weapon simply by pointing his aircraft at the enemy. Armed with this device, the French pilot Roland Garros shot down five aircraft in April 1915 before he was himself forced down in German-held territory. The Germans then asked Anthony Fokker,

AIR FIGHTING OVER THE WESTERN FRONT

1 *A Fokker E I (Eindecker or monoplane), powered by an 80hp Oberursel rotary engine and armed with a single 7.92mm LMG 08 machine gun. Aircraft of this type revolutionised air fighting. During the winter of 1915-1916, Allied observation and bombing aircraft could no longer cross the lines with any degree of security, and Royal Flying Corps pilots and observers began to refer to themselves as 'Fokker fodder'.*
IWM: Q 69222

2 *The charred bodies of the crew of a British Armstrong Whitworth FK8 two-seater, shot down by von Richthofen near Mericourt on 28 March 1918. The photograph is a grim reminder of the realities of the air war over the Western Front. In the RFC and RAF only balloon observers were issued with parachutes during the First World War, and pilots and observers of single-seater and two-seater aircraft stood little chance of survival if their machine was set on fire or suffered severe structural damage in air combat.*
IWM: Q 58049

as the Albatros D.III. The British Royal Flying Corps (RFC) paid an increasingly high price for the offensive policy which its commander, Major-General Hugh Trenchard, was determined to maintain. In April 1917, known to the RFC as 'Bloody April', the British lost 150 aircraft and 316 airmen. By then air combat was a matter of team fighting rather than lone scouting, the best patrol leaders always trying to manoeuvre their formation into a position above the enemy before attacking. Once the attack had been made, formations broke up into the so-called 'dog fight' and pilots chose their own targets as fleeting opportunities occurred among the wheeling mass of machines. The scale of the land fighting in 1917 and 1918 led the opposing air services to assemble ever larger formations over the battlefield. In June 1917 the Germans grouped four *Jagdstaffeln* together to form the first *Jagdgeschwader* (fighter wing), under Manfred von Richthofen. Created to win local dominance as German strategy dictated,

3 *Sopwith Camels of No.203 Squadron RAF at Izel le Hameau on 10 July 1918. The nearest machine was successively flown by Lieutenant-Colonel Raymond Collishaw (60 victories), Captain L.H. Rochford (29 victories) and Major T.F. Hazell (43 victories). By the Armistice Camels had shot down 1,294 enemy aircraft, a total which surpassed that achieved by any other single fighter type during the war.*
IWM: CO 2859

4

5

4 *Rittmeister (Cavalry Captain) Manfred Freiherr von Richthofen, the top-scoring fighter pilot of the First World War with 80 victories. By mid-1917 his fame and prestige were such that his mere presence at the front was of great value to the Germans in terms of inspiration and morale-boosting alone. Aloof, disciplined and ambitious, he was nevertheless a fine marksman and an astute tactician and organiser. He was killed near Vaux sur Somme on 21 April 1918.*
IWM: Q 107381

5 *Capitaine Georges Guynemer with his Spad S7* Vieux Charles. *Guynemer had become a popular hero in France by 1917. He was frail in physique but was credited with 54 victories after 660 hours' flying and more than 600 combats. He failed to return from a patrol on 11 September 1917 and no trace of him was ever found.*
IWM: Q 64213

6 *Captain Albert Ball VC, DSO, MC, one of the first British fighter pilots to achieve national fame. This photograph shows him as a Second Lieutenant and was taken shortly after he had obtained his Royal Aero Club Pilot's Certificate in October 1915. Credited with 44 victories, he crashed following an air combat in May 1917 and died of his injuries.*
IWM: Q 69593

6

7

7 *Captain Edward V. Rickenbacker of the 94th Aero Squadron, United States Air Service. Rickenbacker was the top-scoring American ace of the war. His victory total was previously thought to be 26, but as a result of recent research this has now been reduced slightly to 24.33, including four German observation balloons.*
IWM: Q 66271

1 *Oberleutnant (Lieutenant) Ernst Udet standing in front of his Fokker D VII aircraft. With 62 victories, he was the second highest-scoring German pilot of the First World War.*
IWM: Q 63153

2 *Hauptmann (Captain) Oswald Boelcke, who, in 1915 and 1916, pioneered many of the air fighting tactics and techniques which were to influence successive generations of fighter pilots. Widely respected by airmen on both sides, this brilliant German fighter leader and instructor had 40 victories to his credit when he was killed in a collision with one of his own pilots in October 1916.*
IWM: Q 63147

1

2

3

4 

5 

3 *Major J.T.B. McCudden VC, DSO, MC, MM, who began his career in the Royal Flying Corps as an air mechanic in 1913 and went on to become one of the RFC's foremost fighter pilots and tacticians. He scored 57 victories before he was killed in a flying accident in July 1918.*
IWM: Q 67600

4 *Capitaine René Fonck, the leading French ace of the war with 75 victories. An excellent marksman, he is seen here firing a carbine on his unit's airfield at Hetomesnil in the early summer of 1918.*
IWM: Q 65794

5 *Lewis guns and ammunition being issued to observers of No.22 Squadron at Vert Galand on 1 April 1918, the day that the Royal Air Force came into being as the first independent air service in the world. It was formed by the amalgamation of the Royal Flying Corps and the Royal Naval Air Service.*
IWM: Q 11994

6 

6 *Lieutenant-Colonel (later Air Marshal) W.A. 'Billy' Bishop VC, DSO, MC, DFC, with his Nieuport 17 Scout when serving at Filescamp with No.60 Squadron RFC in August 1917. Bishop, a Canadian, was officially credited with 72 victories.*
IWM: CO 1751

the unit's brightly-coloured aircraft and its movements up and down the line prompted the Allies to name it 'Richthofen's Circus'. Between April and July 1917, however, a series of outstanding Allied fighters, including the SE5 and the Sopwith Camel, started to reach the front, helping the Allies to establish a general superiority which they held until the end of the war.

By November 1918 many fighter pilots had attained the coveted status of 'ace'; a term which was first coined by the French and was widely used to describe any pilot who had destroyed at least ten enemy aircraft in combat. Thirty Allied and German airmen were credited with scores of forty or more victories. Some, like the British ace Captain Albert Ball, the brilliant Canadian Lieutenant-Colonel W.A. 'Billy' Bishop, and the French pilot Capitaine Georges Guynemer, were individualists who preferred to hunt the enemy alone. Others, such as Major Edward 'Mick' Mannock and Major James McCudden from Britain, or the top-scoring German pilot Baron Manfred von Richthofen, were distinguished tacticians and formation leaders.

1918
CRISIS AND CONCLUSION

Previous page: *Prisoners taken by the British Fourth Army in the offensive at Amiens, pictured here at Abbeville on 27 August 1918. Rawlinson's troops had captured 439 German officers and 18,061 other ranks in the four days from 8 to 11 August. The prisoners in this photograph are almost certainly from the German Second Army.*
IWM: Q 9271

THE GATHERING STORM

By December 1917 it was evident to the Allied political and military leaders that they must anticipate a major German offensive effort on the Western Front early the following year. In the first few days of December, both Russia and Romania suspended hostilities with the Central Powers, enabling Germany to accelerate the transfer of divisions to the west. Thirty-three such divisions had augmented the German forces in France and Belgium before the end of the month. While German strength on the Western Front was increasing, the Allied armies were experiencing manpower problems. French manpower resources were certainly dwindling. Three divisions were broken up and another six sent to Italy, bringing the number of French infantry divisions on the Western Front down to 100. Pétain announced that even these were each to contain no more than 6,000 infantry. The BEF, too, was running short of men, a situation that was to generate enormous controversy and caustic debate in later months and years. Put in simple terms, Haig asked for reinforcements totalling 334,000 and received just over 174,000 by 21 March 1918. There can be little doubt that Lloyd George, who had to ensure that Britain's industrial and military stamina could both be sustained, saw the withholding of men as a means of controlling Haig's profligate offensives. Haig could also claim that too many troops were deployed in what might be considered peripheral theatres. Recent research, however, suggests that it was Robertson and the War Office, rather than Lloyd George, who actually kept the general reserve back in Britain and that Haig's own assurances that he could resist a German attack for at least eighteen days with his existing forces were partly responsible for this policy.

1 *The Kaiser is received by General Otto von Below during a visit to the Western Front. Von Below was to command the Seventeenth Army in the German offensive in March 1918.*
IWM: Q 52751

One practical effect of the British manpower problem was the reduction in strength of most of the BEF's infantry divisions from twelve battalions to nine in February and March 1918. Of the British units in France and Belgium, 115 battalions were disbanded, 38 more were amalgamated to form 19 units, and seven were converted into Pioneer battalions. The New Zealand Division, like the five Australian and four Canadian divisions in France, retained a twelve-battalion organisation. Only 130,000 American troops were in France on 1 December and all Pershing's divisions would need three months' further training on arrival, so no immediate help could be expected from that quarter. The Germans would, therefore, enjoy a brief period at the beginning of 1918 when they would outnumber the Franco-British armies on the Western Front by 192 divisions to 156.

Knowing that the introduction of the convoy system was enabling Britain to survive the U-boat campaign, the German military leaders resolved to seek a decisive victory in the west in 1918 before the Americans could make their presence felt. Accordingly, Ludendorff planned a *Kaiserschlacht*, or 'Imperial Battle', consisting in essence of a series of closely connected blows aiming to bring about the eventual collapse of 'the whole structure' of the Allied armies. Calculating that if the British were beaten the rest would surely follow, Ludendorff took the potentially fruitful, if risky, course of directing the principal blows at the BEF. From the various alternatives discussed during the winter, three operations emerged as strong possibilities. One, codenamed *George*, would pierce the front in Flanders, near Armentières, and thrust towards Hazebrouck to take the British forces in the north from the flank and rear, in conjunction with a subsidiary attack (*George II*) which would cut off the British in the Ypres Salient; a second, called *Mars*, was based upon an attack at Arras; and the third, *Operation Michael*, was an offensive against the British Third and Fifth Armies, between Arras and La Fère, on either side of St Quentin. The ultimate object of this latter operation, once a breakthrough had been achieved, was to wheel to the north to roll up the BEF and press it back against the sea.

On 21 January 1918 Ludendorff made his choice, opting for *Operation Michael* as the main spring offensive. The proposed Flanders attack needed dry weather and might not be viable until April or May, while Arras – with the British holding Vimy Ridge – was

2

3

thought to be too difficult a sector for the first assault. Over the next few weeks the detailed plans for *Michael* were drawn up, and 21 March was selected as its starting date. On the right wing, the German Seventeenth Army, under General Otto von Below, and the Second Army, under General von der Marwitz – both from Crown Prince Rupprecht's Army Group – were to attack south of Arras, pinching off the salient which the British had occupied at Flesquières, near Cambrai, since November. These two armies would then advance towards Bapaume and Péronne and across the old Somme battlefield, to a line between Arras and Albert, before swinging northwest in a gigantic left hook, enveloping Arras in the process. On the left wing, General Oskar von Hutier's Eighteenth Army, from Crown Prince Wilhelm's Army Group, was to advance beyond the River Somme and the Crozat canal to protect the flank of the offensive, defeating any French reserves which came up from the south and driving a wedge between the French and British forces. If necessary, von Hutier could also assist the Second Army around Péronne. As soon as a significant tactical success had been achieved south of Arras, *Mars* could be launched. Planning for *George* was also allowed to proceed, as the Flanders operation might yet be required to salvage Ludendorff's aspirations if *Michael* failed.

At Ludendorff's instigation, the cutting edge of the German Army was sharpened during the winter of 1917-1918, a big retraining programme being implemented in an effort to bring more units up to the standards set by the special assault battalions, or storm troops, in the past two years. Around a quarter of the German infantry divisions were redesignated as *angriffsdivisionen* ('attack divisions') and given the pick of new equipment, including light machine guns. The remaining three-quarters, mostly containing older men, were chiefly concerned with holding the line and were classed as *stellungsdivisionen* ('trench divisions'). Stormtroopers were to have a vital role in the coming offensive, seeking out weak spots in the opposing defences and causing maximum confusion

2 *Crown Prince Rupprecht of Bavaria. Having commanded the original German Sixth Army in the campaign in Lorraine in August 1914, he was transferred to the Somme-Flanders area to head a new Sixth Army during the 'race to the sea'. Rupprecht stayed on this part of the Western Front, facing the BEF, for the rest of the war. In the summer of 1916 he was given command of the Army Group which bore his own name. Among the very best of Germany's military leaders, he opposed Ludendorff's policy of deliberate devastation during the withdrawal to the Hindenburg Line in the spring of 1917, and thereafter relations between the two deteriorated. Although Crown Prince Rupprecht's Army Group performed well in the opening stages of both the* Michael *and* Georgette *offensives of March 1918, and again fought hard in the defensive battles of the final autumn of the war, Rupprecht himself had become increasingly pessimistic about Germany's prospects of victory, and he favoured an early peace. He died in 1955, aged 86.*
IWM: Q 45320

3 *General Oskar von Hutier (left), whose tactical success at Riga, on the Eastern Front, in September 1917 led to his transfer to the west to command the German Eighteenth Army in the* Michael *offensive.*
IWM: Q 23904

in the rear by deep penetration and envelopment tactics. The artillery, probably the most important element in the initial assault, would employ the tactics developed and honed at Riga, Caporetto and Cambrai by gunnery experts such as Colonel Georg Bruchmüller, who was himself attached to the Eighteenth Army but whose ideas guided the whole artillery preparation for *Operation Michael*. Bruchmüller's carefully-orchestrated fire plans were built around short, hurricane bombardments of immense weight and intensity, using predicted shooting. They incorporated a high proportion of gas shells to neutralise and silence enemy gunners, and they paid particular attention to the disruption of communications and assembly areas far behind the lines.

1

2

1 *German infantry moving up to the trenches.*
IWM: Q 88092

2 *A muddy communication trench at Essigny, near St Quentin, in the sector held by the 12th (Service) Battalion, Royal Irish Rifles – part of the 36th (Ulster) Division – on 7 February 1918. This sector had only recently been taken over from the French.*
IWM: Q 10681

The BEF, its morale lowered by the frustrations of 1917 and recent disbandments, and with many of its units now made up predominantly of conscripts, was not in the best state to withstand the imminent storm. The dour but single-minded Haig was still in command, though several members of his staff, including Charteris, had been replaced. Back in Britain, Robertson resigned as CIGS in February over Lloyd George's attempts to curtail his powers by proposing Sir Henry Wilson as British representative on an 'Executive War Board' of the Supreme War Council. In the end it was Wilson who succeeded Robertson as CIGS, with effect from 18 February. On the Western Front both Pétain and Haig, in December, had ordered the preparation of flexible defence systems in depth, not unlike those instituted by the Germans in 1916-1917. In the British case, the intention was that the system would comprise Forward, Battle and Rear Zones, each with several successive lines – either continuous trenches or groups of trenches – as well as mutually-supporting strongpoints and machine gun emplacements for all-round defence. However, partly owing to labour shortages and lack of time, the new positions were by no means complete, while the BEF as a whole, having got out of the habit of big defensive battles, needed much longer to retrain and adapt to these fresh tactical concepts. The problem was complicated by the fact that the BEF, already thinned down by the despatch of five divisions to Italy under Plumer, beginning in November 1917, took over an additional stretch of the line in France in January 1918, bringing its right flank to Barisis, well south of St Quentin.

This southernmost sector was occupied by Gough's Fifth Army, which had only twelve infantry divisions and three cavalry divisions to defend a front of 42 miles, whereas Byng's Third Army, to its left, had fourteen divisions to cover 28 miles. The defences inherited from the French Sixth Army by Gough's divisions were rudimentary, and not all of Gough's subordinate commanders fully understood the principles of elastic defence, with the result that the Forward Zone was too densely held. Haig deliberately – and, in the final analysis, wisely – kept the bulk of his

strength to the north, guarding Flanders and the Channel ports, although he does appear to have misjudged the likely weight and direction of the German attack, to have underestimated the danger to the weaker Fifth Army, and to have been over-confident about the BEF's *current* ability to resist. Similarly, while it is true that there was more space behind Gough's front for the Fifth Army to manoeuvre and fall back, the suggestion that this was the real reason why Haig was willing to leave the Fifth Army weak smacks of justification after the event.

3

3 *General Sir Hubert Gough, commander of the British Fifth Army. While his tactics on the Somme in 1916, and at Bullecourt and Ypres in 1917, have often been called into question, he fought a skilful defensive battle under extremely difficult circumstances in March 1918. Ironically, just as the* Michael *offensive began to lose momentum, Gough was singled out as the main scapegoat for the BEF's retreat. He was relieved of his command on 27 March, although Rawlinson did not arrive until the following day to supersede him.*
IWM: Q 35825d

4

4 *Stormtroopers crossing a wire entanglement during training at Sedan in 1917.*
IWM: Q 55021

1 *Troops of the German Eighteenth Army concentrating in the wrecked streets of St Quentin in March 1918, immediately prior to the opening of the German offensive in Picardy.*
IWM: Q 55479

2 *A German 21cm howitzer being dragged into position. The effort involved in redeploying the German 'battering train' before each successive operation influenced both the timing and direction of Ludendorff's various offensives in 1918.*
IWM: Q 23822

3 *British and German wounded being removed from a British ambulance train near Bapaume on 22 March 1918. Bapaume was evacuated by the British two days later.*
IWM: Q 10290

1

2

3

OPERATION MICHAEL: THE GERMAN MARCH OFFENSIVE

The storm broke over the BEF around 4.40am on 21 March 1918, when the Germans launched *Operation Michael* with a shattering bombardment from 6,473 guns and 3,532 trench mortars. Five hours later the German infantry assault began, covered almost everywhere by a thick fog. Forty-three divisions of the German Second and Eighteenth Armies assailed Gough's front and 19 divisions from the Seventeenth Army attacked the British Third Army sector. Outnumbered, with their communications badly affected by the deep-ranging German fire, and with their own artillery batteries largely neutralised by gas shells, most of the defending units in the Forward Zone were quickly overwhelmed, the British front falling apart in many places like a sand castle before an incoming tide. The short bombardment and the extensive use of gas shells by the Germans left the ground relatively uncratered, helping rapid movement, while the fog was heaven-sent for the infiltration tactics of the storm troops. But for the poor visibility the attackers would have been much more exposed to artillery and machine gun fire as they approached and entered the Battle Zone, where the British expected the main fighting to occur. As it was, the defenders were blinded and the garrisons of the strongpoints and redoubts were isolated and unable to assist each other with effective covering fire. The situation was particularly critical on the Fifth Army's right, in the weak sector which it had recently taken over from the French. Here the Germans broke clear of the Battle Zone, persuading Gough to withdraw the British III Corps to the line of the Crozat canal. On other sectors the Germans were less successful. They had decided not to attack the Flesquières salient frontally but, even so, they failed to pinch it out as planned. Von Below, with his key role on the German right wing, made disappointing progress against the better-prepared and more strongly-held positions of Byng's Third Army, and von der Marwitz's units were also denied the hoped-for breakthrough along much of the German Second Army's front of assault.

Nevertheless, by the evening it was obvious that the BEF was facing one of its worst crises of the war. Although the first day's operations had cost the Germans nearly 40,000 casualties, the British had lost over 38,000 men, together with up to 500 guns. The fact that the British casualty figures included some 21,000 who had been taken prisoner showed that many tired British battalions had temporarily reached the limits of endurance and resistance. On 22 March the situation continued to deteriorate for the British. A misunderstanding about Gough's intentions led the experienced and usually far-sighted General Maxse to order an over-hasty retirement of his own XVIII Corps to the River Somme, forcing XIX Corps, on his left, to fall back in turn. Similarly, in the broader context, the right of the Third Army's position was increasingly threatened by the crumbling of Gough's front to the south. Without being too unfair to Byng, he was perhaps unwise, in these circumstances, to

4 *A British Mark IV tank passing through Péronne on 23 March 1918. In the background are a burning store building and an abandoned Expeditionary Force Canteen. A dead horse lies at the side of the road.*
IWM: Q 10838

5 *Men of the British 20th Division and the French 22nd Division in hastily-dug rifle pits at Billancourt, covering a road near Nesle, on 25 March 1918. Although some French reinforcements arrived that day, the barrier of the River Somme was lost by the British Fifth Army. The 20th Division fell back slowly from the Canal du Nord and rallied on the French 22nd Division in the afternoon. However, at 4pm, the French lost Nesle and the British, with their flanks exposed, had to retire from these positions.*
IWM: Q 10812

delay the evacuation of the vulnerable Flesquières salient as he did, since this not only subsequently led to the unnecessary sacrifice of troops of the 2nd Division and 63rd (Royal Naval) Division, but also caused a bigger gap to open at the junction of the Third and Fifth Armies.

By 23 March parts of the Fifth Army had been driven back over twelve miles, and von Hutier's forces were pushing on westwards to seize crossings over the Crozat canal and the Somme. At this point Ludendorff allowed the apparent tactical opportunity presented by von Hutier's impressive progress to deflect him from his declared strategy – a tendency which bedevilled the German high command throughout the war. Instead of strengthening his right to ensure the success of the wheel to the northwest, Ludendorff reinforced his left and issued new orders, which directed the Seventeenth Army towards St Pol and Abbeville and the Second Army westwards to Amiens. Von Hutier's Eighteenth Army, which had originally been given the subsidiary flank protection role, was to thrust southwest towards Noyon and

1 *A British 60-pounder Mark II gun in action in the open near La Boisselle on 25 March 1918.*
IWM: Q 8618

2 *A German transport column advancing along the Albert-Bapaume road in March 1918. Note that the transport is almost entirely horse-drawn.*
IWM: Q 60474

3 *Medium Mark A or 'Whippet' tanks moving past New Zealand infantry at Mailly-Maillet on 26 March 1918, the day on which Whippets first appeared on the battlefield. The Whippet, designed for an exploitation rather than an assault role, had a top road speed of just over 8mph compared with the 3.7mph of the Mark IV tank. It carried four machine guns and a crew of three.*
IWM: Q 9821

Montdidier in a much more clearly-defined attempt to separate the British from the French. Far from being concentrated for the big left hook, the armies would be advancing in divergent directions, like a hand with the fingers spread wide.

Ludendorff's new orders presupposed that the British Third and Fifth Armies were almost beaten. This was a false assumption, although the crisis was not yet over for the BEF. Péronne was abandoned to the Germans on 23 March, followed by Bapaume the next day. As the Fifth Army retreated across the 1916 battlefield, Albert fell on 26 March. The Third Army was compelled to pull back its right to maintain touch with Gough's left while standing firm around Arras. Haig was now much more alive to the Fifth Army's plight and the danger to the railway junction of Amiens, the retention of which was vital to the British. He had therefore become doubly alarmed at what he felt was an inadequate amount of support from the pessimistic Pétain, who feared that the Germans were still likely to deliver a major blow against the French in Champagne, and who was also prepared, if required, to withdraw southwest to Beauvais – away from the British – in order to cover Paris. In Pétain's defence, he, in turn, was probably correct in believing that, if all else failed, the BEF might well retire to the north. Largely at the urging of Haig, who swallowed his previous reservations about a unified command, an

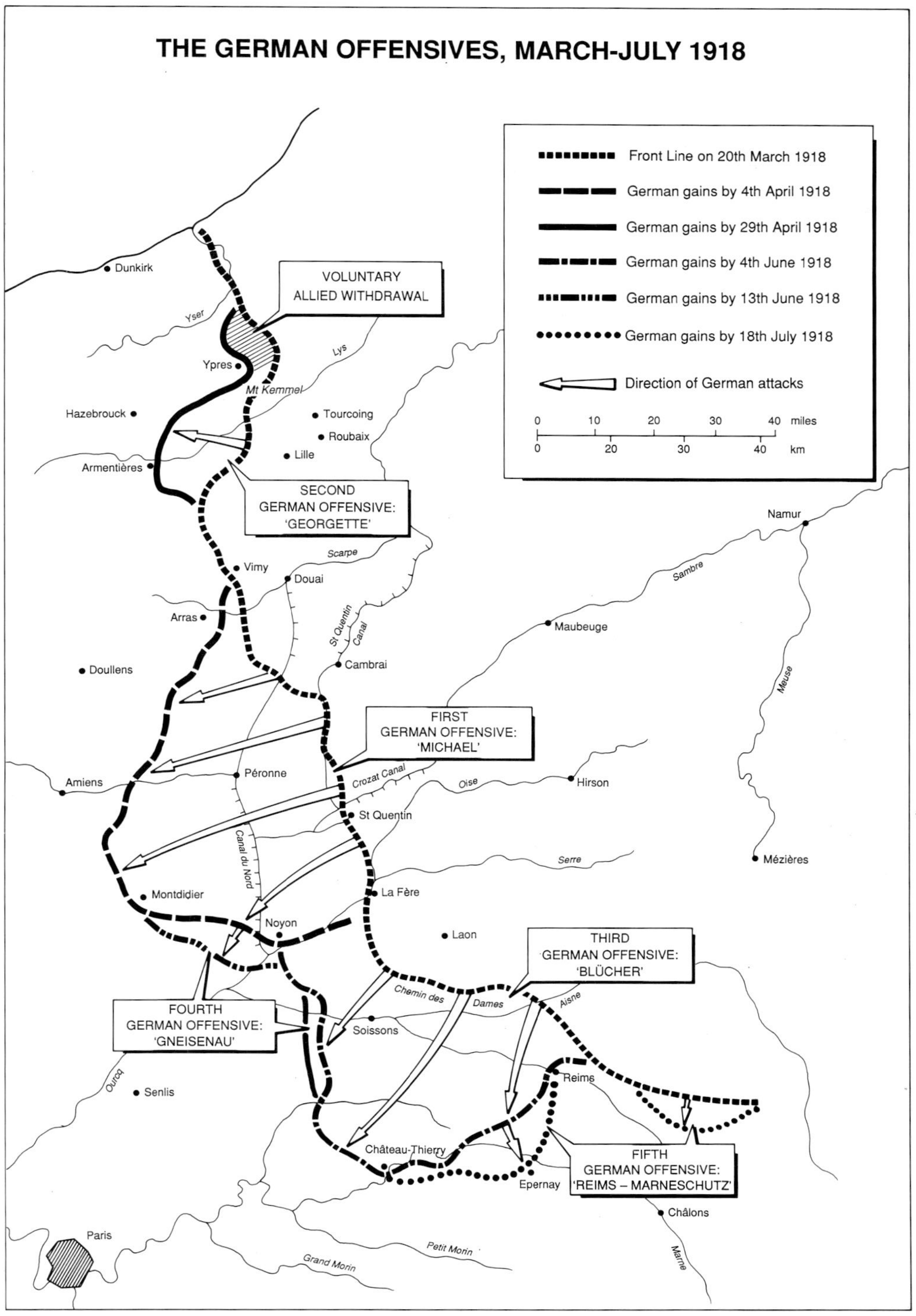

inter-Allied conference was held at Doullens on 26 March, when the energetic Foch was appointed, over Pétain and Haig, to coordinate the operations of the Allied Armies on the Western Front. The appointment did not immediately solve all the problems of the Allies as, for a few days more, the German Eighteenth Army continued to advance, forcing the French out of Montdidier. However, Foch's positive attitude gave the Allies an invaluable psychological boost and, while French reserves took time to arrive, there was no longer any doubt about the French commitment to the protection of Amiens.

On 25 March Ludendorff had sent out revised orders, reversing those issued two days earlier and shifting the main emphasis of the offensive back to the centre and right, where the Second and Seventeenth Armies had stalled. *Operation Mars* was launched

1 *General (later Marshal) Ferdinand Foch at his headquarters at Sarcus on 17 May 1918. At Doullens on 26 March, at the height of the German offensive in Picardy, Foch had been made responsible for coordinating the Allied armies on the Western Front. On 3 April his powers were further defined when he was entrusted with the strategic direction of Allied military operations, though the French, British and American Commanders-in-Chief retained full tactical control of their respective armies. Foch was given the title of General-in-Chief of the Allied Armies in France on 14 April.*
IWM: Q 48178

against Arras on 28 March but was repelled with heavy losses. The motive power of the German offensive was, in fact, running down. The mobility of the attacking armies was governed by the pace of their foot soldiers, since the German forces in the west had few tanks, no armoured cars and comparatively little cavalry. Even their available motorised and horse-drawn transport left much to be desired after years of blockade. Growing casualties among the stormtroopers also accentuated the differences in quality between the élite assault units and other formations. The high level of professional ability of the German General Staff must be acknowledged, yet it can equally be argued that its frequent obsession with short-term operational and organisational detail had merely produced a lopsided Army that was fundamentally ill-suited to its overall strategic purpose. By the end of March 1918 the German infantrymen involved in *Operation Michael* were becoming exhausted and, as on the British side, there were increasing instances of looting and drunkenness. Ludendorff tried to revive his flagging offensive by changing his orders for a third time, reducing his once ambitious objectives to the limited one of seizing Amiens. The thrust was blocked at Villers Bretonneux, some ten miles east of Amiens, on 4 and 5 April by the 9th Australian Brigade and the British 14th and 18th Divisions. This latest check was enough for Ludendorff. On 5 April, the sixteenth day of the offensive, he called off *Operation Michael*.

Despite having advanced about 40 miles, and having recaptured a great deal of the ground they had occupied in 1916, the Germans had not yet administered the mortal blow which Ludendorff had sought. The British had lost 178,000 men since 21 March, including 70,000 prisoners, and French casualties numbered around 77,000. German casualties in *Operation Michael* were approximately 250,000, the losses among the storm troops being particularly hard to replace. The offensive also cost Gough his command. Although he had fought a skilful defensive battle against great odds and in extremely disadvantageous circumstances, he was singled out as the scapegoat for the Fifth Army's misfortunes and relieved on 27 March. He was succeeded by Rawlinson, fresh from a brief spell as British Military Representative at Versailles. The Fifth Army was officially renamed the Fourth Army on 2 April, as if to remove the temporary and somewhat undeserved stain on its reputation.

BACKS TO THE WALL: THE GERMAN LYS OFFENSIVE

Before cancelling *Michael*, Ludendorff had given orders for the projected offensive in Flanders to proceed. The plan was a modified and smaller version of the original, its new codename of *Georgette* reflecting its diminished size. General Ferdinand von Quast's Sixth Army was to attack between Armentières and Givenchy on 9 April, pushing forward in a northwesterly direction across the valley of the Lys towards Hazebrouck, an important railway centre behind the junction of the British First and Second Armies. On 10 April the German Fourth Army, under General Sixt von Arnim, would attack further north, advancing on Messines. The defences along this front were superior to those Gough's Fifth Army had occupied a month previously, but the March fighting had left Haig dangerously short of reserves. The Germans were also feeling the side effects of the recent titanic struggle in Picardy. Over half of their assault units for *Georgette* were 'trench divisions' as opposed to 'attack divisions'.

Preceded by a typical Bruchmüller bombardment, the German attack made good progress on 9 April, brushing aside the weak and dispirited 2nd Portuguese Division near Neuve Chapelle and penetrating about three-and-a-half miles with relatively light casualties. The next day, when the German Fourth Army joined the offensive, Messines village and some of the Messines-Wytschaete Ridge was lost, and Armentières, which lay between the converging German attacks, was evacuated by the British. Haig's appeals to Foch for help at first seemed to fall on deaf ears, a

2

2 *Portuguese troops holding a line of breastworks near Laventie, north of Neuve Chapelle, early in 1918. When the German Lys offensive began on 9 April 1918, the 2nd Portuguese Division had only three weak brigades in the front line to face four German divisions.*
IWM: Q 60288

3 *Men of the 55th (West Lancashire) Division, suffering from the effects of gas, at an advanced dressing station near Béthune on 10 April 1918. The 55th Division was in the line between Givenchy and Laventie when the German Lys offensive opened. Although the Portuguese troops to their north fell back, elements of the 55th Division held Givenchy for five days before being relieved.*
IWM: Q 11586

3

1 *British shells bursting in Armentières on 11 April 1918, the day after British troops had evacuated the town.*
IWM: Q 61032

2 *Field-Marshal Sir Douglas Haig (second from right) talking to the French Prime Minister, Georges Clemenceau, at Doullens station on 13 April 1918. At a conference at Abbeville the next day, Haig made an urgent appeal for the French to take a more active part in the fighting in Flanders.*
– IWM: Q 363

3 *British walking wounded returning from the front near Merris in Flanders on 12 April 1918.*
IWM: Q 10293

1

2

3

disconcerting development so soon after the Doullens agreement, although Foch himself was still having trouble persuading a churlish and reluctant Pétain to free reserves. In a sense, Foch was paying the British a curious, backhanded tribute in assuming that the BEF would be able to halt the Germans in Flanders without much assistance, yet, with the Germans only five miles from Hazebrouck, Haig had real cause for anxiety. On 11 April he issued a special Order of the Day which included the words: "There is no other course open to us but to fight it out. Every position must be held to the last man: there must be no retirement. With our backs to the wall and believing in the justice of our cause each one of us must fight on to the end".

The easing of the crisis on the Lys during the next few days probably owed less to Haig's stirring battle cry than the arrival in Flanders of the British 5th and 33rd Divisions and the 1st Australian Division. On 14 April Foch was named General-in-Chief of the Allied Armies, and this additional step towards genuine unity of command gave him more power – especially over Pétain – to dictate the deployment of reserves. One of his immediate measures was to institute a system of *roulement*, or rotation, whereby weary British divisions could take over quiet sectors of the French line and so release French units for the threatened sectors of the front. By 19 April the French had relieved the British along a nine-mile stretch in the centre of the Second Army's sector. This aid came a little too late to enable Plumer, now back from Italy, to hold on to the positions won so dearly in 1917. As the Germans tightened their grip on Messines Ridge, he took the heartbreaking but necessary decision to relinquish Passchendaele Ridge and retire to a more secure perimeter just east of Ypres – much as he had done in May 1915. Once the decision was made the withdrawal was carried out with the Second Army's customary thoroughness.

It was symptomatic of Ludendorff's growing desperation and strategic inconsistency that the next serious German attack, on 24 April, was another strike towards Amiens, away to the south in Picardy, and it began with a second bite at Villers Bretonneux. The short preliminary bombardment was heavily laced with mustard gas shells, and the attack was notable for the appearance of thirteen German tanks. Though clumsier than British models, they helped the Germans to rip a three-mile gap in the defences and capture Villers Bretonneux. Near Cachy, three of the German tanks met an equal number of British machines in the first tank-versus-tank duel in history. Without French assistance, Rawlinson launched a daring counterattack that night, and the 13th and 15th Australian Brigades, supported by the British 18th and 58th Divisions, retook Villers Bretonneux in an operation characterised by Australian dash and gallantry. Back in Flanders, the British were dismayed when the French lost Mount Kemmel to the German

4

5

4 *German A7V tanks of the type that fought in the first-ever tank-versus-tank action at Cachy, near Villers Bretonneux, on 24 April 1918. The A7V tank was armed with a 57mm gun and six machine guns, and had a crew of eighteen. Ludendorff was sceptical about tanks and their production was not given high priority in Germany. Only about twenty of these clumsy machines were built, although the Germans made as much use as possible of captured British tanks.*
IWM: Q 37344

5 *Villers Bretonneux, as it looked from the German lines in 1918.*
IWM: E(AUS) 2812

Alpine Corps on 25 April, but that was the last German success in the *Georgette* offensive. Hardening resistance and the recurrent difficulties of bringing artillery forward after the initial assault had again slowed the advance. A final lunge against the British and French positions between Ypres and Bailleul on 29 April made minimal gains, and late in the evening Ludendorff terminated the offensive. Ypres and the Channel ports, as well as Amiens, had been saved once more.

LUDENDORFF GAMBLES AGAIN: THE AISNE AND MATZ OFFENSIVES

Rather like boxers after two close and punishing rounds, the opposing armies were glad of the brief lull in major operations which followed the abandonment of *Georgette*. For both sides the question of manpower remained a nagging source of concern. The British had lost nearly 240,000 men since 21 March, the French around 92,000 and the Germans some 348,000. In terms of available divisions on the Western Front at the beginning of May, the Germans, with 206 against 160, retained the advantage. Of the British divisions currently on the Western Front, ten were judged to be worn out, and eight of these were temporarily reduced to cadre strength, with only ten officers and 45 other ranks in each battalion. The long-term answer for the Allies rested, as it had for some time, with the American Expeditionary Force, which had 430,000 officers and men in France on 1 May 1918. American divisions, each containing 28,000 men, were double or treble the size of British and French divisions but, at present, only the US 1st Division was actually in the line. With the help of British shipping, the arrival rate of American reinforcements increased in May, and by the end of the month the AEF's strength in France had risen dramatically to more than 650,000. While the various crises of the spring and early summer caused some relaxation of his stance, Pershing, on the whole, continued to resist attempts to incorporate American troops in French and British formations, and to insist on keeping the AEF as a distinct component of the Allied forces until it could carry out an offensive as a national army under its own officers. As it would be weeks, perhaps months, before the AEF, as a unified body, was in genuine fighting trim, the Allies knew that there were more crises yet to be faced.

There were, of course, other factors to consider apart from numbers. If the BEF had been badly mauled in March and April, it had nonetheless withstood – mostly on its own – the hardest blows that Ludendorff could muster, emerging from the ordeal with a renewed

1

2

1 *German infantry advancing near the Aisne canal during* Operation Blücher *in May 1918.*
IWM: Q 55009

2 *German troops working their way forward through the village of Pont Arcy, which they captured on 27 May 1918. These men are probably from the German 33rd Division which had crossed the Aisne near Pont Arcy by 10.15am that morning.*
IWM: Q 55010

3 *The crossing of the Ailette by German units in May 1918 during the* Blücher *offensive. Reserves are resting on the bank while other troops move off towards the fighting front.*
IWM: Q 55313

4 *Burning buildings in Soissons following its capture by the Germans on 28 May 1918. Soon after Soissons was taken, most German troops were temporarily withdrawn from the town. This was ostensibly because French forces were reported to be assembling to the south and southwest. Other sources, however, claim that the step was taken because the German commanders feared a breakdown of discipline if the troops got hold of provisions and luxuries accumulated in Soissons. The town was recaptured by the French early in August that year.*
IWM: Q 61028

4

optimism and resilience which provided a good foundation for future success. Ludendorff, on the other hand, recognised the deterioration in quality and discipline of some of his troops, as revealed by the reluctance of certain divisions to attack during the Lys operations, and by the persistent tendency of soldiers to linger around captured supply dumps. Some influential officers, such as von Lossberg, were already dubious about the value of further offensives. Ludendorff himself accepted that it was no longer possible to sustain two big attacks at the same time, and that delays between offensives were unavoidable as the German 'battering train' was redeployed, but he was also aware that the transient German numerical advantage was a fast dwindling asset. More attacks were, therefore, essential if the Germans were to achieve their desired victory before the scales tipped, past the point of recovery, in favour of the Allies. Ludendorff's principal objective remained the defeat of the British in Flanders, though he now judged that he must first entice the French reserves away from that region so that they would be unable to support Haig when the moment came for the main event.

To this end, Ludendorff decided that the next attack would be against the weaker French defences in the Chemin des Dames sector. Here the commander of the French Sixth Army, General Duchêne, had misinterpreted Foch's call for 'defence foot by foot' – which actually applied to the front north of the Oise – and thus crowded his forward positions with troops, ignoring Pétain's system of elastic defence and making the task of the Germans easier. Five British divisions had been sent to the sector to recuperate under Foch's *roulement* scheme and, by another of war's savage twists of fate, three of them were in the front line. On the German side, the artillery plan for the attack was, as before, entrusted to Bruchmüller, now

1 *Germans using an improvised stretcher to carry a wounded man back for treatment. They are passing through a reserve line near Soissons early in June 1918.* IWM: Q 55014

2

3

nicknamed *Durchbruchmüller* ('Breakthrough Müller') by the German troops. The offensive on the Aisne, known as *Operation Blucher*, commenced on 27 May with a 4,000-gun, 160-minute bombardment that could justly be described as Bruchmüller's masterpiece. Within a few hours the Germans had crossed the Aisne and destroyed the best part of eight British and French divisions. After advancing up to twelve miles on the first day – phenomenal progress, even by the new standards of 1918 – the German Seventh Army, under General von Boehn, was beyond Soissons by the evening of 29 May and reached the Marne near Château-Thierry, barely 56 miles from Paris, at the beginning of June.

So far *Blucher* had exceeded all expectations, tempting Ludendorff to lose sight of the offensive's original diversionary aim and to exploit its initial success, but at this juncture the German onrush was stopped. Significantly, the United States 2nd and 3rd Divisions fought alongside the French in the defence of Château-Thierry, and on 6 June the 2nd Division counterattacked the Germans at Belleau Wood. Dazzling as von Boehn's advance had been, the Germans were now in a deep salient which, because of the damage to roads and railways, was tricky to supply and which, with its long flanks, was difficult to defend. To expand the salient, draw in more French reserves and establish an improved defensive line, Ludendorff launched von Hutier's Eighteenth Army on a fourth offensive, known as *Gneisenau*, towards the Matz between Montdidier and Noyon. When the attack started on 9 June the French Third Army's commander, General Humbert, was still trying to satisfy the rather contradictory defence requirements of both Foch and Pétain, and repeated the mistake of having too many troops in the most forward zone. Again the Germans made stunning early gains, progressing six miles on the first day. On 11 June General Mangin delivered a counterattack with five divisions, backed by tanks and low-flying aircraft, against von Hutier's right flank, and yet another German offensive ground to a halt. The options open to Ludendorff and the German Army had almost run out.

2 *Troops of the German Eighteenth Army advancing over a captured trench as they attack positions held by the French Third Army in the Montdidier-Noyon area in June 1918.*
IWM: Q 55013

3 *Field-Marshal Paul von Hindenburg, Chief of the German General Staff, reviewing troops on the Western Front in June 1918.*
IWM: Q 52199

1

1 *Lieutenant-General Sir John Monash, who commanded the Australian Corps on the Western Front from May 1918. His plans for the attack at Hamel typified his attention to detail. He was also determined that each participant should be fully briefed about his individual role in the battle, a procedure that was subsequently more widely adopted in the BEF as a whole. Under Monash the Australian Corps was a spearhead formation of the BEF in the offensive at Amiens, in the capture of Mont St Quentin and Péronne, and in the breaking of the Hindenburg Line.*
IWM: E(AUS) 2350

2 *Men of the American 33rd Division resting in the shade of some trees at Corbie on 3 July 1918, the day before they went into action with the Australian Corps at Hamel. Despite General Pershing's reluctance to allow them to take part, four companies of Americans were incorporated by platoons in the attacking Australian battalions. Out of 1,000 Americans who went into action, 6 officers and 128 other ranks became casualties in the highly successful operation.*
IWM: E(AUS) 2694

3 *Some of the ground across which the Australians attacked at Hamel on 4 July 1918. The view is down the slope towards Pear Trench, the chalk parapets of which are visible on the left. On the farther slope are (from the right) Hamel, Vaire and Accroche Woods, the last-named being on the left centre of the horizon. The objective in this sector ran between Vaire and Accroche Woods. It was here that ammunition was dropped to forward troops from aircraft. Two of the parachutes can be seen in the picture.*
IWM: E(AUS) 3840

THE TIDE TURNS

Even though the German Aisne and Matz offensives had been checked, neither Foch nor Pétain had much reason for self-congratulation. The loss of the Chemin des Dames, only a few weeks after Foch's appointment as General-in-Chief, was a chastening experience for the French, and Pétain's general gloominess and slow reactions were becoming increasingly irritating to the younger and more impatient members of Foch's staff. Having themselves suffered humiliation and near-disaster on the Aisne, the French had less cause to be disparaging about the British performance in March and April, and the prestige and influence of Haig and the BEF grew accordingly during the following months, with important consequences for the overall Allied effort on the Western Front. Meanwhile, Ludendorff's problems multiplied. Like other German and Allied commanders before him, he had allowed himself, on more than one occasion, to be misled by spectacular early gains and had continued his offensives too long in an attempt to extract the maximum success from brilliant initial penetration. This disregarded the clear evidence from the war to date that modern railways invariably enabled the defenders to rush reserves to a threatened sector faster than attackers could push reinforcements forward across a battlefield to exploit a breach. The German Army had shown itself to be still capable of superhuman endeavours, but each failed offensive contributed to the gradual erosion of its spirit and motivation. To add to its tribulations, the terrifying Spanish influenza epidemic of 1918-1919 began, in June, to sweep through units already physically weakened by food shortages, further reducing the rifle strength of German infantry battalions.

In a small but symbolic attack on 28 May – the first American offensive operation of the war – the US 1st Division took Cantigny, near Montdidier, at the tip of the German-held Amiens salient. By 26 June the Americans had also secured Belleau Wood. The AEF's debut in battle at Cantigny, Château-Thierry and Belleau Wood cost it over 11,000 casualties, and Pershing's men had displayed the same blend of raw courage and tactical naivety as had the units of Kitchener's Army on 1 July 1916, yet the important fact was that they had taken on seasoned German troops and won. For those with eyes to see it, however, the minor operation which promised most for the future was the model attack carried out by the Australian Corps, under Lieutenant-General Sir John Monash, at Hamel on 4 July.

Formed in November the previous year from existing Australian divisions in France, the Australian Corps had been commanded by Monash since May 1918, when he had succeeded General Sir William Birdwood on the latter's elevation to lead a reconstituted Fifth Army. Born in Melbourne of Jewish parents, Monash was a noted civil engineer before the war, and now showed himself to be one of the outstanding corps commanders in the BEF, particularly in the depth and imagination of his operational planning. The essence of Monash's approach was embodied in his description of a modern battle plan as a score for an orchestral composition, with each instrument, or component – infantry, artillery, tanks and aircraft – playing a precise part in creating the harmonious whole. In preaching the virtues of teamwork and the smooth cooperation of all arms, Monash had a staunch champion in the Fourth Army commander, Rawlinson, a general who had truly profited from the bitter lessons of 1916 and who was to perform as impressively as anyone in the dramas yet to be enacted.

The objectives of Monash's small-scale attack were to capture the village of Hamel and iron out a dent in the British line between Villers Bretonneux and the Somme, thus establishing a straighter barrage line for subsequent operations, and also robbing the Germans of the observation they currently had over Australian positions to the north of the river. The battle plan duly reflected Monash's belief that the infantry should not have to expend themselves in heroic and possibly futile assaults, but should be helped forward by the maximum array of 'mechanical resources' in the form of artillery, machine guns, mortars, aeroplanes and tanks. Sixty of the new Mark V fighting tanks and twelve supply tanks were allotted for the operation. The special combined training given

2

3

1 *German dead near Pear Trench at Hamel on 5 July 1918.*
IWM: E(AUS) 2671

2 *Stormtroopers ready to go into action during the German Marne offensive in July 1918.*
IWM: Q 55371

3 *A soldier of the 5th Battalion, The Duke of Wellington's Regiment, advancing through the Bois du Petit Champ in the Forest of Reims, on 22 July 1918. The British 62nd (West Riding) Division, to which the battalion belonged, was then serving in the area of the French Fifth Army and was involved in the Allied counterattack aimed at pinching out the German salient between Soissons and Reims. The 5th Duke of Wellington's Regiment only partly cleared the wood of German machine gun posts on that day, taking some 200 prisoners and 40 machine guns but suffering over 150 casualties in the process.*
IWM: Q 11092

1

to the assault formation, the 4th Australian Division, restored the Australian trust in tanks which had been so sadly undermined at Bullecourt. As a result, Monash was able to economise on infantry, assigning only eight battalions to a 6,000-yard attack frontage. Moreover, Monash decided that in this assault the tanks, whose secret assembly would be concealed by the noise of aircraft and artillery fire, would advance level with the infantry behind a creeping barrage. Four companies of infantry from the American 33rd Division, which had been training with the Australians, were due to participate but, to everyone's dismay, Pershing withheld his consent. Monash and Rawlinson stood their ground, persuading Haig to countermand

Pershing's order so that the operation could proceed as planned. On the day the Australians and Americans took all their objectives in just over ninety minutes, capturing 1,472 Germans and 171 machine guns at a cost of less than 1,000 casualties to themselves. Among the innovations which made the Hamel operation the prototype for future large-scale attacks by the BEF was the dropping of ammunition by parachute to machine gunners in forward positions. The only sour note afterwards was sounded by Pershing, who became even more determined to resist British or French control of his units.

Realistically, Ludendorff should now have been concentrating on defence but, in the hope of securing at least a negotiated peace on terms favourable to Germany, he resolved to strike another offensive blow. Still intending eventually to defeat the BEF in Flanders, but knowing that the Allies remained too strong there, he made one more attempt to draw off Allied reserves by attacking either side of Reims on 15 July. On the German right, von Boehn's Seventh Army crossed the Marne east of Château-Thierry and, despite some vigorous opposition by the US 3rd Division, established a bridgehead. East of Reims the French Fourth Army, under General Gouraud, had fully applied Pétain's ideas about elastic defence and inflicted a severe reverse on the German First and Third Armies. On 18 July, in a huge counterstroke prepared by its commander, General Mangin, the French Tenth Army – with the Sixth Army on its right – attacked the western side of the German salient between the Marne and Aisne. The US 1st and 2nd Divisions were in the spearhead of the Tenth Army's surprise assault, which was itself supported by 225 tanks, many of them the new Renault light models. In two days Mangin advanced about six miles. By 6 August the Germans, after losing 168,000 men, including 29,000 prisoners, and 793 guns, had evacuated Soissons and withdrawn behind the Aisne and the Vesle. Ludendorff's last throw had failed.

2

3

1

1 *An under-strength platoon of the 29th Australian Battalion, part of the 5th Australian Division, being addressed by an officer during a pause in the advance towards their second objective near the double village of Warfusée-Lamotte on 8 August 1918. The morning mist, which helped the attackers on the first day of the Battle of Amiens, is still evident in this photograph. Despite its diminished size, the platoon seen here has three Lewis guns, an indication of the higher proportion of light machine guns being used by the BEF's infantry units by this period of the war.*
IWM: E(AUS) 2790

2 *A Canadian 60-pounder battery in action on 10 August 1918 during the Battle of Amiens.*
IWM: CO 3006

THE BATTLE OF AMIENS: THE BEF STRIKES BACK

For the Allies the long crisis was over; for the Germans it was just beginning. Having finally surrendered the strategic initiative, Ludendorff, like Moltke four years earlier, came near to nervous collapse at the end of July. Increasingly erratic, paralysed by indecision and losing touch with military reality, he was loath to admit that all hopes of offensive victories were gone, and he rejected Lossberg's sound advice that the German Army should pull out of the Amiens salient and retire to the better-fortified Hindenburg Line. During the first week of August he recovered his composure to some extent, outlining a future policy whereby the German Army would adopt a posture of strategic defence, progressively weakening the Allies by sudden, small-scale attacks launched, in selected areas, from positions of great strength. Ludendorff was given no opportunity to put the policy into effect. The indomitable Haig now sensed that Germany could be beaten before the winter, and had obtained Foch's approval for a larger version of the Hamel operation, with the primary aim of driving the Germans away from Amiens and its vital railway links. On 8 August 1918, Rawlinson's Fourth Army and the French First Army, under General Debeney, struck the German Second and Eighteenth Armies east of Amiens.

The Australian and the Canadian Corps, two of the finest fighting formations in the BEF, played a crucial part in the attack. Both corps had gained immeasurably in morale and tactical experience from having their divisions kept together in national groups, rather than being shuttled between different corps and Armies as so often happened to British units. The Germans would have known an offensive was imminent near Amiens if the presence of the Canadian Corps had been detected, so two Canadian battalions were left behind in Flanders, producing false signals traffic in a way that foreshadowed the deception plans for *Operation Overlord* a quarter of a century later. The mixture of secrecy and bluff with which Rawlinson assembled the mass of men, weapons and equipment needed for the attack was a further demonstration of the giant strides the BEF had made in its overall tactical ability since 1916. At Amiens, much wider use was made of wireless to improve battlefield communications. Aircraft not only carried out their standard reconnaissance and spotting duties, sending back a flow of valuable information, but also added teeth to the offensive in a ground-attack role. Armoured cars and motorised machine guns and mortars of the so-called Canadian Independent Force gave the Fourth Army extra mobility. Backed by 120 supply tanks, some 342 Mark V fighting tanks led the attack with the infantry, while 72 of the lighter Medium Mark A

'Whippet' tanks – which had first appeared at the front in March – were available to work with the cavalry in the exploitation phase. Infantry platoons, with their bombers, rifle grenadiers and Lewis gun sections (as advocated earlier by Maxse and Stephens) were at last more self-contained and better-adapted to the tactical conditions of 1918. Underpinning everything, as at Hamel, was the emphasis which Rawlinson placed on teamwork and the integration of all arms.

3 *German prisoners bringing in wounded in blankets on the Amiens-Roye road near Beaucourt, 9 August 1918.*
IWM: CO 2991

3

1 *Field-Marshal Sir Douglas Haig (left) congratulating troops of the 85th Canadian Battalion (Nova Scotia Highlanders) on their part in the Battle of Amiens. The photograph was taken at Domart on 11 August 1918.*
IWM: CO 3015

2 *A Canadian soldier offers cigarettes to men of the French First Army near Roye, 12 August 1918.*
IWM: CO 3065

3 *Pioneers of the 3rd Australian Division on the Somme Canal at Chipilly on 13 August 1918. They are repairing a bridge which had been blown up by the Germans as they fell back during the Battle of Amiens.*
IWM: E(AUS) 2906

4 *Part of 'A' Company of the 21st Battalion, Australian Imperial Force, during the storming of Mont St Quentin on 31 August-1 September 1918.*
IWM: E(AUS) 3126

Accompanied by a ferocious surprise bombardment from 2,070 guns, orchestrated by Major-General Budworth – the Fourth Army's answer to Bruchmüller – Rawlinson's forces attacked in a thick mist at 4.20am on 8 August. On the opening day the relatively fresh Canadians, who had not been involved in the spring disasters, advanced up to eight miles. The Australian Corps, on their left, pushed forward some six miles. On the assault front of the British III Corps, the Germans had dislocated preparations for the offensive when, on 6 August, they had responded to a previous Australian raid by mounting a counterattack near Morlancourt. The Germans were, therefore, more on their toes in this sector but, all the same, III Corps achieved a two-mile penetration. Although French progress to the south was generally less incisive, the Fourth Army on 8 August inflicted losses of 400 guns and 27,000 men, including over 15,000 prisoners, on the Germans, suffering only 9,000 casualties itself. During the next few days, almost inevitably, the advance slowed. Cooperation between the Whippets and the cavalry was disappointing, with the latter generally outpacing the former, and only six tanks in all remained in action by 12 August.

However, it was the manner of the Allied victory at Amiens, not its scale, that counted most. As the BEF grew in confidence and stature, the accelerating deterioration of the German Army was correspondingly apparent. Defences were no longer constructed with the old skill and care, and while many individual divisions continued to fight bravely and stubbornly, a kind of morose lethargy was replacing professional drive and dedication in the Army as a whole. German troops coming into the line were called 'blacklegs' or were greeted with cries of "You're prolonging the war!" by those they relieved.

Even Ludendorff could not escape the stark facts. As he subsequently wrote, 8 August 1918 "was the black day of the German Army in the history of this war".

APPROACHING THE HINDENBURG LINE

Soon after the setback of 8 August, Ludendorff, who was bereft of hope and inspiration, let alone solutions, offered to resign. The offer was rejected by the Kaiser and Hindenburg, although Wilhelm II agreed with Ludendorff that the war must be ended. At an Imperial conference at Spa on 14 August the Foreign Secretary, Admiral von Hintze, was instructed to make peace overtures through the Queen of the Netherlands. On the face of it, Germany seemed to retain some strong bargaining counters, particularly the fact that her forces still occupied large tracts of French and Belgian soil. However, even this militated against the adoption of a reasonable policy, since it only hardened Ludendorff's resolve to hold the existing front, while his continued insistence that Belgium should stay under Germany's influence would be a certain stumbling block in any negotiations. Senior German staff officers such as Kuhl and Lossberg were beginning to despair about Ludendorff's refusal to withdraw to a more defensible line, a step he had been only too willing to take in 1917.

4

5

5 *Group photograph taken during the visit of King George V to the British Fourth Army headquarters at Flixecourt on 13 August 1918. In the front row, from left to right, are: General Sir Henry Rawlinson (commander of the Fourth Army); General Debeney (French First Army); Marshal Foch (General-in-Chief of the Allied Armies); King George V; Field-Marshal Sir Douglas Haig; General Pétain (French Commander-in-Chief); and General Fayolle (French Reserve Army Group). In the second row, immediately behind them, are, from left to right: General Weygand (Foch's Chief of Staff); Lieutenant-General Sir Herbert Lawrence (Haig's Chief of Staff); Major-General H.C. Holman (Deputy Adjutant and Quartermaster General, Fourth Army); Major-General R.U.H. Buckland (Chief Engineer, Fourth Army); and Sir Derek Keppel (Equerry to the King). The two bareheaded officers towards the back are Major-General C.E.D. Budworth (commanding the Fourth Army's artillery) and Major-General A.A.Montgomery (Chief of Staff, Fourth Army).* *IWM: Q 9251*

The BEF's senior commanders had a much firmer grasp of military realities. Two years earlier their answer to stiffening resistance would normally have been to apply additional pressure in the same sector. Now, as progress became more difficult at Amiens, Rawlinson recommended shifting the main weight of the attack to another part of the front, so keeping the Germans off balance by denying them the ability to settle in new defensive positions or concentrate their reserves at one point. Haig's endorsement of these views meant that the long and vain quest for the elusive strategic breakthrough was a thing of the past; the BEF would no longer exhaust itself in 'dead' offensives, and would henceforth exert more effective pressure with a rolling succession of punches in different sectors. Foch, who wanted the British Fourth Army to go on attacking without a pause, needed some persuading but eventually acquiesced. This, in itself, was a tacit acknowledgement that Haig and the BEF were setting the pace of Allied operations.

Throughout August the general performance of the French in attack was sluggish, a conspicuous exception being Mangin's Tenth Army, which carried out preparatory operations between the Oise and Soissons on 18 and 19 August before gaining two to three miles, and taking over 8,000 prisoners from the German Ninth Army at the start of the Battle of Noyon the next day. On 21 August, in accordance with Haig's revised strategy, the BEF's offensive was extended northwards to the Third Army's sector between the old Somme battlefield and Arras. Byng's troops pushed the Germans back some 4,000 yards and, on 22 August, the Fourth Army recaptured Albert, yet Haig, with the scent of victory in his nostrils, felt that extra vigour was required, stressing "the necessity for all ranks to act with the utmost boldness and resolution in order to get full advantage from the present favourable situation". The Third and Fourth Armies responded by attacking with renewed energy along a 33-mile front on 23 August. They were joined three days later by Horne's First Army which, with the Canadian Corps again under its wing, struck eastwards from Arras, covered by the Rivers Scarpe and Sensee on its left. Under this rain of blows, Ludendorff was forced to order the withdrawal of the Army Groups of Crown Prince Rupprecht and von Boehn to an intermediate line stretching from east of Bapaume – which the New Zealand Division entered on 29 August – to the heights northeast of Noyon. At the same time the Germans pulled out of their salient on the Lys, giving up most of the ground they had won in April. Mount Kemmel once more passed into British hands and the Second and Fifth Armies were able to move forward to a line from Vormezeele and Ploegsteert to Neuve Chapelle and Givenchy.

The month's achievements were crowned by further remarkable exploits by the BEF's Dominion formations. On 31 August the 2nd Australian Division stormed and held the daunting German defensive bastion of Mont St Quentin. With this protective bulwark gone, Péronne fell soon afterwards, its suburbs being cleared by noon on 2 September. Not

1 *The stricken mule in this limber team has just been hit by a shell splinter. The picture was taken in the British 4th Division's sector near Remy during the attack on the Drocourt-Quéant Line.*
IWM: Q 7031

2 *The village of Quéant on 7 September 1918. Five days earlier the British 52nd, 57th and 63rd Divisions had broken through the southernmost part of the Drocourt-Quéant position in this sector.*
IWM: Q 7048

3 *Men of the Lincolnshire Regiment holding a captured reserve trench beyond Epéhy, 18 September 1918.*
IWM: Q 11327

to be outdone, the Canadian Corps that day attacked the *Wotan Stellung*, or Drocourt-Quéant Line, breaking out into open country beyond. This latest blow at last compelled Ludendorff to sanction a retirement to the Hindenburg Line, as Lossberg and others had been urging for weeks. A growing number of German soldiers had by now lost all faith in their leaders. Crown Prince Rupprecht noted in his diary that the inscription "Slaughter cattle for Wilhelm and Sons!" had been seen on a troop train at Nuremberg. Even so, the German Army was still able to summon up enough professional pride, patriotism and tactical expertise in its ranks to ensure that the Allies would pay a high price for almost every local success. As the BEF approached the outpost system of the Hindenburg Line, it found itself confronted by tough units such as the Alpine Corps, which were known to be reliable and which were specially picked by the German high command to hold these important positions at all costs. During the second and third weeks of September,

4

4 *A wounded British 'Bantam' bringing in a German prisoner during the Battle of Epéhy on 18 September 1918.*
IWM: Q 11329

5 *The 45th Australian Battalion following a creeping barrage onto their final objective overlooking Ascension Valley, near Le Verguier in France, on 18 September 1918.*
IWM: E(AUS) 3259

6 *Germans in the act of surrendering to men of the 45th Australian Battalion who were advancing beyond Ascension Farm, near Le Verguier, 18 September 1918.*
IWM: E(AUS) 3274

5

the BEF overcame the strong outpost defences around Havrincourt and Epéhy to get within assaulting distance of the main Hindenburg system. Since 8 August Haig's forces had advanced some 25 miles along a front of 40 miles, but losses of 180,000 were a salutary reminder that more hard fighting lay ahead.

The contribution made by British divisions to these operations has, perhaps, been too often obscured by the undeniably brilliant feats of the Australian and Canadian Corps. The part played by Maxse's old division, the 18th – now commanded by Major-General R.P. Lee – provides a perfect case in point. Serving with III Corps in Rawlinson's Fourth Army, the 18th Division was heavily involved in the opening stages of the Battle of Amiens. Next, between 22 August and 5 September, it pushed its way forward

6

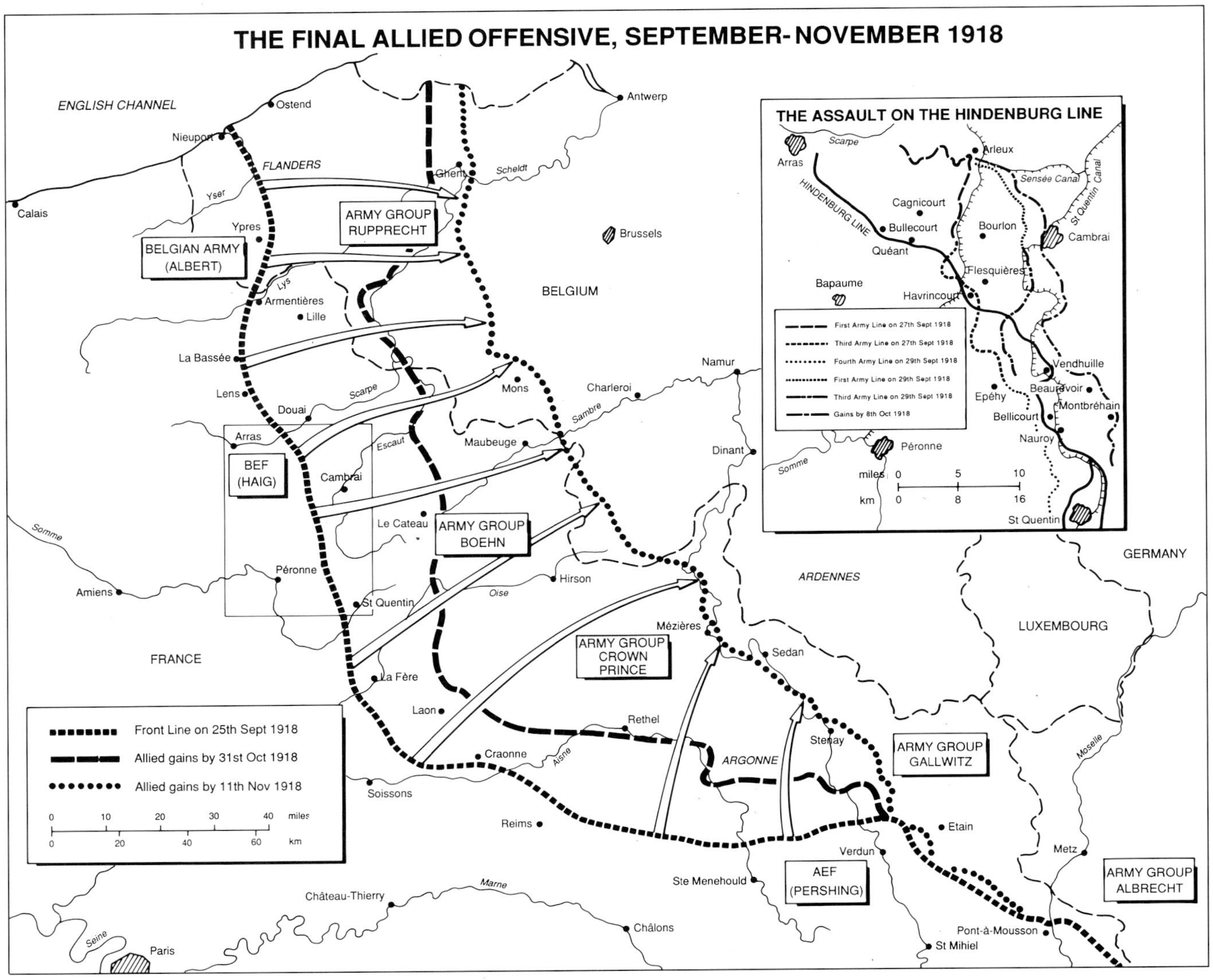

across the devastated 1916 battlefield, recapturing Albert, the Tara and Usna Hills, the La Boisselle craters, Montauban, Bernafay Wood, Trones Wood, Leuze Wood and Combles, as well as securing Fregicourt, St Pierre Vaast Wood and Vaux Wood. In this period, at a cost of 2,852 casualties, including 21 officers and 330 other ranks killed, it advanced 17 miles, taking 2,464 prisoners. The division then had a fortnight's rest before several days of bitter fighting for the Hindenburg Line outposts at Ronssoy, Lempire, The Knoll and Tombois Farm. In the latter series of actions, between 18 and 24 September, its soldiers were exposed to murderous artillery and machine gun fire, and were frequently called upon to engage in savage close-quarter fighting in order to gain any ground. By the end of this phase the 18th Division, with a high proportion of young conscripts in its units, was extremely weary and its battalions were depleted, the average strength of a company being down to seventy men. The division may by then have lost its earlier zest, but not its persistence and powers of endurance, arguably the two outstanding qualities of the British soldier in the First World War. It should be remembered that, while the élite German storm divisions in March, April and May had made spectacular progress at the beginning of each offensive, they also had little real bite left after only a week or so. In contrast, the standard British division in August and September 1918 had the capacity to maintain the pressure on the enemy over a prolonged spell of five or six weeks. It was this relentless and constantly-shifting pressure, rather than dramatic, rapier-like thrusts, which did much to bring about the ultimate defeat of the German Army.

One possible explanation for the solid achievements of divisions such as the 18th is that the men of the BEF – whether they were young conscripts or wary veterans – now had a great deal more trust in their commanders who, in turn, were finally in a position to exercise more flair and imagination in their planning. A second ingredient was the consistently high level of performance of the Royal Artillery, which lay at the heart of the vastly improved cooperation between infantry and gunners in the summer and autumn of 1918; even the rawest newcomers could be shepherded onto their objectives by creeping barrages of great weight and accuracy. The third reason for success was almost certainly the emphasis placed on teamwork. Quite simply, the BEF had become infinitely better balanced, and therefore more flexible as a fighting force, than the German Army. If one of its components failed, a combination of others could usually see the operation through to a satisfactory conclusion. This was why it was not a catastrophe when the tanks, having played a leading role in the assault at Amiens on 8 August, were reduced to a

1 *Foch (left) and Pershing (right) confer at Chaumont in the summer of 1918. The two were not always in agreement regarding the strategic role of the American Expeditionary Force on the Western Front.*
IWM: Q 58390

on 24 July was principally designed to eradicate the salients resulting from Ludendorff's offensives, and to free the Paris-Amiens and Paris-Nancy railways from German interference. Foch's plan was, in some ways, surprisingly unambitious for a soldier with his innate attacking spirit, but he did agree to Pershing's proposal that the newly-formed American First Army should help to make the Paris-Nancy railway secure by reducing the long-standing German salient at St Mihiel.

In August Foch signally failed to exercise the degree of tactical and strategic coordination expected of a General-in-Chief. Apart from Mangin, the perennial firebrand, the French generals were not pulling their full weight, the performance of Debeney's First Army, on Rawlinson's immediate right, being particularly lacklustre. Foch, created a Marshal early in the month, had not yet imposed his authority on Pétain, who seemed temperamentally incapable of injecting greater drive and urgency into his armies. Foch's constant demands for further pressure from the BEF

2 *Mark V tanks moving up near Bellicourt on 29 September 1918 for the Battle of the St Quentin Canal. They are carrying 'cribs' – a lighter version of the earlier fascines – to enable them to cross the trenches of the Hindenburg Line. The Mark V tank, first used operationally at Hamel in July, had a more powerful engine and was more manoeuvrable than previous models, though its ventilation left much to be desired.*
IWM: Q 9364

mere handful by direct hits, damage and breakdowns after five days. At last the formula was right, and the sum of the BEF truly mattered more than its individual parts.

THE WIDENING ALLIED OFFENSIVE AND THE BREAKING OF THE HINDENBURG LINE

As Generalissimo, Foch had been anxious for several weeks to broaden the scope of the Allied offensive effort. The scheme he had presented to Haig, Pétain and Pershing at his headquarters at Bombon Château

on the toughest sectors of the Western Front were, therefore, all the more unjustified. In truth, the BEF was already shouldering the biggest burden of active attacking operations. Haig, who saw the opportunities for outright victory in 1918 more clearly than anyone, was, like Rawlinson, finally coming into his own now that the BEF was on the move. Haig's use of a headquarters train to take him to the areas where his forces were most heavily engaged at the time showed how much closer he was to the progress and 'feel' of the battle than he had been in previous years. During the last week of August he expressed the opinion to Foch that the Americans should be assuming a more positive operational role. Pershing and his staff

1

was essentially echoing Haig's recent suggestion in calling for all the Allied forces to be brought into play "in one great convergent attack". The problem for the American Commander-in-Chief was that, whilst he saw the strategic sense of an advance towards Mézières, he strongly opposed Foch's proposal that some twelve to sixteen American divisions should join the French Second and Fourth Armies in attacks between the Meuse and Argonne and astride the Aisne. Pershing quickly told Foch that he could not agree to any scheme which meant dispersing his divisions among the Allied armies: "I do insist that the American Army must be employed as a whole ... not four or five divisions here and six or seven there". He was also concerned about the effects Foch's change of plans would have upon the cherished St Mihiel operation.

After four days of sparring, a compromise was reached. The St Mihiel attack would proceed, but with limited objectives, so that it would go no further than the German defence line, known as the *Michel Stellung*, running across the base of the salient. The Americans

2

3

1 *The St Quentin Canal, near Bellenglise, where the British 46th Division crossed in its successful assault on 29 September 1918.*
IWM: Q 9510

2 *The barbed wire entanglements which formed part of the German Hindenburg Support System defences near Gouy, in the 3rd Australian Division sector, 3 October 1918.*
IWM: E(AUS) 3481

3 *An ammunition column on the Arras-Cambrai road on 30 September 1918, during the First Army's advance towards Cambrai.*
IWM: CO 3322

regarded the elimination of the St Mihiel salient as a possible preliminary to an offensive eastwards against the powerful fortress of Metz. Haig, however, believed that richer rewards would be gleaned if the Americans attacked northwestwards, up through the Argonne and the Meuse valley towards the rail centre of Mézières, thus converging with the BEF's planned thrust against and beyond the Hindenburg Line near St Quentin and Cambrai.

Haig's advice, contained in a letter to the Generalissimo on 27 August, appears to have been decisive in altering Foch's entire concept of the Allied offensive. It is surely more than a coincidence that, from this point on, with the slogan *Tout le monde à la battaille!* ('Everyone into battle!'), Foch began to think in terms of a series of violent and interrelated hammer blows with more lethal intentions than merely eliminating salients or freeing railways. In a note left with Pershing following an inconclusive and occasionally ill-humoured meeting on 30 August, Foch would then switch their main effort to the Meuse-Argonne sector where, under their own commander, they would play an appropriate part in the overall Allied offensive which Foch was preparing. Having won the vital point, Pershing did allow some American divisions to remain with other Allied formations elsewhere on the Western Front. On 12 September, preceded by a four-hour bombardment from 3,000 guns – half of which had American crews, though most of the weapons were French – seven American and two French divisions assaulted the southern and western sides of the St Mihiel salient, while additional

4 *Brigadier-General J.V. Campbell VC addresses men of the 137th Brigade from the damaged parapet of the Riqueval Bridge over the St Quentin Canal, 2 October 1918. The North and South Staffordshires of the 137th Brigade had crossed the Canal three days earlier. Some soldiers are still in the lifejackets which they wore in the assault.*
IWM: Q 9534 4

French units attacked its 'nose'. Although the Germans, through poor Allied security, knew an attack was imminent and had started to withdraw, this first major American-led operation was an incontrovertible success for the AEF, reducing the salient in thirty hours and netting 15,000 prisoners and 460 guns at a price of approximately 7,000 American casualties. Even more noteworthy was the ensuing transfer of 600,000 troops to the Meuse-Argonne region in less than a fortnight. This rapid movement of men and equipment owed much to the organisational skills of George C. Marshall, then a colonel in the First Army's

1

1 *American transport struggling along a rough road in the Argonne on the morning of 1 October 1918.*
Bettmann Archive Photo

Operations Section but destined one day to become US Chief of Staff and a Secretary of State.

By 23 September, the various Commanders-in-Chief had drawn up the detailed plans for the operations to be carried out by their respective armies in the general Allied offensive decreed by Foch. While the final preparations were being made, cheering news was coming from other theatres. In Salonika the Bulgarians were about to request an armistice following a powerful Allied attack which had begun on 15 September. In Palestine the Turks were in retreat as a result of Allenby's breakthrough at Megiddo between 19 and 21 September. On the Western Front, four separate but coordinated blows were to be delivered by the Allies within a week. First, on 26 September, the big Franco-American attack would take place between the Meuse and Reims. Next, on 27 September, the British First and Third Armies would strike towards Cambrai. The third day of this rolling offensive would see the start of a drive in Flanders by a force comprising the Belgian Army, nine French divisions – three of which were cavalry – and the ten divisions of Plumer's Second Army. This force was commanded by King Albert of the Belgians and had a French Chief of Staff, General Degoutte. Last, but not least, the British Fourth Army, with the French First Army on its right, would assault the Hindenburg Line near St Quentin on 29 September.

The Meuse-Argonne offensive, involving the US First Army and the French Fourth Army, began on schedule and the Americans gained up to three miles on the opening day. German opposition then hardened, the carefully-sited defensive positions adding to the natural obstacles presented by the steep and densely-wooded countryside between the Meuse and the Argonne Forest. Severe supply problems soon arose in this difficult terrain and casualties mounted. The considerable courage of the American troops did not compensate for their tactical inexperience or failures of staff work and, after five days, the Allies had only progressed some eight miles at the deepest point of penetration.

The attack by the British First and Third Armies west of Cambrai on 27 September was initially more effective. Here the Canadian Corps, as the right wing formation of Horne's First Army, had the task of crossing the Canal du Nord. The canal, under construction in 1914, still had dry stretches and, to take advantage of one of these and thereby avoid a direct assault on the tougher sector in front of him, the commander of the Canadian Corps, Lieutenant-General Sir Arthur Currie, obtained approval to sidestep to the south, push his troops across on a narrow front and then spread them out fanwise on the farther bank. Currie's bold plan worked. In two days the First and Third Armies penetrated six miles. Again German resistance stiffened and arduous fighting followed, but the Canadian thrust across the Canal du Nord prepared the way for the later capture of Cambrai. In Flanders the pattern of progress was much the same. By nightfall on 28 September the Allied forces under King Albert had burst out of the former Ypres Salient, driving the Germans from Passchendaele Ridge and back beyond the boundaries of the BEF's advance in 1917. On the second day, Plumer regained possession of the Messines-Wytschaete Ridge and reached Warneton on the Lys, while the Belgians got to within two miles of Roulers. The first phase of the Flanders offensive carried the Allies forward about nine miles, but the arrival of German reserves and the customary problems of rain and mud caused the pace to slacken, especially on the left, where the French and Belgians were hampered by Degoutte's inadequate arrangements for the transportation of supplies across the swampy and cratered terrain of the old Salient. An air drop of thirteen tons of food supplies to advanced French and Belgian troops provided another foretaste of future warfare. However, it became necessary to halt the Flanders offensive temporarily in order to overhaul the administration of the support services and re-establish proper lines of communication.

Rawlinson's turn to attack the Hindenburg Line on a 12-mile front between St Quentin and Vendhuille came on 29 September. Opposite the Fourth Army's right-hand formation, the British IX Corps, lay the St

Quentin Canal, which was some 35 feet wide and had cuttings with steep, almost vertical banks up to 60 feet high in places. The key assault – by the Australian Corps, with the US 27th and 30th Divisions attached – was therefore to be made on a three-and-a-half-mile sector further north, between Bellicourt and Vendhuille, where the canal ran underground through a tunnel. Unfortunately for the Fourth Army, the green American 27th Division was unable to take three remaining German outposts in a preliminary operation on 27 September, partly because the troops lost purpose and direction when their few company officers became casualties. Rather than risk hitting any Americans who might still be out in front, the US 27th Division started 1,000 yards behind the barrage when the big attack was launched two days later. On this occasion the accompanying tanks were not a great help, as the Germans were displaying increasing skill in countering them with field guns and anti-tank rifles. Hence the 3rd Australian Division, which had been given an exploitation and not an assault role, was embroiled in a fierce struggle much earlier than anticipated. To the right the US 30th Division made better initial headway but experienced problems in the complex network of trenches of the main Hindenburg system, whereupon the 5th Australian division, following up, also had to fight hard to push on with the Americans through Bellicourt to control the southern end of the tunnel and reach Nauroy, a joint advance of nearly 4,000 yards.

A day of some disappointment was saved for Rawlinson and Monash by the magnificent performance of the Territorials of the 46th (North Midland) Division. Their success was founded upon a daring plan submitted by Lieutenant-General Sir Walter Braithwaite, the commander of IX Corps, and also upon painstaking preparations. On 29 September, the division's Staffordshire Brigade, hidden by fog, stormed the defences of the St Quentin Canal near Bellenglise, crossing the canal itself on footbridges which the Germans had neglected to destroy and with the aid of rafts, mud-mats, lifelines, collapsible boats and life

2

2 *A battery of the American 108th Field Artillery in action at Varennes in the Meuse-Argonne offensive, 3 October 1918.*
IWM: Q 70711

3

3 *View over the Beaurevoir Line, the last reserve trench system of the Hindenburg defences, in October 1918.*
IWM: E(AUS) 3582

jackets, either provided by the Royal Engineers or requisitioned from Channel steamers. After capturing the enemy trenches on the far bank, the attacking troops, together with the 32nd Division and a few Whippet tanks, swung to the right to outflank and take in rear the German defences along the eastern arm of the canal and on the high ground to the south. The deepest inroads achieved by the Fourth Army on 29 September – between three and four miles – were in this sector, with the 46th Division capturing 4,200 out of the day's bag of 5,300 prisoners.

FORWARD TO VICTORY

The war was already lost in the hearts and minds of the German high command when the Hindenburg Line was pierced. On 28 September, a few hours before the Bulgarians laid down their arms – the first of Germany's allies to capitulate – Ludendorff told Hindenburg that Germany must sue for peace and ask for an armistice without delay. In Ludendorff's words, the two officers parted that evening "like men who have buried their dearest hopes". The following day they were both displeased to hear from von Hintze that he had so far taken no action about the proposed peace moves through the Queen of the Netherlands, and were even more shocked by the Foreign Secretary's assertion that revolution could only be averted by the introduction of parliamentary government. An emissary, Major von dem Bussche, was despatched to Berlin to inform the Reichstag of the situation, and on 3 October the liberal Prince Max of Baden, a known advocate of peace, agreed to succeed von Hertling as Imperial Chancellor. While the party leaders in the Reichstag were still reeling from the sudden revelation of the country's true military plight, peace notes were sent by Germany and Austria-Hungary on 4 October to President Woodrow Wilson of the United States. Wilson's Fourteen Points, a series of conditions for peace which had been set before the US Congress in January, would serve as a basis for negotiations but, even now,

1 *A Canadian patrol entering Cambrai on 9 October 1918.*
IWM: CO 3373

The breach in the Hindenburg Line on the Fourth Army front was narrower and shallower than planned, but it was a breach all the same, and was sufficiently wide to give Rawlinson the leverage he needed and enable the French First Army to his right to re-enter St Quentin. On 3 October the Fourth Army opened a six-mile gap in the Beaurevoir Line, the last substantial support system of the *Siegfried Stellung*. The village which lent the Beaurevoir Line its name fell on 5 October, along with the stronghold of Montbréhain, where the Australians brought their distinguished fighting record on the Western Front to a notable end with another victory. Rawlinson was the first to admit that the breaking of the Hindenburg Line might well have proved impossible had it been defended "by the Germans of two years ago" yet, whatever qualifications he and others cared to make, the strategic and even political ramifications of the BEF's most recent offensives would be no less profound for all that.

Hindenburg and Ludendorff baulked at the idea of giving up Alsace-Lorraine or any territory in the east which they considered to be rightfully German.

During October the Allied advance continued, though not with the speed which either side might have expected. German machine gunners and artillerymen, in particular, remained capable of tenacious resistance, in spite of the fact that the field strength of German infantry battalions was draining inexorably away. An average strength of between 450 and 550 men per battalion had only been maintained by disbanding more than twenty divisions. Some battalions were down to 150 all ranks. On 8 October the British Third and Fourth Armies, with the French First Army on their right, attacked on a 17-mile front stretching south from Cambrai, progressing four miles and taking 8,000 prisoners. Early on 9 October Canadian patrols from the First Army entered Cambrai itself to link up with elements of the 57th Division from Byng's Third Army. Even Lloyd George at last felt compelled, after these recent events, to offer Haig tardy congratulations on "the greatest chapter in our military history", but within another forty-eight hours the Germans had managed to make a stand on the line of the River Selle near Le Cateau, obliging the British to pause in this sector in order to prepare a fresh attack. The improvement of communications in Flanders, however, permitted the Allies to resume the offensive there on 14 October. The French formations under King Albert's command again made a weak contribution, leaving the Belgians and the British Second Army to deliver the most telling blows. Turning a blind eye to orders which would have restricted his role to that of flank guard, Plumer pressed on energetically across the Lys. The Second Army's progress helped the neighbouring Fifth Army, under Birdwood, to liberate Lille on 17 October, the day on which the Belgians recaptured the important prize of Ostend, and the British First Army, to the south, occupied Douai. Two days later Belgian units freed Bruges and Zeebrugge while Plumer's troops took Courtrai. By 20 October the Allies had reached the Dutch border and the British Second Army was eight miles beyond the line it had held the previous week. Crown Prince Rupprecht, whose Army Group faced the Allies on this northern flank, reported to Prince Max that the morale of German troops had suffered seriously, that their powers of resistance were diminishing daily, and that they were surrendering in hordes whenever the Allies attacked.

The diplomatic thumbscrews, too, were being tightened. On 8 October President Wilson had replied to the German peace note, affirming that the evacuation of all occupied territory would be the first condition of any armistice discussions. Barely had the Germans declared themselves ready to comply with Wilson's terms than the American President, on 14 October, insisted that the U-boat campaign must be stopped and also indicated that the Allies would only negotiate with a democratic German government. Largely disregarding Ludendorff's objections, Prince Max once more signalled Germany's willingness to meet Wilson's conditions. The response was brutal. In a third note, on 23 October, Wilson demanded what would amount to unconditional surrender on Germany's part. Wilson had not always fully consulted his allies before presenting his terms, and not everyone agreed with the increasingly harsh line being taken. Haig, for example, sagely commented to his wife that the statesmen should "not attempt to so humiliate Germany as to produce a desire for revenge in years to come". For Ludendorff, Wilson's latest conditions were the last straw. On 24 October a telegram, in Hindenburg's name but almost certainly drafted by Ludendorff, proclaimed that the American President's reply was "unacceptable to us soldiers" and "a challenge to continue our resistance with all our strength". The text of the telegram leaked out before it could be withdrawn and provoked a furious reaction in the Reichstag the following day. Out of step with the new policies of the German government, and badly misjudging the real mood of the Army and the people, Ludendorff could not ride out the storm and resigned on 26 October. He was succeeded by General Wilhelm Groner. Hindenburg stayed on as Chief of the General Staff.

On the Allied side, Haig was more anxious than ever to reach a conclusion in 1918. He knew that the Americans were not yet completely battle-fit, that the French Army was probably incapable of a decisive offensive, and that the BEF was tired and short of

2 *Canadian troops – probably from the 12th Canadian Brigade – entering Valenciennes across the Scheldt Canal on 1 November 1918. The crossing was made, under machine gun fire, by means of some lock gates and a ruined bridge.*
IWM: CO 3504

1 *Winston Churchill (centre), the British Minister of Munitions, watching the March Past of the 47th (London) Division at the ceremony to mark the official entry of the Allies into Lille, 28 October 1918. Standing immediately in front of Churchill is Lieutenant-Colonel B.L. Montgomery (later Field-Marshal Viscount Montgomery of Alamein). Montgomery was then Chief Staff Officer (GSO1) of the 47th Division.*
IWM: Q 11428

2 *Admiral Sir Rosslyn Wemyss, the First Sea Lord and Head of the British Delegation at the Armistice negotiations at Compiègne, is seen here in the centre of the front row of the group posing for the camera beside the railway coach in which the Armistice was signed. Wemyss is flanked by Foch (right) and General Maxime Weygand (left), Foch's chief of staff.*
Hulton-Deutsch Collection: 3L 884

1

2

reinforcements. On the other hand, he had no wish to allow the Germans any chance of establishing a solid defence line during the coming winter. Haig therefore tried to keep the Germans off-balance and on the retreat while he simultaneously recommended moderate armistice terms to encourage them to surrender. The British Fourth Army opened the attack on the German positions on the Selle on 17 October, Haig's target being a line from the Sambre and Oise Canal to Valenciennes, so bringing within artillery range the communications centre of Aulnoye, where the Mézières-Hirson railway linked up with that running back to Germany via Maubeuge and Charleroi. Rawlinson's assault on 17 October was made on a ten-mile front south of Le Cateau. The Selle was crossed without major problems and, although German opposition then became more stubborn, the right wing of the Fourth Army advanced some five miles to the Sambre Canal in three days, with the French First Army for once keeping pace alongside. The British First Army had also pushed forward about six miles, to bring it abreast of the Third Army in time for a joint night attack across the Selle north of Le Cateau early on 20 October. Here, as elsewhere, the Germans had used the time earned by their determined rearguards to strengthen their positions beyond the river with thick wire entanglements, and it took Byng's and Horne's units all day to progress two miles and attain their immediate objectives. The BEF grimly maintained the pressure with a combined attack by the Fourth, Third and First Armies which began at

1.20am on 23 October. A further gain of six miles in two days was achieved as the Fifth and Second Armies, to the north, approached the line of the Scheldt. Another pause was now necessary to coordinate the next sequence of Allied attacks. By and large, October had proved a successful month for Haig's forces, but the going had not been easy. In the four weeks since they had broken through the Hindenburg Line they had covered just twenty more miles and had suffered some 120,000 additional casualties.

Had the front line soldiers only known it, their long ordeal would be over in less than a fortnight. After five weeks of bitter fighting in the Meuse-Argonne sector, the US First Army penetrated the last main German defence line on 1 November, cutting the vital Lille-Metz railway two days later. In the BEF's area of operations, the Canadian Corps captured Valenciennes on 2 November as a preliminary to a bigger attack by the First, Third and Fourth Armies. Supported by only 37 tanks, this was launched on 4 November along a 30-mile front from Valenciennes to the Sambre, on either side of the Forest of Mormal. That day, men of the New Zealand Division scaled the outer and inner ramparts of the walled town of Le Quesnoy in a mediæval-style assault to force the surrender of the German garrison. The storming of Le Quesnoy was almost a microcosm of the overall strategic and political situation, for the whole war effort of the Central Powers was now crumbling. Turkey had signed an armistice with the Allies at the end of October, followed on 3 November by Austria-Hungary. In Germany, sailors of the High Seas Fleet mutinied on 29-30 October rather than put to sea for a desperate last sortie; by the evening of Monday 4 November Kiel was in the hands of the mutineers and revolution was beginning to spread its tentacles throughout the country, a Bavarian Republic being declared in Munich on the Thursday of that week. During the night of 7-8 November a German delegation crossed the front lines to negotiate an armistice face to face with Marshal Foch.

Although the end was very near, the Allied advance went on. By Saturday 9 November two American corps were on the heights above Sedan and the French Fourth Army was close to Mézières. On the northern flank, Allied patrols were crossing the Scheldt as the Germans withdrew to the Antwerp-Meuse line. Plumer's Second Army would soon be over 50 miles from its old battleground around Ypres. It was on this fateful Saturday, when the Kaiser's abdication was prematurely announced by Prince Max, and a German Republic was proclaimed from the Reichstag, that Wilhelm II relinquished the Imperial throne before slipping away to Holland and exile. At approximately 5am on 11 November, the Armistice was signed in a carriage of Foch's special train at Rethondes, in the Forest of Compiègne. As dawn broke the Canadians brought the wheel of war virtually full circle by clearing Mons of German rearguards. At 11am, after 1,568 days of war, the roar of the guns ceased and peace and silence finally descended on the Western Front.

3 *Crowds outside Buckingham Palace, celebrating the signing of the Armistice on 11 November 1918.*
IWM: Q 56642

AFTERMATH AND LEGACY

While news of the Armistice was the cause for wild celebrations in Paris, London and New York, the reaction at the front was generally more muted, most fighting men welcoming the end of hostilities with a feeling of weary relief rather than heady excitement. Even the advance to victory had cost too much blood for the rejoicing to last very long. Between 8 August and 11 November the BEF, for example, suffered some 350,000 casualties. In the Argonne offensive, from 26 September onwards, the Americans lost 117,000 men in 47 days. It is impossible to calculate the precise cost of the war in human lives. French casualties are normally estimated at nearly 5,000,000, including 1,385,300 dead and missing; German losses numbered at least 1,808,545 dead and 4,247,143 wounded; and 115,660 Americans died out of a total of 325,876 United States casualties. The overall losses of the British Empire were 3,260,581, including 947,023 dead and missing. As we have already noted in this book, the BEF's battle casualties on the Western Front alone amounted to 2,690,054, of whom 677,515 died or went missing and 1,837,613 were wounded.

To talk loosely of a whole generation of young men being wiped out in the First World War is sometimes a trifle misleading. Although many had lost limbs, had been blinded, or carried psychological scars which would stay with them for life, over 80 per cent of those who served in the British forces survived the conflict. Thus one might argue that the term 'maimed generation' would be more accurate. Conversely, recent research by Dr J.M. Winter has confirmed that over 70 percent of fatal British casualties were under the age of thirty, and that the proportion of casualties was notably higher among

1

1 *Allied political leaders at Versailles in 1919. They are, from left to right: David Lloyd George, the British Prime Minister; Vittorio Emanuele Orlando, the Italian Prime Minister; Georges Clemenceau, the French Prime Minister, and Woodrow Wilson, President of the United States.*
Hulton-Deutsch Collection: 3L 886

2

2 *A street party in England after the First World War.*
Hulton Deutsch Collection: CP 278-5

junior officers than among other ranks. Many of these junior officers came from well-off families and were the products of public schools and universities, so in the sense that a disproportionate share of the casualties may have been borne by this particular social group, one can still correctly use the phrase 'lost generation'. Whatever the statistics demonstrate, it is also reasonable to surmise that there was scarcely a family or household in any of the belligerent nations that was untouched by death and bereavement. The war memorials in cities, towns and villages throughout countries such as France and Britain stand as mute but striking testimony to the mind-numbing scale of sacrifice and grief.

The peace settlement imposed by the Treaty of Versailles on 28 June 1919 solved little. New frontiers were drawn in Europe, new countries were created and a League of Nations was set up to prevent future wars. However, the economic, military and territorial penalties demanded by the victorious Allies left

Germany weakened and resentful – a condition that would soon be exploited by Hitler and the Nazis. The latter conveniently ignored the reality that the German Army was essentially a beaten force by November 1918, and that an even more overwhelming defeat would surely have followed in 1919; the fact that the Army was still fighting on the Western Front when Germany had collapsed internally instead gave them a tenuous excuse to propagate the myth of the 'stab in the back'. In Britain and France, war-weariness – accentuated by the literature of disillusionment and disenchantment in the 1920s and early 1930s – undoubtedly contributed to the mood and policies of appeasement, sapping resolve and inhibiting a firm stand against Hitler until it was too late to stop the slide into the abyss of another major conflict.

Nature and the hand of man have combined to heal most of the physical scars of the First World War in France and Belgium. Today there are relatively few traces of the widespread devastation that once defaced huge areas of these countries. The battered walls of Fort Douaumont at Verdun, the enormous mine crater at La Boisselle, and the grass-covered trench lines at Beaumont Hamel are among the more obvious features to be seen, but the most potent reminders of the events of 1914-1918, and of the suffering which occurred on the Western Front, are unquestionably the many war cemeteries dotting northern France and Flanders. The Commonwealth War Graves Commission now maintains 1,665 such cemeteries in France and 385 in Belgium, which wholly or predominantly contain the remains of men from Britain and the Empire who fell in the First World War. Beautifully kept, and in many ways resembling pleasant English gardens, they serve as appropriately peaceful resting places for the legions of the dead. It is difficult not to be profoundly moved by them or by the great memorials to the missing. The present Menin Gate at Ypres, designed by Sir Reginald Blomfield and unveiled by Plumer in 1927, bears the names of 54,896 British and Commonwealth soldiers who went missing in the Salient before 15 August 1917 and who have no known grave. The Last Post is still sounded here every evening by buglers of the local Fire Brigade. In the vast Tyne Cot cemetery near Passchendaele is another memorial, listing 34,888 officers and men missing at Ypres between 16 August 1917 and the end of the war; 73,412 of those who died on the Somme, and who similarly have no known grave, are commemorated at Thiepval on the imposing monument designed by Sir Edwin Lutyens, this being the largest British war memorial anywhere in the world.

If the dead are rightly remembered so many decades after the war, the actual deeds of the soldiers of both sides, and the nature of the fighting on the Western Front, are too often forgotten or distorted by myths and half-truths. In Britain at least, the collective folk-memory of the Great War continues to be dominated by images of stupid and incompetent generals or of bloody and futile attacks for a yard or two of Flanders mud. Comparatively few people, apart from old soldiers, military historians or members of the Western Front Association, could even identify the war in which the crossing of the St Quentin Canal took place, let alone name the month or year in which it occurred. Yet, as John Terraine has stressed on a number of occasions, the period known as the 'Hundred Days' – between the Battle of Amiens and the Armistice – was the only time in British history that the British Army has defeated the *main* body of the *main* enemy in a continental war. Whereas Montgomery faced thirteen divisions, eight of which were Italian, at El Alamein in 1942, Haig's BEF, from August to November 1918, fought up to 99 German divisions, some more than once. In recognising this one begins to place the BEF's successes in 1918 in their proper perspective. Of course there were bungling generals and many instances of almost criminally wasteful assaults on the Western Front. But these did not represent the entire picture. Other generals learned to master the new technology and, by applying it in different ways, eventually broke the trench stalemate which that same technology had largely helped to establish in 1914. When criticising Foch for his conduct of operations in, say, 1915, or when castigating Haig for his mistakes on the Somme and at Passchendaele, one should also give them due credit for their victories in 1918. Equally, to recall *only* the tragedies and horrors of the conflict and to overlook the courage, comradeship and achievements of the average front line soldier is to do an immense disservice to all those who fought, endured and died during those terrible years.

3 *The ossuary and war cemetery at Douaumont near Verdun. The ossuary, which was built between 1922 and 1932, contains the remains of over 130,000 French and German soldiers. Another 15,000 are buried in the adjacent cemetery.*
Hulton-Deutsch Collection: Key 2/876736

INDEX OF ILLUSTRATIONS

Day and Night *Animals*

Contents

Day

When can you see a butterfly?

Night

When can you see a moth?

Day

When can you see a blackbird?

Night

When can you see an owl?

Day

When can you see a squirrel?

Night

When can you see a bat?

Day

When can you see a chicken?

Night

When can you see a fox?

Day

butterfly

blackbird

squirrel

chicken

Night

moth

owl

bat

fox

Index